CONTENTS

ACKNOWLEDGEMENTS

I would like to thank my friends and colleagues in the Department of English and American Studies at Manchester for their continuing help and support as this project moved towards completion. My colleagues in the British Association for American Studies have offered tireless assistance and advice over the years and in particular I would like to thank Simon Newman, Marina Moskevicz, Jon Roper, John Dumbrell, Iwan Morgan and many more who have all heard or commented on parts of this book at some time or another. I also want to thank countless numbers of students on my Film and Politics course over the years who year on year have always contributed something new, illuminating and inspiring in their work for me to go away and think about. I want to thank my family and friends for their support, especially Rick, Kevin, Dave, Steve and Chris, all of whom I have known for more years than any of us would care to mention but who have always been there to support and offer good advice, usually involving trips to the pub! I want to acknowledge the hard work and constant encouragement of all the staff at Edinburgh University Press, including Esme Watson and especially Vicki Donald for her patience and perseverance with this second edition of the book.

LIST OF ILLUSTRATIONS

For Helen

INTRODUCTION:
'WE'RE LIVING YOUR SCRIPTS'

As the 2008 presidential primary election season began to kick into gear, the Democratic campaign quickly drew attention to itself: not just for the war of attrition that was starting to unfold between Senators Barack Obama and Hillary Clinton, but also because news pundits and casual watchers alike seemed to be hit by a wave of déjà-vu about the ensuing battle. Here was an election that seemed very familiar. Haven't we seen this campaign somewhere before? they cried. This sense of recall did not, however, emanate from another time in American political history. This was not a rerun of 1960 when John F. Kennedy defeated Hubert Humphrey; nor a similar scenario to 1976 when Jimmy Carter emerged from obscurity before the primaries began that year to claim the nomination and then the White House. No, the similarity about this race came from television: specifically the seventh and final season of the acclaimed NBC political drama, *The West Wing*, in which aspiring but largely inexperienced Latino congressman, Matthew Santos (Jimmy Smits), beats Vice-President Bob Russell (Gary Cole) to the Democratic nomination before going on to triumph narrowly over a moderate Republican from the West, Arnold Vinick (Alan Alda), in the November general election.

If all of this were nothing more than the coincidental coming-together of art and life, it would be pretty interesting to begin with. The fact that one drew inspiration from the other, however, shows the reality of the Hollywood/entertainment/Washington nexus within American political culture in the early twenty-first century. For when Elie Attie, a former speechwriter for Al Gore in 2000 and then a writer and producer on *The West Wing*, approached Obama aide David Axelrod in the summer of 2004, asking about the background and life of his boss, the two men set in train a sequence of events that saw the fictitious show uncannily predict the real-life action as it unfolded two years after the final season of the series had been screened in the United

1

States. 'We're living your scripts,' joked Axelrod in an e-mail to Attie as Obama's campaign gathered momentum and the real possibility of following in Santos's footsteps took hold in early 2008.[1]

For his part, as Jonathan Freedland reports, when Attie heard Obama's speech at the 2004 Democratic convention in Boston, he was convinced that he should use the prospective Senator's tone, style and rhetoric as a basis for his construction of Matt Santos in the programme. 'After that convention speech, Obama's life changed,' commented Attie. 'He was mobbed wherever he went. He was more than a candidate seeking votes; people were seeking him. Some of Santos's celebrity aura came from that.'[2]

Of course, Attie is not the first former political speechwriter to make his way to Hollywood and rewrite at least some piece of political reality for the big or small screen. He was following in the wake of people like Jeremy Larner, Gary Ross and even Dee Dee Myers – the latter a long-time script/story adviser on *The West Wing* and former press secretary in the Clinton White House – who have penned political stories and added a touch of insider perspective, with some success. But the real impact of this fiction/reality crossover lay not just in highlighting a tradition that goes back many years, nor yet in uncovering the links between politics and speechwriters who have made their way into Hollywood filmmaking. The real importance of this tale lay in the long-standing success of *The West Wing* as a political drama in the early 2000s, and in a changing era for cultural representation of politics that few could have predicted only a couple of years before.

Back in 2000, with the millennium having come and gone and the Clinton era drawing to a close, the feeling in Hollywood was that films about politics were becoming harder to 'green-light' and that no studios really wanted to touch stories about political institutions and politicians that included strong ideological remits and challenging questions for the audience and wider society. Outside of the historical drama, *Thirteen Days* (released in 2000 in the US but 2001 in the UK, which director Roger Donaldson and star and co-producer Kevin Costner admitted had taken years to bring to the screen in any case), the example of Rod Lurie, writer and director of *The Contender* (2000), virtually the last film to appear before the first edition of this book surfaced, seemed to confirm the premise. His experience making this picture about a female senator chosen to succeed a dead vice-presidential incumbent indicated that political movies were becoming increasing box-office anathema for studios – Lurie had gone abroad to get most

Josiah Bartlet is succeeded by Matt Santos as The West Wing *series draws to a close*

of the money, a lot from the French company Studio Canal – and the audience were neither taken with it nor invigorated enough to consider the consequences of such material in the wider political culture. Made on a modest budget of $20 million, the film recouped less than $18 million at the box-office in America.

Lurie's competition for political drama and public engagement came from an unlikely source in these years. After all, the Clinton White House had turned into an even bigger soap opera than many a scriptwriter could have conceded, and much of the early drama of the Clintons' race to the White House had already been portrayed in loose form through Mike Nichols's *Primary Colors*, released two years before Lurie's film. Nevertheless, Joan Allen's portrayal of Senator Laine Hanson rightly won her an Oscar nomination and *The Contender* was awarded some decent reviews, even rich acclaim, especially in Europe; perhaps its combination of sexual politics, brokered deals behind closed doors, and open warfare among Republican and Democrat ideologues was better appreciated from a greater distance, as something of a commentary on if not indictment of the later Clinton years, framed as they were against the backdrop of the Newt Gingrich-inspired Republican revolution of the mid-1990s. But the film's moderate box-office business in America seemed to confirm a fate that had befallen other political films in the second half of the 1990s. Oliver Stone's *Nixon* (gross $13.5 million from a $50 million budget), Peter Guber and Jon Peters's *My Fellow Americans* (gross $22 million), and Warren Beatty's *Bulworth* (gross $26.5 million from a $30 million budget) – all films with biographical, satirical or comedic intent, all with some merit and worth, and all released in the second half of the 1990s – caused only murmurs at the box-office, and the genre seemed to have run its course for the time being.[3] At the beginning of 2001 one wondered how long it would be before Hollywood returned to a drama set in the White House or on Capitol Hill.

But while Hollywood political movies set around institutional characters and locations did indeed whither on the vine for a time after 2000, politics found alternative avenues in which to channel drama, comedy and provocative social comment. Naturally, a good deal of this renewed vigour and enthusiasm for documenting and examining public life has to be laid at the door of events that shook the world to its very core in September 2001. In the aftermath of these events, a distinctly assertive foreign policy ethic appeared in Hollywood, perhaps to no great surprise, characterised initially by patriotic endeavours like Phil Alden Robinson's *The Sum of All Fears* (2002), *Tears of the Sun* (2003, directed by Antoine Fuqua), *Behind Enemy Lines* (2002, John Moore) and Sidney Pollack's *The Interpreter* (2005). As Jean-Michel Valantin argues, the reasons for the clarity of the agenda and the force of the messages in such movies were quite unambiguous. In November 2001, the long-time head of the Motion Picture Association of America (MPAA), Jack Valenti, met with President George Bush's Deputy Chief of Staff, Karl Rove, in Hollywood. The subject of the meeting was the way the coming 'war on terror' could be portrayed in motion pictures and the general measure of support that Hollywood could and would give the administration in up-coming productions. The force of the impact of September 11th was so great that nothing could be left to chance and Hollywood had to be made to understand its position and influence on society, both at home and abroad.

Thus films such as those mentioned above broached America's rapport with the world and its continuing mission to protect democracy in a not so discreetly lopsided ideological manner. The stakes were so high, asserts Valantin, that a measure of the reciprocal arrangement between Hollywood and Washington, played out in the understanding forged by Valenti and Rove, was the fact that two prominent productions were delayed, rescheduled and, certainly in one case, adapted to a different storyline in the months after the terrorist attacks in New York and Washington.[4] The two films were *Collateral Damage*, starring soon-to-be-governor-of-California Arnold Schwarzenegger and directed by Andrew Davies, and *The Sum of All Fears*.

The latter had originally been part of the Tom Clancy series of novels centred around CIA operative Jack Ryan, two of the books having been filmed in the 1990s with Harrison Ford in the role (see Chapter 6). This latest novel told the story of the acquisition of an Israeli nuclear device by Palestinian terrorists, who then use it against the US. The movie version, on the other hand, utilised Russian criminals, intent on restarting the Cold War and working in tandem with European neo-Nazis, as the basis for the plotters of all-out Armageddon. Robinson as director even went as far as personally writing to the Council on American–Arab Relations (CAIR) to assure them that the movie had no intention of pillorying Muslims or Arabs by placing them at the centre of the narrative.[5] Yet such an act itself only served to underscore the highly charged atmosphere of the time and the political ramifications of the movie as a commentary on America's diplomatic state. But even accounting for this change, *The Sum of All Fears* and the other

movies mentioned above rather obviously adopted particular forms of
the gung-ho, spirited, against-the-odds nationalism that is frequently
Hollywood's wont, particularly in times of national crisis, while political figures, policy rhetoric and institutional ideals rarely made more
than an fleeting appearance. Even in a 'political thriller' construct that
is as blatant as the Clancy-adapted Ben Affleck vehicle (finally released
nine months after 9/11), and despite displaying remnants of the novelist's deep-seated conservatism, American politics was not the object of
The Sum of All Fears, even though a presidential character is central to
the action (Bob Fowler, played by James Cromwell). Saving the world
from disaster was the object of the film, and that made it and at least
two of the other movies above about as 'purely political' as those 1990s
multiplex favourites, *Independence Day*, *Men in Black*, *Deep Impact* or
Armageddon.

Pollack's movie was somewhat different. Gaining full-blown access
to the United Nations' headquarters in New York for the first time,
The Interpreter was a murder mystery starring Sean Penn and Nicole
Kidman that was wrapped up in a tale of murky African politics, UN
diplomacy, and American legitimacy within the organisation. While
not perfect by any means, the film nevertheless pointed towards a
much more deep-rooted concern with the tangled underbelly of institutional and world politics than Hollywood had allowed itself to portray for a decade or more. In many respects, poorly matched up though
it was in comparison to the pictures that followed it, *The Interpreter* was
a significant signal of intent on the part of Hollywood filmmakers that
the post-9/11 shock and complicity highlighted by Valenti and Rove's
'arrangement' back in 2001 were giving way to a questioning, critical
and ideologically charged filmmaking era in the remaining years of the
decade.

In the wake of Pollack's film, movies like *Rendition* (2007) and *Lions
for Lambs* (2008), as well as more ostensibly military-based pictures
like *Jarhead* (2005) and *Redacted* (2007) and the 'returning vet' drama,
In the Valley of Elah (2007), all led to the widely acclaimed and Oscar-
winning *The Hurt Locker* (2009), as well as action film *Green Zone*
(2010), and painted a wildly unstable picture of modern combat, its
effects on the participants, and the preconceptions and misjudgements
that were beginning to affect a nation under whose name the wars
in Iraq and Afghanistan were being fought. These were very different
presentations of America's role in and reaction to the world from the
models concocted in the immediate aftermath of 9/11, and their mixed

reception at the box-office and among critics testified to a film culture and wider society that were divided over America's position in the post-9/11 environment, and also over the way that cinema was dealing with those questions and complications.

Of course, this kind of reactionary historical periodisation is quite familiar in Hollywood's history, even if wars had been subject to revisionism largely after the fact rather than during the conflict, as increasingly became the case with Iraq. Whether it was the legacy of World War One, the backdrop to the Depression and then World War Two, the instigation of the Hays Office, the investigations by the Dies Committee and then later the House Committee on Un-American Activities (HUAC): all have been characterised by a form of review and re-assessment in later Hollywood treatments of their actions and influence. But while the second edition of this book revisits many of those moments and reflects on the political films that emerged from these times, something did appear different in the post-9/11 era and is worth reflecting upon. It was not only the speed of response to events at home and abroad that seemed to increase after 2005; nor the vehemence with which some films attacked their subject, and were themselves criticised for their unapologetic approach to both the attitudes and the ideology of the American government after 2001. The Channel 4– and Film 4–backed *Death of a President* (2006), for instance, was called on to be banned in America by the Bush Administration, for its fictionalised 'mockumentary' approach to the putative shooting of Bush in the 'near future'. It was, in fact, the change in Hollywood attitudes that was critical, though not necessarily subtle, touching not only the manner and focus of the filmmaking but also the means by which production companies, directors and stars broached their subject material and publicised their efforts.

And yet this change was signalled before 2005 and prior to Hollywood's spirited riposte to the Bush doctrine. Its emergence could be traced directly to those years just before and after the terrorist attacks of 2001, a time when Hollywood film at least dithered and/or reacted in predictable fashion to the new 'age of terror'. For the mantle of reactionary, critical focus in the cultural arena shifted in these years to American television, a place that could rarely be counted on for hard-hitting ideological or institutional agendas, but where drama in general, and political drama in particular, altered beyond all recognition at this time. In the early 1990s politics and the political system had become something of a counterpoint to series like *Dark Skies* and especially *The X-Files* (see Chapter 4), in which government cover-ups and political manœuvrings were the narrative mandate upon which, in the tradition of Hollywood conspiracy narratives, rogue, lone, heroic individuals battled forces they knew little of, and with hardly any support set out to uncover the fabric of a concocted 'big lie' about history, aliens, corrupt leaders and new technology. *Dark Skies* (a conspiracy narrative disproving the whole of post-war American history and set in the Kennedy-era 1960s) survived only one series while *The X-Files* proved to be an international smash hit, only losing some of its momentum in the seasons that followed the first cinematic outing (commonly referred to at the time as *X-Files: Fight the Future* but now known just as *The X-Files*), made at the height of the drama's popularity in 1998. Added to this was the emergence of other much grittier television dramas using cinematic production values, and visual techniques gleaned from the likes of MTV and taken up by emerging cable companies like Showtime and HBO. Series like *NYPD Blue*, *Homicide: Life on the Street* and *ER* paved the way for later, even more strident shows such as *The Sopranos*, *Boomtown* and *The Wire*.

By the end of the 1990s, and even more surprising than the success of *The X-Files* and the originality of *Dark Skies*, came two very different politics-based programmes. The first, beginning in 1999 (2000 in the UK), was NBC's *The West Wing*, to be followed in 2002 by the phenomenon that became *24*, made by Fox Television. The two could not have been more different. One was a televisual experiment in the ways of manipulating and reinventing the thriller genre, the other a slow-burn, wordy, intellectual drama about beltway insiders working for a liberal president. Yet both in their own ways rewrote the rule-book on political drama, on what could and could not be expressed and the ways in which the traditions of that drama and the new technological advancements in filmmaking could be reconfigured to make compelling television. The initial seasons of both these shows would prove to be their zenith and yet their continued popularity beyond four, five and even six seasons of television testified to the quality of their production values, the strength of their scripts (in *The West Wing*'s case, anyway) and the level of action and excitement (in *24*'s). While this new edition of the book is by no means a shared analysis of film *and* TV portrayals of politics in America, the very scale of the impact made by these and other series (*Lost* and *Commander-in-Chief*, as well as the aforementioned *The Wire*, to name only a few) means that analysis of the first decade of the twenty-first century must include some recognition of their impact as a way to interrogate and theorise the complex ideological volte-face in American entertainment attitudes towards political themes.

It is for these reasons that Chapters 4 and 7 have been expanded and a new Chapter 6 inserted for this edition to take account of the post-9/11 era and to examine the ways in which entertainment culture in general – not just Hollywood particularly, though the two are largely interchangeable in the modern era – has reshaped attitudes and ideas towards the presentation of politics on screen. Chapter 1's examination of the theories and formulas that have infused political movies is also brought up to date, complementing the examination of values, ideals and beliefs that stretch back into the early history of the republic. Chapter 2 revisits the 1930s and 1940s, and attempts to build upon the notions of historical evolution and ideological construction in political movies that Hollywood focused on at this time. It acts as a companion piece to Chapter 7's analysis of films of the 1990s and 2000s, with its focus on the reflection of real political events taking place and of real people existing outside of the theatre as a backdrop to the fictional action, and the changing nature of the Hollywood/Washington relationship, which are woven together to demonstrate how the 1990s both parodied and revisited traditional values and approaches to political comedy especially. But the 1990s analysis has also expanded to take account of some of the developments in television, as well as to interpret a number of the films just appearing at the time of the first edition, notably *The Contender, Thirteen Days* and *Spartan*.

Chapters 3, 4 and 5 build upon the sub-generic formations that the first edition of the book laid out. Election movies are reconsidered and updated as a vital part of the political movie canon, incorporating new analysis of 'classic' productions like *Bob Roberts* and *The Candidate*, as well as offsetting these in comparison to and with consideration of later election films like *Man of the Year* and *Swing Vote*. Remakes in the shape of *All the King's Men* (1949 and 2006) and *The Manchurian Candidate* (1962 and 2004) are plotted out as a Hollywood exercise in revisiting and extending its own historical reference points for political culture. Paranoia, adventure and action films, colloquially gathered under the banner of political thrillers, are also reinterpreted and added to with a host of productions that have arisen in the intervening years, notably the above-mentioned *Thirteen Days, Shooter, The Sentinel* and *Vantage Point*. Chapter 5 also uses television as a comparative effect for the way political biography has been shaped and developed, and looks at how a recent text like *Bobby* stands up in comparison to the ideals and cinematic layout of past biographical features.

It is clear, as the first edition stated, that Hollywood and Washington are closer bedfellows than ever before. They collaborate on and work towards an emphasis on the efficacy of the American polity, a facet even more crucial in the second decade of the twenty-first century. While it is also true that, over the longer historical period, Hollywood has often been accused of simplifying democratic debate, the film industry has nevertheless been crucial in opening up wider social and cultural awareness of the ways in which institutions operate in America. Hollywood has also served to ground many of the fundamental principles and beliefs of the nation in the consciousness of its citizenry through symbolic as well as pedagogic means. This second edition of the book demonstrates not only the way these dual tracks have run their course throughout cinematic history, but also the manner in which they have shifted and renegotiated themselves in the early twenty-first century, and the messages of change and re-evaluation that they have for America's political culture and its entertainment heart.

NOTES

1. Jonathan Freedland, 'From West Wing to the Real Thing', *The Guardian*, 21 February 2008 at: http://www.guardian.co.uk/woprld/2008/feb/21/ barackobama.uslelections2008/.
2. Jonathan Freedland, 'From West Wing to the Real Thing'.
3. One might counter this premise with the success of movies like *Air Force One* and *Enemy of the State*, though both belong to the more 'high-octane' action thriller category than the movies cited.
4. Jean-Michel Valantin, *Hollywood, The Pentagon and Washington: The Movies and National Security from World War II to the Present Day* (London: Anthem, 2005), pp. 90–1.
5. Jean-Michel Valantin, p. 93.

Chapter 1

FILM, IDEOLOGY AND AMERICAN POLITICS

In the first edition of this book, I attempted to distinguish films about politics from political films. The reason why I thought the distinction was so important was because a number of implicit definitions of political movies had been incorporated into other texts and scholarship over the years – with a myriad of other cultural and ideological agendas – and as such, a key, perhaps definitive, interpretation seemed to be necessary. Subsequent writing has begun to address this issue more forcefully in the last few years, notably the work of Terry Christensen and Peter Hass. In their book, *Projecting Politics*, Christensen and Hass outline a typology whereby 'pure political movies' – the ones I was initially trying to pin down – are set in a 'recognizably political environment', while 'politically reflective movies' include clearly defined political characters but are films that are not intentionally peddling an obvious agenda or ideology.[1] In fact, the overriding and very useful aspect of their work has lain not in the way they have re-asserted the purity of certain political texts, but in the way they handled more oblique, often allegorical interpretations of politics. Their crucial contribution in many ways has been in explicating what they describe as 'the political aspects of inexplicitly political films': in essence, those messages to be found in the films inhabiting the last two categories of their typology, 'auteur political movies' and 'socially reflective movies'.[2] Many more films, they assert, follow a sublimated agenda, not unlike the ideas put forward by James Coombs and Dan Nimmo, to the effect that films from science-fiction to horror to westerns offer up analogies and metaphors as part of an on-going critique of the political times and context.[3] This is not fundamentally different from the pattern of presentation that a critic like Richard Maltby sees as part of a mirroring process for cinema. 'Politics' in American society exists in a 'parallel universe', he suggests, where echoes of the world outside the movie theatre infiltrate the stories on screen, sometimes through newspaper headlines, events happening to peripheral characters and so on. Whatever the equation might be for these types of pictures, though, each of the scholars is nevertheless keen to parade politics, not as 'trivial' or 'irrelevant', but as part of a structure that informs the movie audience's pervasive world-view.[4]

In short, Christensen and Hass, while deeply interested in definitively political films, also provide a way of seeing the 'political' in movies that metaphorically or allegorically add weight to ideological themes or periods, obviously and notably in examples as diverse as *Invasion of the Body Snatchers* (1956) and, more recently, *The Passion of the Christ* (2004), but which clearly need to be differentiated from 'purer' forms of Hollywood political representation. They see the 'political' in many texts, in other words, but some films still remain more 'political' than others. They are perhaps the movies that offer politics with a capital rather than a small 'p', we might suggest.

Following on from Christensen and Hass, Michael Coyne's work, meanwhile, does focus on what we might term 'pure' or 'strictly political' movies. But *Hollywood Goes to Washington* does this by grouping the major films together into six key phases that 'correspond to a period of considerable drama in American political, social and cultural history', as Coyne puts it.[5] He therefore reads Hollywood's political film history as a parallel track running side by side with the country's actual evolution, sometimes reflecting, occasionally dictating the moods and momentum of the nation's political scene as it has unfolded across the century.[6]

One theory concerning the location of political movies in certain periods of film history, and what they contributed as cultural tracts in these eras, is provided in a summary of Hollywood as it developed through the 1980s and early 1990s. Some scholars not only pointed out the dearth of political-themed pictures in this era, but also criticised the scale of ambition and moral rectitude within Hollywood generally. Michael Medved's notorious 1992 text, *Hollywood v America*, has often been held up as the thesis upon which – predominantly right-wing – criticism of the industry rested in these years because of Medved's focus on violence and promiscuousness as a provocation to the young and impressionable. Film critic Tom O'Brien added to this clamour with *The Screening of America*, his book that appeared at the end of the 1980s and attacked Hollywood for its ever-increasing reliance on these themes at the expense of daring and intelligent cinema. But O'Brien's motivation was two-fold: to reject the baser instincts of some

Hollywood producers and directors who saw money to be made in vulgarity for sure, but also to re-assess the claim to social and political messages within the best and most serious of Hollywood pictures of the time. O'Brien cites films like *Chariots of Fire* (1981), *The Last Emperor* (1988), *A Dry White Season* (1989) and *Mississippi Burning* (1988) as his examples: quality pictures, major directors, serious topics, he thought.[7]

These films also fall into the final two categories of the Christensen and Hass typology so they confirm the premise that the social and political can be found and discussed in a variety of texts. But in many ways, an undercurrent running through these books was that Hollywood had apparently lost its political will in these years and thus the search for meaning and contemporary signification was being played out in pictures that, historically and/or allegorically, referenced the contemporary period but did not address 'pure' political themes or characters at all. By the later 1990s and certainly into the 2000s any concern about Hollywood's political intent in this respect had been washed away and the movies that subsequently appeared sought to reflect this in a variety of fashions.

So Christensen and Hass, Coyne and other works have proved immensely informative in the 2000s, which if anything became recognised as an era when American politics was perceived as having become even more 'Hollywoodised' than was the case during the last couple of decades of the twentieth century. That morphing of the two cultures was almost certainly aided by the fact that the controversies and the overwhelming nature of the events that shook the US between 2001 and 2009 have been utilised more and more in the name of drama and entertainment. In a way, my attempt to define the political film initially at the end of the 1990s, as well as touching upon the themes these authors have subsequently taken up, was also a ploy to locate the genre that dare not speak its name. If anything, the array of movies that filled the screens in the first decade of the new millennium made some of that task harder but the debate ever more intriguing.

Genre criticism in film studies has for a long time recognised, even if some have not necessarily agreed, that a singular, contextualised definition of gangster films, *film noir*, horror, science-fiction and/or musicals in American film – to name only some of the most prominent – has disappeared by the wayside. As Barry Langford has observed, genre is by its very nature an evolutionary term: 'genre is a *process* rather than a fact.' And that process has splintered generic categories and broken them apart every inch of the way, not only in terms of subject matter, but also across time, authorial influence and even geographic position. Langford goes so far as to reveal that what passes for generic categorisation in academic film scholarship may be, and often is, very different from what is considered a genre out in the mainstream world of DVD rental houses, internet retail sites and multiplex cinema culture. Who in academic or serious film scholarship, he asks, relies on genres such as 'classics' (anything pre-1975 available on DVD) or 'family' (anything by Disney and/or much that is classified as PG or U by the British Board of Film Classification (BBFC)) outside of Blockbuster, Amazon and HMV?[8]

If this sounds dreadfully pejorative, Langford and others are quick to point out that there is plenty of method in the seeming madness of such broad-sweeping delineation, not least the commercial imperatives that inform much of the film industry's operations. And to be fair, even the commercial and retail organisations that have benefited from the widespread release and re-release of a host of features in the low-cost DVD era that were barely available beforehand, have offered up lists of movies that are every bit as interesting as they are contentious. One of internet retail site Amazon's targeted sales pitches for 'political films', for example, constructed a fascinatingly diverse and debatable bunch of texts. While it was a pleasant surprise to see the likes of *Breach*, *Vantage Point* and *The Good Shepherd* line up next to 'classics' like *Mr. Smith Goes to Washington*, *The Parallax View* and *All the President's Men*, the inclusion of *Blood Diamond*, *Hotel Rwanda* and *The Last King of Scotland* could only make one wonder why Amazon would not go the whole way and simply describe any film with an African setting as somehow being politically encrypted, as though that continent offered an obvious sub-genre of political movies that might just as well be created there and then.

In fact, this example is well chosen. Political films have never really had a working definition to speak of in any form, so why not seek to be as inclusive as possible? As Phillip Gianos says:

> To look at a genre is to look at the society that generates and sustains it; genre analysis is as much social as aesthetic. For that reason it is significant that nothing approaching a developed political film genre has ever taken root in the United States.[9]

If Gianos too hints at a phrase that has been perceived as pejorative within film theory and culture, it is no coincidence that the term 'political film' has been eyed with some suspicion also in Hollywood, for both its ideological and, perceptibly more importantly, its financial prospects. Hence the genre of political movies has for a long time floated around the subject of certain pictures (and certain filmmakers) without anything like the kind of debate that characterised how we might define or recognise more staple, and often better-received, categories like westerns, musicals and horror films. In fact, political movies have often found themselves acting as the cornerstone of 'action' or 'thriller' categories, and even that has not prevented a number of them from entering the 'comedy' or 'melodrama' genre too. Indeed, as the Amazon example testifies to, political films have also been subject to a certain geographical inference, and one that only adds to the dilemma of definition if one is to accept the political component of a film like *The Last King of Scotland* (as excellent a piece of cinema though it is) as somehow comparable to, say, *The Constant Gardener.*

Further obfuscation is to be found amongst a variety of directors who have acquired the sobriquet of 'political filmmaker' as their careers have moved in particular directions not necessarily associated with the kind of films included in this book. A good example, and a noticeable one among the current luminaries of Hollywood, is Stephen Spielberg, whose films *Amistad* and *Munich* are the only ones spoken about at any length in the pages that follow, but who has periodically been defined as a 'political director' for an array of efforts including *The Color Purple, Saving Private Ryan, Minority Report* and, perhaps most poignantly and particularly, *Schindler's List.*

Finally, one might simply look at the way the word 'political' has been used to describe a whole set of films released in the years since the turn of the millennium, from *Fahrenheit 9/11* (2004) (obviously a political movie but also a documentary and thus something belonging in yet another sub-generic form, as we will consider in more depth) and *The Constant Gardener* (2005) (ecological thriller with institutional figures and hence much more cautiously definable as 'political'), by way of *Good Night, and Good Luck* and *Munich* (both 2005) (both of these films with historical settings and easily identifiable 'real' events as their 'political' backdrop) to *United 93* (2006), *The Kingdom* (2007), *State of Play* (2009) and *Edge of Darkness* (2010) (the last two being Hollywood interpretations of 'classic' British television drama, their 'political' context therefore 'transferred' to an American setting). All of these movies, indeed all the ones cited in the preceding few pages, are of course 'political' in some way, in much the same sense that Spielberg could be read as a 'political' filmmaker. Some offer up politicians and institutions within their plots, at least as an implicit characterisation of the period and events being spoken of, and they tackle important social, cultural, economic and historical issues from contemporary as well as more far-sighted perspectives. The debate they have generated within the public arena could by itself nominate the films as political texts, highlighted in 2005 by the Israeli Consul General of Los Angeles, who was moved enough by the contents of Spielberg's *Munich* to comment thus: 'As a Hollywood movie, I assume that it will be defined as a well-made film, but from the standpoint of the messages it sends, the messages are problematic.'[10]

But while all of the films mentioned immediately above have strong ideologies and issue-orientated ideas to speak of (to the extent that they provoke responses from those in power, as outlined in the *Munich* example, a theme developed in this book), what do they actually present or even perceive as the ideas and agenda at the heart of American political culture? How are institutions portrayed and what kinds of political figures are constructed? In fact, some of these films offer what we might determine to be the background or peripheral subtext to Hollywood's concern with the actual internal and insular constituent parts of the institutional fabric of the nation, something akin to Christensen and Hass's 'politically reflective' movie category. In other words, these films and a number of others like them do what Hollywood has always done; they offer historical perspectives and re-enactments, social concerns and global polemics that either allegorically reference the American polity or simply skirt its boundaries.

This book is interested in a slightly more precise definition of the phrase, and thus in films that are related to but also somehow different from the list above. We are principally concerned with films that have very direct settings, characters and/or references to politicians, political institutions and political history. The aim here is to define, even re-articulate what films about politics (and more specifically, American politics) are about, how we recognise them and, crucially, what this particular set of texts says about the state of relations between Washington and Hollywood. We are attempting to discover whether this relationship has become ever closer over the last 90 years or so, or whether it has merely been a marriage of convenience that looks a lot cosier than it sometimes is but does not amount to as much as we might think.

These rhetorical questions are really rather important for, if one were to group the films together that have so far been referenced, a broad interpretation would probably gather them under the collective adjective 'liberal'. Whether one employs the dictionary definition (progressive, generous in temperament, tolerant) or accepts the political goals inherent in the word (advance equal opportunity, promote a creative and productive society), the films are primarily acting upon these ideas, even if one were to ignore the reactionary content of such movies that seemingly target the politics of the contemporary society in which they were made. For example, *Good Night, and Good Luck* from a historical perspective, *The Constant Gardener* from an ecological, multi-national corporations perspective, and *Lions for Lambs* from a straightforward ideological position have all been 'read' as stridently anti-George W. Bush and/or his administration. Daniel Franklin goes so far as to assert that Hollywood is broadly liberal and secular because its core audience is the same and thus, as he says, 'you are what you pay to see'; Hollywood therefore caters for its clientele from a social and ideological point of view.[11]

This political position worked as a form of criticism implied in Medved and O'Brien's texts: that Hollywood movies of the 1980s and early 1990s actually tended to be far too progressive and tolerant in their attitudes to things like sex, drugs and violence, though where that would leave their criticism and Franklin's critique of movies as stridently nationalistic as the *Rambo* series begs further questions about Hollywood's ideological agenda then and now. This duality, however, actually becomes the focal point of one particular movie considered in this book: Warren Beatty's *Bulworth* (1998) and its openly confrontational position between the two communities of cinema and politics (see Chapter 3). And yet while these movies and many others to be discussed do seem to have locked perceptions of the film industry at the very least into an ideological and philosophical straitjacket that has always somehow interpreted Hollywood as being liberal and left-leaning in its persuasion, many pictures, whether they are conscious of it or not, still manage to uphold the traditions and philosophies that conservative thinkers, and even the Bush Administration of 2001–9, hold so dear. Why and how could and would that be so?

This new edition is not typically going to examine all of the broader political movies above and especially all those that have emerged since 2000, though it would be foolish simply to ignore them or to imply that they have no influence on all manner of other political movie-making. Clearly they do have an influence, and indeed the likes of

Munich, United 93 and *The Constant Gardener* have been chosen not least for the impact they have had on wider public discourse, and the inspiration they have provided for similarly engaged filmmakers looking to initiate projects that were not always well received within the studios or wider Hollywood movie-making machine, but who have been re-energised and repoliticised by the events at the beginning of the twenty-first century.

In particular, their tale is reminiscent of the way that filmmakers in other eras of Hollywood's history have been galvanised into action and impulse. Indeed, a sense of authorship that is encapsulated within this proposition – that the same or similar directors return to political themes again and again – does pervade the history of Hollywood's political landscape. From Frank Capra on through Alan J. Pakula to Oliver Stone, Michael Moore and Paul Greengrass, the context for and analytical investigation of political directors will actually underpin a number of important discussions in the book about political movie style, rhetoric and subject matter.

So the films so far mentioned are important for two principal reasons that occupy much of the investigation here. The first reason can be broached as a question we have to ask ourselves after we have decided what a film about politics is: namely, are these movies important, to the film community and to wider society? The attention garnered by certain political films provides at least a partial answer. Clearly art and culture do have the capacity to shape thoughts and ideas in society. The movies also provoke debate and bring forgotten historical moments back to public consciousness, even to the pages of news media not concerned solely with entertainment – a service the editors of one film journal thought was worthwhile in its own right amid the furore that surrounded Spielberg's *Munich*.

> Here at *Cineaste*, we welcome the adoption of movies as topical subjects by our 'hard news' journalistic colleagues [they said]. At its best such spirited and informed discussion promotes broader public debate on important issues. And if the argument sometimes gets emotionally overheated, that may be the clearest indication that filmmakers are not only exploring provocative social issues but may also have broached some uncomfortable home truths.[12]

As Christensen and Hass also assert, quoting director Costa-Gavras's maxim that movies cannot change countries, 'they [can] make a contribution, however. They inform and educate. They provide catharsis.'[13]

So, if it is possible to assert that political movies do have a value and indeed a role beyond the industry and wider film culture, the second issue to consider is the films' aesthetic quality, the way they are made, and the techniques and stylistic nuances employed that make them stand out from other films and other categories. These are important features because they not only hint at another maxim that is often associated with this 'genre' of movie-making – that political films are often well made, stylish, intelligent and therefore worthy artefacts – but also suggest the way history and ideology cut a swathe across the visual foundations of political movies reflected in the way they have been made and presented throughout Hollywood's history. This is ideology as cinematography, and in this second edition of the book, I believe that the visual pretence of this type of film – 'iconographic political movies', we might call them – is even more important in many respects than it was before the turn of the century, for the weight of political movies that have come along that rely ostensibly on signs and signals as a means to convey messages and principles. Subliminal politics is therefore a vital component of the way Hollywood works, and the means by which the traditional and enduring values of America's political culture continue to operate.

HOLLYWOOD AND THE PORTRAYAL OF AMERICAN POLITICAL IDEAS

First of all, films about politics are trying to convey ideas: in short, the values, beliefs and identity that are wrapped up in the ideology of the American creed. Hollywood has always taken its role very seriously in this respect. It has often been perceived as the champion of democracy, and has become an active participant in the debates that have engulfed American political life. Sometimes those debates have been sparked by the tone and content of certain films (*The Birth of a Nation, JFK, Fahrenheit 9/11*), while at other times cinema has been caught up in discussions about the simplification, or 'dumbing down', of ideals and values (*Mr. Smith Goes to Washington, Dr. Strangelove, Air Force One*) that have supposedly been gleaned from popular movies; the latter list, however, also demonstrates the extent to which the political elite in particular are less enamoured of the criticism, irony or satire directed at them than of the actual quality of cinematic presentations like these.

But even where movies are standard-bearers for change within the polity (and Frank Capra's *Mr. Smith* is a good example of this), they still frequently preach a reverence for the Founding Fathers, for the Declaration of Independence and the Constitution, and for the ways in which American political culture is perceived to operate. Liberalism, democracy, pluralism and populism, to name the most obvious elements: they are all there within the typical political movie, sometimes overtly characterised, at other times more discreetly proposed.

As we will see, one of the reasons why Hollywood returns again and again to its greatest leaders, for instance, is because somehow these people have enveloped all these ideals, all that is 'best' about American politics. From Washington to Roosevelt and Kennedy, by way of Jefferson, Jackson and of course Lincoln, Hollywood has been drawn to these figures throughout its history because they are men who represent moments when American democracy suffered critical tests or was subject to re-evaluation. Hollywood has offered their words and deeds as explanations for the endorsement of these ideological traditions, as well as providing a convenient reading of their interpretations of American philosophical thought.

Liberalism and democracy are two such traditions that have constantly been reiterated in Hollywood films about politics from the very beginning, but which offer potentially contrasting inspirations for the American system that are not necessarily teased out in a cultural medium as blunt as cinema. On the one hand, American liberalism draws its influence from the law of natural rights as envisaged by seventeenth-century philosopher John Locke. Locke took on board the individualist argument of Thomas Hobbes, together with the egalitarian thoughts of Hobbes's contemporary, James Harrington.[14] Knitting these strands together, Locke foresaw the property-owning classes as having the means to control legislative power but also stipulated that a 'contract' needed to be established between the governed and the government. Hence a relationship was quickly drawn out between liberalism as an ideology, capitalism as an economic system, and natural rights as a bulwark of American democracy and inspiration for the Founders of the republic.[15]

So instrumental has liberal thought been in American society that, by the 1950s, Louis Hartz, in his famous book, considered the 'liberal tradition' in the US to have been the pervasive theory in its ideological evolution. Hartz attributed the strength of liberalism, acting indeed almost as a countervailing force against other strident values, as a contributing factor in the failure of socialism in America.[16] Later work by, for example, pre-eminent political philosopher John Rawls in *Political Liberalism* also equates reasonable and reciprocal relationships in society with a strong and self-regulating political system. As Andreas Hess points out, Rawls saw reason as a precondition of liberalism; by this he meant the extension of rights and guarantees not just as a judicial or constitutional concern, but also as a 'larger project' that liberal democracy was widely concerned with in America.[17]

On the other hand, American democracy has always been a source of tension in comparison to liberalism, rather than the oft-perceived complement to it, because it has feared the kind of majority rule that strikes down minority thought and opinion. The Founding Fathers sought to maintain both these ideas within a single framework when they wrote the Constitution in 1787, and Hollywood films have grappled with the consequences ever since the moving image's inception. Especially in times of crisis, when liberalism is challenged and the democratic system has to be seen to enforce regulation, balancing freedom with fascism is a tricky cinematic manœuvre, an ideological balancing act perhaps best represented by, among others, Gregory LaCava's important 1933 film, *Gabriel Over the White House*, Capra's *Meet John Doe* from 1941, and John Frankenheimer's *Seven Days in May* (1965).

Egalitarianism is another intrinsic part of the American ideological and philosophical make-up. In J. R. Pole's view, equality has been central to democratic beliefs in the US.[18] How are the poor, the needy and the disenfranchised to be represented in public life? What of the role of women and minorities? In asking such questions, there is also a note of caution to be struck. Somewhat endorsing the themes of Hartz, egalitarianism is one of those principles that can be seen to endorse the view that America's ideology is precisely to eschew ideology, or as Richard Hofstadter's famous phrase has it, 'our fate as a nation is not to have an ideology, but to be one.'[19] Hollywood films, not unlike America itself, have more often than not refused to confront the key ideological tensions at the heart of the republic: noticeably, the core schisms of race and gender. Instead, America has sought to defuse these controversies, and obfuscate them into a set of solutions that have constantly sought 'healing', 'redemption', 'forgiveness' and 'closure' for the sins and or inequities of the past.

American political films, it should be stressed, do have critical beliefs and ideas historically, and a will to examine the American experience, even if this is more likely conceived with the plan of finding

satisfactory, not to say happy solutions to chronic malfeasance or structural defects. Indeed, it is this very outlook that is probably responsible
for Hollywood being far more cautious about certain ideas than others,
lest they not find the adequate solutions desired. Especially on questions of race and gender, therefore, here have been endemic matters of
grave consequence that have proved very difficult areas for American
political movies to tackle or even to want to address, no doubt as a
result of the kind of shadow that such issues have cast over Hollywood
as a business, as much as an art form, throughout its history. One only
has to see how a historical epic like *Glory* (1989) works in comparison
to a more preachy, worthy but ambiguous historical and also strongly
political text like *Amistad* (2002) to know how the political genre has
so desperately failed to appreciate the subtleties of the debate. *Kisses
for my President* had a female in the Oval Office as early as 1964, and
women Vice-Presidents were in place in Hollywood by the late 1990s
(*Air Force One* and *The Contender*), but in a whole host of other films,
women have been relegated to stereotypical versions of the politician's
wife (*The Seduction of Joe Tynan, Murder at 1600*, and even in a movie
as interesting and thoughtful as *The Candidate*). So it is with only a few
notable exceptions that the majority of the chief protagonists in the
movies about to be discussed are principally white, male and wealthy/
privileged/middle-class (itself an accurate and acute commentary on
the state of both Washington and Hollywood).

    In a way it should be seen as natural that Hollywood does this with
movies. That controversial and provocative statements about society
and its evolution are subsumed in a variety of morally and ideologically ambiguous guises mirrors much of the way American society
has approached issues and events of troublesome countenance. As
Richard Maltby has said, Hollywood is a 'social institution' and therefore it is understandable that it should reflect society's hopes, fears
and beliefs.[20] The complexity of certain cultural and historical ideas
is therefore relinquished for ever-greater and more optimistic leanings towards a better future, redemptive endings, and a saviour or
prophet coming to rescue the troubled nation. In films about politics
we see good triumph time and again; democracy wins the day, and
the underdog, or the 'little fella', smashes the big corporations. Films
about politics have their roots in the way institutions perform, how
politicians behave and the ways in which corruption and deceit ('graft',
as it was known in the heyday of the studio era!) can be excised from
the system. Even in the most brutal critiques of the political culture,

this hopeful and often simplistic redemption is never far away, perhaps best exemplified in a brief comparison of the way American film and TV present its politics and how Britain does it.

Critical, cynical and corrupt are only some of the more positive attributes that certain filmmakers have adopted for their examination of the machinations of British politics. One only has to think of television series such as *Yes Minister, House of Cards* and *The Thick of It,* political dramas like *The Politician's Wife, A Very Social Secretary* or *State of Play,* and certainly films like *Hidden Agenda, Defence of the Realm, Scandal, Michael Collins* and *The Constant Gardener,* again, to know that British penchant for thoroughly denouncing those at the heart of institutional authority. As Dominic Sandbrook so eloquently puts it in *Never Had it So Good,* his cultural history of the nation in the 1950s and 1960s, talking of the writing and cinematic realisation of the novels of John Le Carré at the time: 'Le Carré used the conventions of popular fiction to dissect the lies and hypocrisies of an enfeebled British elite struggling to come to terms with their fall from international preeminence.'[21] Sandbrook's description, if it was applicable to Le Carré's breakthrough novel of those years, *The Spy Who Came in from the Cold,* is equally attributable to a later book of his, *The Constant Gardener,* which was so ably transferred to the screen by rising Brazilian director, Fernando Meirelles.

In the US by contrast, and even in a series as successful and lauded as, say, *The West Wing* (1999–2006), in which harsh indictments of the American system did frequently appear, the oft-quoted refrain of hope, expectation and a certain wilful optimism was often on show, wound up in narratives where the system, terminally in crisis in shows from Britain, could nevertheless be cured, bettered or redeemed in America. And the pattern is consistently reproduced across Hollywood's history, from the Depression-fuelled anxiety of James Cruze's *Washington Merry-Go-Round* (1932) to the liberal paean to tolerance and activism in post-9/11 America in Robert Redford's *Lions for Lambs* (2008).

Ultimately, liberalism is often the banner under which most commentators – and especially those on the right in American life, as already indicated – believe Hollywood political movies operate. As contemporary indictments of certain regimes, incidents or eras of controversy and change, that is possibly right, but it is to ignore the underlying, and temperate, nature of movies (and moviemakers) that self-consciously re-articulate the messages of hope and expectation that American politics has lived and breathed for the better part of

200 years. As the following pages make clear, the post-9/11 era has created a rich new vein of political filmmaking that, on the face of it, is inflamed, accusatory and polemical. But at the same time it is filmmaking that is arguably conditioned to rebranding the traditional values and beliefs of the American experience for the twenty-first century; it is iconic representation of a system that can somehow still be redeemed, can still triumph against the cynicism and manipulation of those in power and those that orchestrate its less accountable operations from beyond institutional power sources. It is, in short, a template first constructed by political movies in the 1930s and 1940s, when the need to believe in the strength of the political system, and the willingness to accept that power could be reclaimed by the people, were an exhortation hotwired into the memory banks of Americans wanting answers to the crisis of that era, and believing the system could and would always overcome its harshest challenges. How, then, do the twenty-first-century examples parade these similar ideals? The simple answer is that they do this with the imagery that passes before the eyes of the watching audience.

THE ICONOGRAPHY OF HOLLYWOOD POLITICS

If ideals, beliefs and theories are important to the presentation of politics in Hollywood, there remains something else that is actually far more pervasive, and something Hollywood does far better when it comes to conveying political messages. As the following chapters explore, where high-minded and often complex ideals and theories have been the principal substance of a political movie, they have tended on the whole to be poorly received, by critics and the public. Movies like Henry King's 1944 biography of Woodrow Wilson, or Otto Preminger's 1962 congressional drama, *Advise and Consent*, rich though they are in meaning and interpretation for the scholar, have tended to be rather dry, quite drab narratives in lots of ways for the casual viewer. Hollywood has often made political films interesting by wedding them to other genres like comedy, satire and conspiracy/paranoia, as already suggested, but even here a consistency of values, ideals and beliefs still resonates, though not necessarily in the most obvious way.

What Hollywood has tapped into more meaningfully has been the mythology at the heart of American democracy. The nation's democratic symbols are as much tied together by its iconic political structures as by other forms of Americanism. Hollywood has been careful to utilise this imagery as a signifier of political discourse in many genres of movie-making. One could list a collection of films that are outside the confines of this book but which nevertheless draw upon the idea of institutional backdrops as a basis for their implicit narrative and social context. With Washington DC operating as the natural environment for such visual presentation to take place, the likes of Alfred Hitchcock's *Strangers on a Train* (1951), Robert Wise's *The Day the Earth Stood Still* (1951), *The Firm* (1993, directed by Sidney Pollack) and *True Lies* (1995, directed by James Cameron) all utilise the nation's capital and its landmarks as significant pillars of establishment or elite power. Hollywood has done this by a recall to iconography: to images, faces, landmarks and features that convey political ideology, form and outlook. The work of culturalist Albert Boime is instructive in this regard. For Boime, key images, and for him especially monuments, convey very precise idealistic standpoints about America, its past and its political culture.

> Those who attempt to control the nation's history through visual representations as well as through texts are regulators of the social memory and hence of social conscience [he says]. In learning about the original history of our national monuments and icons, Americans can come to understand that the democratic rhetoric surrounding them has been manipulated for political purposes.[22]

In Boime's mind, then, iconography is ideology; and it is a powerful tool in sensory perception for the viewer and scholar. In fact, the historical origins of this intercourse, as Boime makes clear, stretch well back into the past, and its extended relationship has served to make iconographic representation a mainstream tool of artistic movements and discourses. Indeed, it has long been the province of America's cultural elite to deconstruct the effigies of American exceptionalism. One only has to think in artistic terms of painters like Robert Rauschenberg or Jasper Johns to appreciate the perpetuation of this tradition. Rauschenberg borrowed the image of John F. Kennedy during the 1960s and 1970s for use in paintings like *Retroactive* and *Signs*, while Johns's series of works centred on the Stars and Stripes interrogated notions of nationalism and symbolism, but within a clear visual template. Indeed, the critic Robert Hughes went as far as to describe the devotion of Johns to the national flag as an 'aesthetic, not patriotic' sentiment: a deconstruction of formalism that is very comparable to the political imagery at work in Hollywood films.[23]

It is not just symbolic forms of identification, however, that Hollywood has used to link scenes of the White House, the Washington Monument or Capitol Dome to a representation of American politics. In Hollywood's language, these structures really do tell the story of America's democratic heritage, and thus literal as well as metaphoric dimensions of discourse sit neatly side by side in the most famous of cinematic presentations.

High up on that list of presentations is certainly *Mr. Smith Goes to Washington* (1939). Made at a time when the malignant effects of the Depression were still painfully raw, and on the edge of a global conflict that would force Americans to re-evaluate their place in the world, Frank Capra's much-vaunted political treatise celebrates liberty, communalism, common sense and love-thy-neighbour rhetoric. In other words, *Mr. Smith* celebrates a vision of American politics that of itself celebrates America. Capra's hero, Jefferson Smith (James Stewart), is chosen to go to Washington to replace one of his state's favourite sons, the recently deceased Senator Sam Foley. Embarking on a trolleybus tour of the capital as soon as he arrives, to see the sights and hear the sounds of the nation's seat of government, Jeff ultimately finds himself – as so many movie politicians have – on the steps of the Lincoln Memorial. The grandeur of Henry Bacon's architectural style and Daniel Chester French's imposing sculpture of the man embody the very essence of iconic symbolism; but what Smith, and through him Capra, are really drawn to is the education of the young boy, accompanied by his grandfather, and followed by the black man who takes off his cap and listens while the child recites the Gettysburg Address on the inside south wall of the monument. The memorial is thus a place of learning as well as worship, something it later proves to be for Jeff also. The boy could go home and read the address in any history book, but being there *is* history, a time and place where the young and impressionable can be at one with those who shaped the direction of the nation. Yet remarkably, what the Lincoln Memorial did for *Mr. Smith* as a film is slight compared to what *Mr. Smith* did for the Lincoln Memorial as a landmark of political reverence. From this moment on it overwhelmed the space for iconic structures, helped along the way by John Ford's use of the monument at the close of *Young Mr. Lincoln* in the same year as Capra's offering, itself a homage to D. W. Griffith's brief presentation at the close of *Abraham Lincoln* (1930) nine years earlier. The former two movies, at least, established the memorial as the pre-eminent site of political affiliation for Americans, even though at this point it was only seventeen years old, having been dedicated as recently as 1922 by Warren Harding. But in Capra's film, it was given the appearance of a monument much older than that. It looked as if it dated far back in time and encompassed within its walls and columns the principles held by Lincoln and his forebears: those who had fought to bind the nation together back in the 1860s, as well as those who had been present at its birth.

For Capra, the focus on the Gettysburg Address at the memorial was also an inbuilt recognition of the nature of the political principles carved literally and figuratively in the imagery of the picture. Capra recognised the need to reinforce 'text' with 'iconography of text', and implicitly to take on board the debates in society concerning the reality and the perception of ideas and principles. *Mr. Smith Goes to Washington* thus created a framework upon which, as Eric Smoodin has argued, the audience were offered not only an aesthetically plausible democracy but also a guide to the rigours of good citizenry.[24]

But it is not only the doctrines underpinning *Mr. Smith* as an aesthetic and ideological piece of work that have stood the test of time in political movies down through the ages; the impressionistic connotations of the film's title and, by implication, its central character, have also been subject to renewed application over and again. Allen Roston has written of 'Mr. Carter Goes to Washington' in equating the Smith persona with the former President, who also saw himself as a kind of Horatio Alger-like figure, coming from the wilds of Georgia to clean up Washington.[25] In Lauren Berlant's analysis of a more contemporary cultural phenomenon, she picks out the *Simpsons* episode, 'Mr. Lisa Goes to Washington' from Season Three, as especially significant, proof for her that the 'activity of national pedagogy' is alive and well, building upon elements of Hollywood's classical history, and finding a reception even in the ironic world of contemporary TV culture.[26] Mimicking Capra's template, Lisa Simpson wins a competition to go to Washington only to uncover corruption and scandal at the heart of power.

Capra's film therefore acts as a dual conduit both for the perceptions of democratic theory that it translates through its imagery and symbols, and for the patented logo of politics that has become inbuilt into the title of the picture and the representation of the principal character. From then until now, Hollywood has attempted to build upon this construct of democracy; it has tried to infuse its output on politics with a sense of history, to proffer a democratic tradition that it claims has no equal. In other words, it has attempted to offer its own version of exceptionalism and manifest destiny.

Back in the 1930s this ideological conviction was critical for a nation that had begun to suspect that, in the face of the Depression, its great democratic experiment might be washed up. Political films during the decade countered this in a way that was part triumphalist, part nationalistic, but almost wholly recognisable as a fragment upon which the edifice of American history had been built: only one reason why Abraham Lincoln cropped up in so many of the features of the time. Even by the 1950s, when any portrayal of political life could be interpreted as a codified attack on American values in the era of HUAC and Joe McCarthy, Hollywood could still allow for a re-examination of the early life of another 'great' president, Andrew Jackson, in Henry Levin's *The President's Lady* (1953, and further discussed in Chapter 5).

So each decade, from the 1930s onwards, has followed almost precisely the same formula of encrypting democratic patriotism within familiar symbols, and has thus constructed a formula for reception and appreciation that few other art forms have been able to touch. But that reception has been crucial in negotiating the way audiences have perceived their political culture to operate. As already stated, and alluded to by a number of scholars, even in the harsh climate of the 1930s, political or social consciousness cinema was often unpopular at the box-office, rejected in favour of escapism from the worst privations of the time.[27] Brian Neve even suggests that films, especially in the second half of the decade, had 'little political or social relevance' for audiences or critics.[28] Box-office statistics certainly support the notion that political films rarely did as well as the staples of westerns, musicals and even gangster pictures. But, as I argue in Chapter 2, Hollywood, while well aware of the financial constraints, nevertheless clearly recognised the political implications of having to support and condition audiences to believe that democracy and America's institutions could survive the present crisis. For that reason it is important to note not only how many political films actually got made, but also why they continued to be produced in an industry where the economic rationale was almost always the first consideration.

Mr. Smith Goes to Washington was one political movie that actually *did* do extremely well for Capra and his studio, Columbia Pictures, in 1939, as befits the most critically and commercially acclaimed director of his generation. It followed a spate of his pictures coming out of the Columbia backlot during that decade that were as socially aware, and popular, as *American Madness* (1932), *Mr. Deeds Goes to Town* (1936) and *You Can't Take it with You* (1938). Amassing takings of more than $3 million in America despite scathing attacks from the establishment (see Chapter 2), *Mr. Smith* remains one of the most commercially successful political movies of all time, and was only surpassed at the box-office that year by *Gone with the Wind*. This fact alone helps to explain why the film has been a template for all manner of political movies as well as ironic animated comedies that have followed in its wake.[29] Capra's 1948 film, *State of the Union*, for example, was in many ways a more recalcitrant and vital examination of politics at the time, but was far less popular and today remains comparatively marginalised in the director's canon.

Likewise in the 1990s, two of Hollywood's most conspicuously light-hearted fables, *Dave* (1993) and *The American President* (1995), did far better at the box-office than the satirical and caustic *Bob Roberts* (1992), directed by Tim Robbins. Popularity and audience reaction are, of course, reliant on a number of factors, but it should come as no surprise to learn that Ivan Reitman's and Rob Reiner's films, unlike Robbins's, contained heavy chunks of symbolic political iconography enveloped within rousing choruses of music and popular patriotic sentiment, no better evidenced than in the opening title sequence to *The American President*. Here, pictures, busts, documents and ephemera pass before the audience's eyes, all enveloped within a patina of stirring music and iconic identification of America's most redoubtable leaders, and broadly only these leaders. The concurrent history this opening title sequence tries to parade, therefore, is not so much a brief potted résumé of presidential succession, so much as a negation of those figures (the Filmores, Arthurs, Coolidges and Tylers) who did not belong in such illustrious company as the cohort on display. What these two films also did in the 1990s was to pay homage to the 1930s screwball cinematic tradition, and update that tradition for contemporary audiences wanting to feel better and more comfortable about their political system once again.

So within these more modern political films of the late twentieth century, it became ever more important to consider nostalgia in the context of iconography, the way Hollywood's own past has been built upon, and re-imagined for contemporary audiences. Postmodern theorists like Fredric Jameson have written of the uses of nostalgia in Hollywood and also considered the way surface or reconstructed cultural icons have contributed to the postmodern condition of 'depthlessness'.[30] Critics such as Christopher Lasch have further warned of the dangers of 'nostalgia culture' for the modern era, an argument that bears some comparison with Warren Beatty's use of the Stars and Stripes as a backdrop to key events in his satirical electoral movie, *Bulworth* (1998).[31] Nevertheless, these arguments deserve and invite a number of responses.

The first is that certain forms of mythic idealisation within Hollywood's history are nothing new. Many of the 1930s films harked back to previous, kinder, reverential eras as much as recent movies have, though granted not with the knowing reconstruction of a cinematic tradition to play with. The second issue is that while Jefferson Smith, along with Dave Kovic, Andrew Shepherd and, more recently still, Josiah Bartlet and Tom Dodds (Martin Sheen from *The West Wing* and Robin Williams in *Man of the Year*, 2006, respectively), are identifiable political figures for the audience because they are in fact the type of politician voters really would like, it should come as no surprise that their words, deeds and actions are in fact composites of long-standing heroes of the American scene in the first place: Kennedy (John and Bobby), FDR, John Glenn, Jack Kemp, even Clinton and latterly Obama. Like their fictional counterparts, these are all people who have benefited from name recognition, heroic status or positive personality traits, and/or from the realisation that style and image matter at least as much as, if not far more than, content and ideology. Did they influence Hollywood visions of an approach to personal campaigning and political governance; or, over time, did Hollywood influence them? As the Obama example outlined in the Introduction shows, in the twenty-first century both angles seem true. Commentators like Allan Lloyd Smith have talked of the 'element of spectacle' involved in American politics and about politicians' desire to create 'scenarios of power and ideology', a sign of the way Hollywood and Washington have increasingly morphed together.[32] As Mark Wheeler further suggests, 'the relations between Hollywood and politicians have been a two-way street as the political classes have realised that stars can help them to appeal to a wider constituency.'[33] This is a scenario that dates back at least as far as the 1960s too. Reflecting on election movies like *The Best Man* (1964) and *The Candidate* (1972), Phillip Davies and Brian Neve comment that, 'just as politicians must become celebrities in order to gain power, so celebrities are halfway to becoming politicians; indeed in a country lacking a debate about public philosophies, style may be everything.'[34]

In short, Hollywood has been acutely susceptible to recognising the media and connecting them to the source of all political messages and personalities in this modern age. In films of the 1930s, the press and radio could be prescribed a detached focus whereby they merely conveyed the ebb and flow of political currents, typified by the presence of earnest fictional reporters in movies like *Gabriel Over the White House*, and the hand of real-life press legends like H. V. Kaltenborn addressing the nation triumphantly but objectively in *Mr. Smith*. But with the rise of television, and now global communication networks emanating from the internet, the media are an intrinsic and integrated part of the political process, not just an observer, a player in the game the public witnesses on their TV and computer screens but seemingly participates in less and less. In Hollywood terms, the rise of fictional media figures goes hand in hand with the real thing; for every Tom Dodds (Williams is a chat show host in Barry Levinson's movie) on film, there is a Fred Thompson or an Arnold Schwarzenegger in real life. Film – Hollywood, American cinema more generally – has also become an integrated source of discourse for the political culture that in some respects now cannot match the thread of events that take place in the real world. Nevertheless, as the argument here is at pains to point out, Hollywood is not, and never really has been, solely about replication and presentation; it is about examination and application. Hollywood exists to legitimate the dominant institutions of the nation state as well as their value systems, an observation Michael Ryan and Douglas Kellner made some time ago in their analysis of the changes in film after the 1960s.[35] How and why that legitimation continues to prosper, and the form in which it does, are the themes of the following chapters.

NOTES

1. Terry Christensen and Peter J. Hass, *Projecting Politics: Political Messages in American Films* (New York: M. E. Sharpe, 2005), pp. 7–10.
2. These two categories in Christensen and Hass's typology, 'auteur political movies' and 'socially reflective movies', both tend to sublimate the political or ideological message through directorial concerns with particular subjects (the environment, history, particular crises or controversies) or by reflecting on socially grounded subjects that are really quite distantly removed from any political character, institution or geographic setting – notably Washington DC (Christensen and Hass, p. 11).

3. See Dan Nimmo and James Coombs, *Mediated Political Realities* (New York: Longman, 1983).
4. Richard Maltby, *Hollywood Cinema* (Oxford: Blackwell, 1995), p. 362.
5. Michael Coyne, *Hollywood Goes to Washington: American Politics on Screen* (London: Reaktion, 2008), p. 19.
6. One might refer to other works published subsequent to the first edition of this book that either have linked Hollywood and politics together, or else have spoken at some length about pure political movies. These include Mark Wheeler, *Hollywood Politics and Society* (London: BFI, 2006); Daniel P. Franklin, *Politics and Film: The Political Culture of Film in the United States* (Oxford: Rowman & Littlefield, 2006); Beverly Merrill Kelley, *Reelpolitik II: Political Ideologies in '50s and '60s Films* (Oxford: Rowman & Littlefield, 2004); Peter C. Rollins and John E. O'Connor, *Hollywood's White House: The American Presidency in Film and History* (Lexington: University Press of Kentucky, 2005).
7. Tom O'Brien, *The Screening of America: Movies and Values from* Rocky *to* Rainman (New York: Continuum, 1990), pp. 16–20.
8. Barry Langford, *Film Genre: Hollywood and Beyond* (Edinburgh: Edinburgh University Press, 2005), pp. 4–6.
9. Phillip L. Gianos, *Politics and Politicians in American Film* (Westport: Praeger, 1998), p. 7.
10. Gary Younge, 'Israeli Consul Attacks Spielberg's *Munich* as "Problematic"', *The Guardian Unlimited*, 12 December 2005. At the time this represented only a small fragment of the debates about the film that were filling the media. Spielberg himself, having previously stated that he wished to let the film speak for itself, then reluctantly backtracked and gave a telephone interview to renowned critic Roger Ebert in which he defended the events and principles in the movie. See Karina Longworth, 'Spielberg Defends *Munich* . . . but is the "Controversy" for Real?', *Cinematical*, 26 December 2005 at: http://www.cinematical.com/2005/12/26/spielberg-defends-munich-but-is-the-controversy-for-real/.
11. Daniel Franklin, *Politics and Film: The Political Culture of Film in the United States* (Oxford: Rowman & Littlefield, 2006), p. 6.
12. 'Editorial, Debating Politics at the Movies', *Cineaste*, vol. 31, no. 2, Spring 2006, p. 4.
13. Terry Christensen and Peter J. Hass, p. 288.
14. Locke's *Second Treatise on Government*, published in 1690, became the work that was to dominate American thinking in later generations. It took its influence from Hobbes's *Leviathan*, published in 1651, and Harrington's *Commonwealth of Oceana* in 1656. See Kenneth M. Dolbeare, *American Political Thought*, 2nd edn (Chatham, NJ: Chatham House, 1989), pp. 19–20.
15. Daniel Franklin, p. 21.

16. Louis Hartz, *The Liberal Tradition in America* (New York: Harcourt Brace, 1955).
17. Andreas Hess, *American Social and Political Thought* (Edinburgh: Edinburgh University Press, 2000), p. 44.
18. J. R. Pole, *The Pursuit of Equality in American History* (Berkeley: University of California Press, 1978).
19. Quoted in Jon Roper, 'A Democratic Polity?', in *Democracy* (London: Hodder & Stoughton, 1994), p. 30.
20. Richard Maltby, *Hollywood Cinema* (Oxford: Blackwell, 1995), p. 361.
21. Dominic Sandbrook, *Never Had it So Good: A History of Britain from Suez to The Beatles* (London: Abacus, 2006), p. 626.
22. Albert Boime, *The Unveiling of National Icons* (Cambridge: Cambridge University Press, 1998), p. 9.
23. Robert Hughes, 'Behind the Sacred Aura', *Time Magazine*, 11 November 1996, pp. 104–6. See also Albert Boime, p. 3.
24. Eric Smoodin, '"Compulsory" Viewing for Every Citizen: *Mr. Smith* and the Rhetoric of Reception', *Cinema Journal*, vol. 35, no. 2, Winter 1996, p. 3.23.
25. Allen Roston, 'Mr. Carter Goes to Washington', *Journal of Popular Film and Television*, vol. 25, no. 2, Summer 1997, pp. 57–67.
26. Lauren Berlant, 'The Theory of Infantile Citizenship', *Public Culture*, vol. 5, no. 3, Spring 1993, pp. 395–410.
27. See, for example, Phil Melling, 'The Mind of the Mob', in *Cinema, Politics and Society*, ed. Philip Davies and Brian Neve (Manchester: Manchester University Press, 1981), pp. 21–4.
28. Brian Neve, *Film and Politics in America: A Social Tradition* (London: Routledge, 1992), p. 2.
29. Joseph McBride, *Frank Capra: The Catastrophe of Success* (London: Faber & Faber, 1992), p. 424.
30. Fredric Jameson, *Postmodernism: or, The Cultural Logic of Late Capitalism* (London: Verso, 1991).
31. Christopher Lasch, *The True and Only Heaven: Progress and Its Critics* (New York: Norton, 1991), pp. 82–119.
32. Allan Lloyd Smith, 'Is there an American Culture?', in *Culture*, ed. Richard Maidment and Jeremy Mitchell (London: Hodder & Stoughton, 1994), p. 307.
33. Mark Wheeler, *Hollywood Politics and Society* (London: BFI, 2006), p. 139.
34. Philip Davies and Brian Neve, p. 16.
35. Michael Ryan and Douglas Kellner, *Camera Politica: The Politics and Ideology of Contemporary Hollywood Film* (Bloomington: Indiana University Press, 1988), p. 1.

Chapter 2

POLITICAL FILMS IN THE CLASSIC STUDIO ERA

> People . . . All of them coming to Washington to get something.
> Why doesn't anybody come to Washington to give something?
> B. G. Brown in *Washington Merry-Go-Round*

The stock market crash on Wall Street in October 1929 changed the United States forever. The ensuing Depression created an era as enriching and vibrant culturally as it was shattering and despondent economically. Historical evaluations ever since have dictated that, in the aftermath of the crash, President Herbert Hoover's response only deepened the crisis at hand, condemned the Republican Party to electoral ignominy, and heralded the arrival of America's saviour: New York Democrat Franklin Delano Roosevelt. Roosevelt's election victory in November 1932 certainly initiated the beginning of a political era the nation had never witnessed the like of, but whether Roosevelt 'cured' the Depression, or indeed whether Hoover was appropriately cast as the villain he seemingly was, has become a source of much greater debate and anxiety amongst historians over the years. 'Hoover was not heartless,' asserts Michael Heale, even if he tended to convey a sense of indifference.[1] Michael Parrish goes even further and takes the clichés, apocryphal stories and songs about the President that circulated at the time and retranslates them for the modern age as distance and perspective have taken a hold. As a result of this re-assessment, Parrish notes, unlike his immediate predecessors, that 'Hoover's reputation has grown with the passing of time. Most scholars now reject the idea of his culpability for the economic collapse of 1929–32.'

But even here, Parrish admits that, while there were initiatives, there were also 'serious limitations', not least Hoover's contempt for other politicians and his retreat into a 'fantasy world, where soothing words were used to paper over the accumulating evidence of disaster' as the Depression intensified.[2] Hoover also just happened to have to campaign against, and then give way to, a man who went on to become one of America's most charismatic leaders of all time.

Fronting an administration that treated communication as a policy tool, Franklin Roosevelt's presidency in particular, and the New Deal in general, became an exercise in pragmatic and, often, dispassionate political management, rather more than the complex Keynesian economics it was linked with, which Roosevelt only vaguely comprehended and largely disavowed. Instead he reinvigorated public faith in political institutions, and he did so with what Phil Melling describes as a 'theatrical style' of presentation in public, but especially on radio and film. This style not only generated a sympathy and support for his presidency but kept more dangerous, reactionary forces at bay too.[3] 'Roosevelt delighted in the open exercise of his personal political skills,' confirms Tony Badger, suggesting how quickly the President understood the need to assert character, style and rhetoric as a political tool in his fight to win over the masses whose support he desperately needed for the schemes on offer from his administration.[4] Politically though, whatever the presentation looked like, Roosevelt's revolution was in fact a much quieter affair than initial summaries allowed for. It was a steady, unrelenting, but more or less conservative reformulation that, as Carl Degler explains, 'purged the American people of their belief in the limited powers of the federal government and convinced them of the necessity of the guarantor state'.[5]

The debate over Hoover's legacy, the rise of FDR and the sea change that took place in American politics in the worst years of the Depression were and are just as important for an appreciation of Hollywood too. They were crucial because the crisis and subsequent election brought into office a leader who knew all about publicity, self-promotion and the means of using the new communications media. But the film industry's contribution to the portrayal, assistance and interpretation of the new politics and society Roosevelt was forging – that was contained in a series of movies made during the decade – was equally pertinent as a signal of the way cinema was becoming a galvanising social and political mechanism that increasingly worked alongside clever political exponents like the President.

Yet when one thinks of the 1930s and the establishment of the classic Hollywood studio era, ideological and social commentary might not be the first thing that springs to mind. This was, after all, the decade of Garbo and *Queen Christina*, of screwball comedy, of classic Marx Brothers movies, of horror and musicals, of Cary Grant, Gary Cooper and John Wayne, of Bette Davis, Joan Crawford and Vivien Leigh. It was an era of lavish spectacle and imaginative faraway worlds, of *Gone with the Wind* and *The Wizard of Oz*.

But Hollywood was also maturing politically and socially in these years as an industry and as a community. A decade that started with D. W. Griffith's biographical portrayal of Abraham Lincoln ended with perhaps the definitive political movie of this or any other Hollywood age: Frank Capra's *Mr. Smith Goes to Washington*. Both films showed that Hollywood was no longer afraid of tackling outright political subjects and/or reliving key moments in the nation's history. Both films told the tale of America's political experiment as it had unfolded since the formation of the republic, but they did so from very different cinematic and ideological positions. One was serious, portentous and historical; the other smart, comedic and modern. But the evolution of these different genres, which coalesced into what we generally term 'political films', was another important signal of Hollywood's determination to regale its audiences with tales of contemporary and/or historic significance, as well as to challenge any overbearing imposition of restriction and censorship of its products.

Outside interference as well as self-regulation had begun early, though. In 1915 the Supreme Court had effectively stated in the *Mutual Film Corporation v Ohio* ruling that the movies did not have the protection of the First Amendment to the Constitution. They could not say whatever they liked, and furthermore they had to be purveyors of ideas and events already in the public domain, not a mouthpiece for their own visions and values.[6] The National Association of the Motion Picture Industry was the self-regulatory arm of this early reach for control that signed up its patrons to rules of taste and decency even before government could leap in. Under its president, William A. Brady, the association introduced its Thirteen Points in March 1921, point nine of which called for the need to avoid stories which 'ridicule or deprecate public officials, officers of the law, the United States army, the United States navy or other governmental authority, or which weaken the authority of the law'.[7]

Later legislation such as the Hudson and Neeley–Pettingell anti-trust bills hammered home this mantra of responsibility and morality upon the studios who had been assuming wider control of their product on screen and off it, and notably attacked their monopoly practice of block-booking within theatres. Indeed, as Richard Maltby reports, an average of 250 bills per year were being introduced across the United States between 1925 and 1940 that aimed to censor or restrict the industry in some fashion.[8] But it was under the later Motion Picture Producers and Distributors of America (MPPDA), headed by former Postmaster General Will Hays, that the censorship of Hollywood's emerging political interest would be subject to most challenge. The Los Angeles office, which effectively ran the code from 1930 until its demise in the 1960s, was known as the Breen Office after its administrator Joseph Breen, who was responsible for the liaison and direction of the industry through the provisions of the more strictly enforced code amendment, the Production Code Administration (PCA), from 1934 onwards. Each individual studio entered into its own dialogue with the PCA and many had created their own regulations to serve as strictures on their personnel, directors, writers and producers in any case: a development that Hays himself had talked of as more desirable than forcing the need for intervention from outside authority at every turn.[9]

It was also true that the Code did not include anything quite as specific as the old National Association amendment that referred to political institutions directly. But it did talk of morals and decency and respect for authority in almost every clause, although this ultimately did not stop many directors and writers from gaining an eye for controversy and subject material that they knew would be politically provocative, relevant and maybe even disturbing for the Breen Office and others. While the Code focused a lot of its early attention on sex and religion, however, the rise of sub-genres like the legalistic or courtroom drama, the popularity of gangster pictures, and most especially the emergence of a small but significant number of Depression-focused films paved the way for the more overt political settings and characters to follow, which then evolved still further as the decade progressed towards the quintessential construction of the political movie in the hands of a cinematic master like Capra.

Even allowing for these larger-than-life personalities who occupied often larger-than-life films throughout the decade and were amazingly popular with audiences, and despite the restrictions on its output that only emphasised how successful and potentially influential the movies were, it is important to recognise that Hollywood was still by no means immune to the economic collapse going on all around it. In 1931 and 1932 both RKO and Paramount studios were put into receivership, and Warner Bros, by now one of the biggest of the majors, lost a combined total of $22 million in just two years, having been in profit to the tune of $24 million during 1929–30.[10]

He was not the sole reason, but Franklin Roosevelt's forging of a relationship with the movie industry after 1932 did pave the way for a remarkable recovery in the fortunes of these and other industry insiders. Even though Jack Warner was the only mogul willing or able to come out in support of the President during the election campaign – taking out a full-page advertisement in *Variety*, the movie trade paper, on one occasion – Hollywood and Washington went on to join hands anyway and enter into an *entente cordiale* that lasted all the way through to the other side of the Depression and the end of the war that followed. 'Together they metaphorically sang and danced through the decade, echoing each other's ringing declarations of confidence and pointing to each other as inspiring symbols of recovery from past troubles and optimism for the future,' notes Colin Shindler.[11] For Kevin Starr, the film industry was a haven of protection if not education for what he calls a 'recently derusticated' population now exposed to the harsh realities of urban and economic life. 'Hollywood helped stabilise the nation by offering intensities of psychological release,' he notes.[12]

There are scholars, however, who are wary of placing too much emphasis on the decade as the instigator of an era of cultural and political consciousness being generated in film audiences who took this relationship as their cue to become politically engaged and vocal. Melling is not at all convinced, for instance, that 'political' movies had enough box-office clout during the decade to make much of a difference to wider public opinion. And Maltby further argues that the studio moguls were often no more than simplistic artisans who ravaged history for the most effective stories and commercial ways to represent America's populist tradition, only then giving it a slightly refined cultural identity.

Yet whether they were commercially successful or not, whether the moguls had a deep-seated political agenda or otherwise, films with political themes, often centred on Washington, did go into production in greater numbers. And whilst these projects may have appeared populist or even escapist in tone, pervasive democratic ideas did seep though their storylines and infiltrated their dialogue and visual spectacle in a concentration sufficient to engage public consciousness and liberate political thought from the shackles of a hitherto rigidly self-imposed Hollywood regulation.

Indeed, the attention afforded audience reception in recent scholarship has revealed a public whose capacity for social and political drama was far more exacting than previously thought. As Eric Smoodin notes in his study of official distribution, exhibitor and fan correspondence with regard to Frank Capra in particular, reaction to a movie like *Mr. Smith Goes to Washington* did not just alert people to the workings of the political process; it opened debates among audiences about the whole efficacy of American democracy.[13] Smoodin makes the very salient point that today and in most recent accounts of Hollywood where *Mr. Smith* has been a part of the undisputed list of great American films, its interpretation as a political text has been 'absolutely unproblematic'. Like Norman Rockwell's paintings, Steinbeck's literature and Jimmy Stewart's 'star' persona, it appears quintessentially to inhabit a '1930s American school of representation', suggests Smoodin.[14]

But back when the film first appeared in 1939, that consensual opinion was nowhere to be found. Members of the federal government were dumbfounded at its presentation of them and their chamber, yet the film started to feature in high-school debates about ethics and citizenship. In addition, the style of American democracy that it put on display was caught up in discussions over the premise, presence and promise of what the republic could deliver, as seen through the lens of the 150th anniversary celebrations (1937–9) of the ratification of the Constitution. As Smoodin concludes, to top it all, no other production from the era researched for its reaction from exhibitors – who were always required to fill out comment and questionnaire sheets about the movies being shown in their theatres – or from audiences – who sometimes filled these out too and/or wrote in, many of them to Capra himself – garnered as much comment as this film. 'It is a mark of the special reaction to *Mr. Smith* that many of the entries run [to] several hundred words,' he says.[15]

Of course, *Mr. Smith Goes to Washington* became one of the great American films because it achieved what many other political movies of that and every subsequent era have admittedly struggled with; it meant lots of different things to lots of people, but it meant *something* to everybody. It was also made by a studio that, up until the mid-1930s, had not been a major player on the Hollywood backlots but which, largely thanks to Capra's endeavours in tandem with a select few writers, did power its way into the company of the majors. That studio was Columbia Pictures and its reputation for taking chances with social and political material should not be easily discounted for its influence and originality. As Bernard Dick remarks:

Capra helped establish a policy that Columbia implemented during the 1930s; it was a policy that combined ingredients that had worked individually and might work even better in combination. If topical movies succeeded at Warners and marital romps at Paramount, Columbia would make marital romps with a social dimension.[16]

It was in that spirit of social conscience, political engagement and, yes, economic reward that an established 'major' like Warner Bros influenced Capra and Columbia by trying to extract some of that social interest from their audience too. They thus added dollops of tension, excitement and verve to their own productions throughout the decade, especially the gangster movies, courtroom narratives and social melodramas that made their name in this era.

Only four months into Roosevelt's Administration, Warners' production of William Wellman's *Heroes for Sale* set the tone for their interest in a strident, uncompromising manner. Richard Barthelmess plays Tom Holmes, a World War One veteran whose heroics in France have not been recognised and who returns to America scarred mentally and physically by his experience. Hooked on morphine, Holmes nevertheless finds the love of a good woman (Loretta Young) and makes a go of his life until the Depression sinks him, his plans and the future into serious despair. Wellman's uncompromising, pre-PCA Code agenda deals with the downtrodden and dispossessed in no uncertain terms, to say nothing of the brutal violence and drug addiction which would be topics at best camouflaged in, if not entirely absent from, even the meatiest of melodramas within a few years of the Code's higher-profile instigation. Perhaps the graphic nature of the picture surprised and repulsed critics and viewers alike, because the film had moderate reviews and pretty poor box-office on its release. Despite this, its reputation has not only survived but has also had new life breathed into it as time has gone by, and the movie today stands as a signal of the studios' intent at the time, and the determination of some not to be deflected entirely from the economic conditions outside movie theatres.

Russell Campbell's assessment of *Heroes for Sale* actually downplays the entreaty to social action. Indeed, Campbell argues that what Wellman's film really achieved – even for those who did not see it but knew of its existence – was the start of an initiative that moulded public perceptions about society at large and began to, in Campbell's words, 'forestall any radical sentiment among the dispossessed'.[17] It preached patience for the measures being enacted, in other words, rather than wholesale change of the system. When King Vidor's *Our Daily Bread* followed up some of the themes and ideals of Wellman's picture only a year later, it was nevertheless clear that some filmmakers *were* willing to challenge the precepts of economic and social thought, and even question the ideological doctrines upon which America itself functioned. If the Depression was this bad, if hopelessness abounded, then was American democracy under threat and failing its populace as well, the movie hinted? It tells the story of a farming couple, John and Mary Sims (Tom Keane and Karen Morley), and their battles to work and irrigate their land, and Beverly Merrill Kelley links the film with decidedly left-wing aspirations. 'The romantic idealism of universal equality that initially drew adherents to communism', as she puts it, was an on-going theme that Vidor himself trumpeted. 'It glorifies the earth, it glorifies helping each other,' he said of the movie.[18]

These and the more overt political movies that circled them stopped short of challenging the robustness of the whole system in quite as bullish a manner as Vidor might have implied, as we will see, but the emerging 'social problem film' did at least explain why, in Peter Roffman and Jim Purdy's words, 'a hungry and insecure audience needed the psychic relief and rejuvenation of entertainment films but also demanded that filmmakers give at least token recognition to the ever-pressing realities of the time'.[19]

It would be wrong to get carried away and perceive the studios as political neophytes who were all of a sudden converted to the cause during these years. Many parts of Hollywood did remain wary of taking social responsibility on board, or feeling that they were in any way obligated to participate in some kind of crisis management at large in the country. But if the studios appeared to remain steadfast in their resolve not just to become propaganda arms of a wider institutional movement that wanted to restore confidence and belief in democracy, individual filmmakers and writers were aware of the changing dynamics of social thought and political ideology. They were also aware that influential writers such as John Dewey had already subjected the notion of community to rigorous examination and forcefully argued for public participation in moving the 'Great Community' on towards a 'Great Society', as Dewey called it. Here was the essence of democracy in his eyes: the widespread participation and interaction of the public in social and organisational functions of the state.[20] It was, of course, a blueprint in many ways for the New Deal to follow.

Richard Maltby therefore describes the service that some studios and a few filmmakers entered into as 'restrained respectability' for society and the democratic system.[21] That might open the door to interpretations, if not accusations, of populist sentimentality in the films that were made, a recollection of times past that was shrouded in mystical reverence and which tended to ignore the most pressing problems at hand. In truth, the distinction that emerged in the set of films and with the particular filmmakers described below was more about a working definition that tried to distinguish between ideology and practice, between the practitioners of policy and the overarching ideas of history and nationhood. In short, the line Hollywood pursued was that the Depression and the crisis at the heart of American democracy – if that was what is was – were more the fault of individuals than they were fundamental flaws in the system itself. And time after time, goodly heroes come to the rescue of that system, so much so that the narrative form employed by such a storyline became a model that became particular not just to 1930s political movies, but to films in the genre across the ages.

In the first instance, however, Hollywood's dive into the political maelstrom was neither a commercial godsend nor a fully-fledged ideological investment. Political awareness initially raised its head, not just with the films described above, but in other genres too, notably the gangster film, as already intimated. The notion of federal power, and of in-fighting at local and state level amongst political machines, gave an authentic tone to *The Public Enemy, Little Caesar* (both 1931), *Scarface* (1932), and later *G-Men* (1935) and *Angels with Dirty Faces* (1938). The latter two movies also signalled a twist for Hollywood as the decade wore on, switching their focus towards authority and the reinstatement of law and order rather than the glamorisation of the hoodlum's lifestyle, as the earlier films had at least perceived it.

As the decade progressed, the effect of the early hard-hitting gangster pictures – which had been a revelation for audiences unused to such violence and behaviour on screen – wore off to some degree, and films across the board were more apt to reinforce the status quo than to present anything quite so radical. Hollywood as an industry too, despite the unionisation of the town and the procession of especially left-wing writers through its midst, reasserted a much more conservative, some might say reactionary, outlook, best exemplified by an attack on one of said writers, Upton Sinclair, and his bid for the governorship of California in 1934.[22]

Sinclair, author of the best-selling and politically influential *The Jungle*, had grown increasingly interested in representative politics during his career and had already twice stood for Congress on the Socialist Party ticket before he founded the EPIC (End Poverty in California) movement. EPIC became the rallying cry and manifesto for Sinclair's attempt to win the 1934 contest, when he stood on the Democratic Party platform and won the primary that year by a healthy margin. Not only Republicans, however, but moderate Democrats too were appalled by Sinclair's 'socialist' philosophy and he was in effect excommunicated from the official party in the run-up to the vote as many fell in behind moderate third-party candidate, Raymond Haight.

Demonised as a free-thinking, communist sympathiser with all manner of crackpot ideas, Sinclair had a vague plan to let the homeless and dispossessed of the Mid-West settle in the state of California, and this was the cue for Hollywood to become involved. He was famously condemned in a series of short films – shown in theatres – that certain industry patrons had concocted themselves; actors were hired to play the part of 'hobos', who citing Sinclair as a man who would help them, just like they did in Russia.[23] The Chair of the California Republican Party, which secured the election of incumbent Frank Merriam on the back of this assault on Sinclair's character – no small feat with the New Deal under way and the Republicans in electoral free-fall – was none other than Louis B. Mayer.

Despite all this, Sinclair secured 37% of the electoral vote in 1934, and if that figure had not been split by the strong showing of Progressive candidate Haight (who captured a respectable 13%), he might have won. The experience told at least two stories. One was that California did have the stomach for more radical politics and different approaches to the Depression, some of which was reflected in films of the time and subsequently. The second point, though, is that this first assertion was tempered by a reaction from the studios, who were determined not to have any radical or (what they saw as) subversive thought infiltrate the backlots; the moguls' view on this especially restricted a great deal of the political engagement that might otherwise have spread more forcefully in these years. Indeed, it was the emergence of influential filmmakers backed in no small part by the authority of the newly established Screen Directors and Screen Writers Guilds during the 1930s that allowed for something of a battle of wills to take place and for political ideas and narratives eventually to flourish in small pockets of the Hollywood studio system. Sinclair's campaign might have been

doomed from a long way out, but its reach and influence for galvanising thought and ideas should not be under-estimated in any manner.

At Columbia, a good example of the toing-and-froing that was
beginning to occur was manifest in Frank Capra and his writers, who
were about to emerge as part of that cohort embarking on a defining
series of socially informed political movies. During 1934, however, the
tyrannical head of the company, Harry Cohn, erected a 'Merriam fund'
barometer in the commissary during the heated gubernatorial campaign, to which every employee was expected to contribute. It was a
sign of their emerging authority – in this studio environment at least
– that Capra and his chief writer, Robert Riskin, were powerful enough
to argue openly with Cohn about the ploy; but they also knew that the
majority of their colleagues had contributed. Out of fear or belief, it did
not matter. Hollywood was now entering into a period of brokering
and delicate negotiations about the kind of material that might go up
on screen. The result was films where the heroes became the guard-
ians of American democracy, alongside the Founding Fathers and the
Constitution; never allowed to become revolutionaries who might tear
down the walls of the sacred palaces, their mission was to vanquish
the powerfully corrupt and venally evil. The words, sentiments and
doctrines of American political thought therefore infuse all of the pictures discussed below; and if, as Hollywood opined, the heroes could
ride in and out of town in time to rescue their honour and fall in love
with the heroine, that did not disguise the fact that the documents of
the republic remained their bible of faith. In essence, the political films
of the 1930s reflected the Roosevelt transformation in politics but they
were also about to become the template for the way the genre has
operated cinematically from that day till this.

INSIDE THE CORRIDORS OF POWER

In its 1932 review of James Cruze's film, *Washington Merry-Go-Round*,
the magazine *Photoplay* described a story that 'tears the veil from conditions in this country' and added that its director 'hammers home
his truths with brass knuckles'.[24] The film created quite a stir when
it was released in America barely a month before the presidential
election was due to take place. Columbia Pictures had purchased the
rights to the title only of a best-selling 1931 novel by popular journalist Drew Pearson and Robert Sharon Allen. The studio then hired
leading screenwriter Maxwell Anderson to write a treatment based

almost exclusively on that title, which subsequently became the basis of Cruze's film. Anderson's story, then scripted by one of the studio's outstanding scribes of the time, Jo Swerling, was transformed into the tale of a crusading ex-serviceman recently elected to Congress, who comes to Washington to root out the bribery and corruption that he sees generated through the political machine that controls his home state. Thus the controversy over *Washington Merry-Go-Round* not only arose from the timing of the piece but was also inherent in its content, characters and ideology. It was a potent mix that, as *Photoplay* intimated, exposed the seedy interior of Washington politics at a time when audiences were looking for reassurances from their politicians that the country would survive the Depression and the institutions of state would not collapse around their ears. Swerling and Cruze, however, concocted a scenario that, on the surface at least, threatened to do all these things and more. Here was a political story with romance and some little comedy, but also ample amounts of deceit, subversion and ideological contention.

Button Gwinett Brown (Lee Tracy) is elected to Congress from an undesignated state with all the history and knowledge of politics that will help him root out the corrupt practices of the political machine in his state, which are, in his words, 'strangling us with bribery'. Brown meets Alice Wylie (Constance Cummings) on the train to Washington via a humorous confrontation in which she comes across a valuable family heirloom that blows into her carriage. The piece of paper is one of only three priceless letters confirming Button Gwinett as one of the signatories of the Declaration of Independence, hence reaffirming Brown's lineage and crusading zeal; Alice tears it up, thinking it nothing more than some casual bit of litter.[25]

Their paths cross again in Washington, as Alice turns out to be the granddaughter of the esteemed Senator Wylie (Walter Connolly), an old-style patrician figure of the upper chamber. This confluence of characters is linked by the relationship Brown and Wylie establish. Brown comes searching for an old friend, Carl Tilden (Wallis Clark), who already works in government as a prohibition official, but he shockingly discovers that Tilden has committed suicide right on the eve of Brown's arrival and delivered a letter to the new congressman containing evidence of the corruption and bribery that have forced his desperate act. Wylie is a friend of the rich and influential Edward Norton (Alan Dinehart), who has business and political interests in Washington and abroad. Norton, it turns out, sponsored Tilden's appointment and then compromised him by bribing him to conceal the extent of Norton's power and duplicity. Tilden's confrontation with Norton at the film's opening, when he declares his intention to reveal the extent of the businessman's influence in Washington, thus provokes his suicide and the chain of events that leads Brown to Norton. Wylie, little knowing it at the time until Brown later reveals the truth, is also being bribed by Norton, albeit surreptitiously every time they play cards together socially. Norton meanwhile has every intention of marrying Alice and making her his 'queen' of Washington.

These various plotlines are brought together when Brown is laughed out of the House during one of his initial speeches for protesting against a corrupt piece of legislation, the Digger Bill, which is nothing but graft for Norton and his cronies. Discovering the murky facts behind the Tilden case and Norton's part in it and then being confronted by the blatant poisoning of Wylie by Norton's henchman in his office, after the aging senator has also accepted the truths concealed behind his regular card-playing activity and threatened to expose Norton, Brown hatches a plan. He enlists the help of his old service buddies, who are in town appealing for their bonus to be paid – a real-time/life comparison to the actual bonus army and Hoovervilles being set up in Anacostia Flats in the summer of 1932 literally as the film was being shot.

Brown and the men collect the evidence over a series of days and then apprehend Norton, taking him to Anacostia and divulging their knowledge of the insider dealings, manipulation and racketeering that the business tycoon has been authorising in Washington. Once finished, Brown offers Norton the same alternative as that given to Tilden at the beginning of the film: face the ignominy of exposure and jail or take a different path. 'Oh, and that's your gun,' remarks Brown, pointing to the open drawer of a table as he leaves Norton in one of the camp's tents during the final, climactic scene. 'The one Tilden killed himself with . . . and it's loaded.' Norton's last act closes the scene and the film as Alice, having resisted the charms of the bullying businessman, falls into the arms of her crusading hero Brown when the fatal shot goes off.

If Cruze was aware of the nature of his ambiguous hero and Brown's tacit acceptance of 'an eye for an eye' in the conclusion, where Norton's own suicide is at least some kind of retribution for his friend Tilden's death, then the director does his best to disguise this salutary lesson by hiding it away within the greater monuments of Washington. Brown constantly reinforces his link to Button Gwinett as a signatory of the Declaration of Independence; the United States Capitol Building is a pervading backdrop throughout the film; and barely a scene goes by without Brown pontificating in front of the document at the National Archive, standing up on the floor of the House to denounce legislative bills filled with graft, and solemnly contemplating his actions at the Lincoln Memorial as he resolves to expose Norton and bring the whole Washington merry-go-round to its knees. The iconographic intent is therefore very carefully registered throughout the film and it should come as no surprise that – coming as it did from the pen of a friend, Swerling, and being produced at the studio where he resided, Columbia – Frank Capra was so taken with the movie as to make it a template for the kind of political story drawn out nearly seven years later in *Mr. Smith Goes to Washington*.

But, just like the later, better-known and better-received Capra picture, the under-rated *Washington Merry-Go-Round* also created one further precedent that became the bane of political movies from here on in: how to resolve the ending. Norton's suicide seems a convenient full stop for the plot and Brown and Alice are brought together by both the death of her grandfather and Norton's demise. But Brown has been suspended from the House; the film implies that graft and deceit are endemic, not just reserved for one power-hungry individual; and the passing of legislation like the corrupt Digger Bill, as well as being the controlling force of a political machine the like of which sent Brown to Washington in the first place, as he himself confesses, appears unresolved and unbroken by the conclusion. Contemporary reviews in publications like *Photoplay*, as well as the *Cinema Booking Guide Supplement* in Britain (where, interestingly, the film was given a more literal title, *Invisible Power*), acclaimed the movie for its 'finely fluid direction' and Lee Tracy's 'vigorous and likeable performance' as Brown.[26] But they were reluctant to engage with the premise that the film did not really provide many answers as to how the quite legitimate institutional and social problems that it marked out were to be solved; only that the bad guy gets his comeuppance in the end.

Washington Merry-Go-Round was released barely weeks before the November 1932 election that brought Franklin Roosevelt to power, and did respectable business. Only a few months before, however, the MGM studio had already tried out the template of melodrama within a political setting with the Lionel Barrymore vehicle, *The Washington Masquerade* (later known as *Mad Masquerade*), directed by British-born Charles Brabin. Barrymore plays Senator Jefferson Keane, a widower

recently elected to Congress. Keane becomes involved with a scheming 'vamp', Consuela Fairbanks, played by Karen Morley; surprisingly,
he resigns from office, giving up the desperate quest for re-election
funds for the love of his faithless new wife, in order to keep her in the
luxury to which she has become accustomed. In a finale where Keane
admits his personal and professional errors, as well as financial impro-
priety, to a Senate hearing, he implies that which is problematic and
failing the American people overall: namely, greed and intransigence.
But the film is about relationships and about men in particular falling
for the wiles of attractive and irresistible women, as much as it is about
the machinations of Capitol politics, and its conclusion can only really
deliver redemption and closure in Keane's personal resolve rather
than any institutional re-adjustment. *Washington Masquerade* might
have provided the jumping-off point for *Washington Merry-Go-Round*'s
setting, but the few short months separating the release of the two
pictures showed how far Hollywood was now willing to go to cast a
spotlight purposefully on the social and institutional problems at hand.

If these early forays into the corridors of power were not yet ready to
contest the underlying issues at the heart of the Washington system,
a picture was already on the way that would open the door to more
controversy and questions. In 1933, *Gabriel Over the White House*,
directed by Gregory La Cava, made a new case for harder and more
discursive political commentary within Hollywood and was not afraid
to court publicity and notoriety along the way. To begin with, its overall premise was that contemporary social dislocation, crime and poverty in America could be cured with a very profound shift in political
authority: that by extending the powers of the President nearly as far
as dictatorial rule, organised crime and even reckless foreign policy
agendas could be averted or even swept away entirely.

A review of the time from *Cinema Quarterly*, with perhaps a nod
towards the Barrymore film from the year before, proclaimed that
'It marks a deliberate breakaway from the comparative trivialities of
individual romance and a concentration of attention on the social and
political problems of the day.' The review notes that the issues are
often dealt with in a superficial manner but, from a 'Hollywood [that]
is often justifiably knocked for the piffling products that come from its
studios, here is surely an occasion for admiration of aim, if not to the
same extent of achievement.'[27] In fact, *Gabriel*'s success and the generally positive notices of the time belie a movement in film circles which
was already beginning to take shape by the time the picture arrived in

theatres in early 1933. In the pages of *Hollywood Spectator*, for example, the paper's editor added to the clamour for La Cava's movie but said also that the 'success of *Gabriel* does not justify the craze for pictures dealing with timely topics'.[28] By craze, the editor no doubt meant principally *Washington Merry-Go-Round* and *The Washington Masquerade* too, implying that this moderate number of political texts was on its way to becoming a flood and that they had become the talk of critics' circles as well as studio boardrooms.

La Cava's picture sees Judson Hammond (Walter Huston) elected as President with the help of an omniscient political machine identified as such in the initial scene of the film: the inauguration party held in the White House. 'Thanks for those votes from Alabama,' comments Hammond. 'Wait till you get the bill for them,' quips one of the political cronies who have helped the new President's career thus far. The President cannot thank his campaign manager and now Secretary of State, Jasper Brooks (Arthur Byron), enough for getting him elected. Don't mention it, he replies; 'by the time they realise you're not going to enact any of your campaign promises, your term will be over.'

Thus defined by the 'party's' corrupt and cynical manipulation of the process, Hammond falls into a routine whereby he simply enjoys the office for the sinecure it is. His more idealistic assistant, Beekman (Franchot Tone), and personal secretary, Pendola Molloy (Karen Morley), attempt to encourage greater ideals in him. But he sees the Depression, bootlegging and gangsterism as 'local problems', as he informs the assembled press at his first news conference. 'Can the president be quoted?' asks one of the hacks. 'The president may not be quoted,' retorts Hammond, and the scene is set. Nothing is on the record, Hammond sees himself as a pawn of the party, power resides elsewhere and he pointedly ignores the pleas of the leader of the self-proclaimed 'army of the unemployed', John Bronson (David Landau), who demands action from the White House in a live radio address. While the broadcast is heard in the background, Hammond continues playing with his young nephew, oblivious to the undercurrent of tension and despair in the nation at large.

In political terms, this opening puts Hammond squarely in the camp of Hoover Republicanism, at least as it was perceived at the time. States' rights are key, is the suggestion, the federal government is limited in its scope, and the Depression will cure itself 'with the spirit of Valley Forge, Gettysburg and the Argonne', as Hammond so succinctly puts it. Then a miracle occurs. Hammond takes his high-powered motor car for a spin and has a near-fatal accident. As he lies in a coma flirting with death, the Archangel Gabriel visits him and provides the chance for redemption in the few brief months of life afforded by the spiritual visitation.

At first seemingly zombified by his impossible recovery, Hammond nevertheless acquires previously unknown levels of resolve and sets out to cure the ills of America. His cabinet are less than convinced by this about-face so he sacks them, Beekman suddenly and inexplicably becomes a military commander in a domestic army/police unit, and Hammond moves to suspend Congress because the threat to the country is so grave he cannot waste time negotiating the passage of bills. He unites himself with Bronson and the army of the unemployed, and critics were right to liken some of Hammond's actions in this passage of the movie to the coming of the New Deal. And for March 1933, when the picture was finally released, it does seem remarkably prescient of the months to come. Hammond lays out a policy of welfare and job creation, and is determined to end the practice of bootlegging that is so crippling the country in the era of prohibition.

But it is in Hammond's personal confrontation with leading gangster Nick Diamond (C. Henry Gordon) that a departure towards something more dictatorial, threatening and even totalitarian begins to be made. Writers Bertram Bloch and Carey Wilson, together with director La Cava, constantly frame the battle with Diamond as a confrontation testing the righteousness of the American cause and positioned in relation to its history and traditions. Diamond is invited to the White House, whereupon he mocks the bust of Lincoln, is looked down upon by a picture of Washington, and is generally made to feel insignificant set against the totems of American history and politics. Hammond unambiguously threatens him as an 'immigrant' who has been invited to America rather than as a 'citizen' on the make, and one who is looking to exploit the American Dream rather than live it. So the pursuit of Diamond after he declares 'war' on the government is thus ruthless and without remorse. Andrew Bergman provides a point of comparison for the adoption of a paramilitary-style police unit in the film, mentioning George Hill's *The Secret Six* (1932), which appeared at nearly the same time as *Gabriel*; in the former film, civic leaders assume masked identities and suspend 'due process in the name of crime-fighting'.[29] Even so, the justice meted out in La Cava's story is stinging and noticeably symbolic. Once the hoodlum and the remnants of his gang are captured, a kangaroo court led by Beekman tries and sentences them;

they face a firing squad in Battery Park, New York, presumably so that an image of the Statue of Liberty can be framed in the background and so rationalise the actions in the foreground, providing yet more solid credentials for America's divine pedigree.

As if this were not enough, in a tacked-on third act, Hammond proceeds to bring all the world's leaders to Washington and preach to them about their responsibilities for reparations after the Great War, condemning their renewed build-up of arms less than a generation on from that terrible conflict. By using new planes that can attack and bomb from the air, Hammond puts on a show of force and has some mothballed ships blown out of the water, which encourages the assembled leaders to accept the President's idea of a Washington covenant and a form of 'peace in our time'. Later, as the covenant is signed and Hammond, now weak and drawn, manages to scrawl his name on the document, he collapses and, a few moments later, passes away. The period of redemption is over, Gabriel visits one more time and Hammond is ethereally whisked off to the heavens. In less than ninety minutes, Hoover, Roosevelt and Wilson have all been evoked by the fictional chief executive come to save America in its darkest hour.

While the heavenly sub-plot is fantastical, the foreign policy coda to the film is at least reminiscent of the thinking of the time. Just as B. G. Brown in *Washington Merry-Go-Round* speaks to the veterans' camp about his service in World War One while questioning whether 'any of us knew what it was all about', so Hammond taps into a mood prevalent by the early 1930s in an America that felt disillusioned by the nation's involvement in European affairs fifteen years beforehand and was resolved never to fall into the same trap again. John Pitney's excellent reading of the film positions the utopian world peace ideals at the end as a counterpoint to the, in effect, fascist principles that are espoused in many other parts of the picture. Because fascism had no use for the sort of peace and responsibility for which Hammond implores the other leaders, suggests Pitney, it acts as a deliberate ploy to rein in the implications of Hammond's wide-ranging domestic clampdown.[30]

But *Gabriel*'s good intentions, even on Pitney's generous reading, leave the audience with as many questions as answers at the end. What is to stop another figure like Hammond being put up by the party machine? What worth had a document like the Washington covenant in a world where fascism was once again on the rise? And, as Roosevelt assumed power, was the film really asserting that martial law was a plausible answer to America's problems? This somewhat restless and mixed ideological message was in part the product of its creators. Producer Walter Wanger, described by Terry Christensen and Peter Hass as the 'major auteur' of the movie, and later involved in further political projects like *The President Vanishes* (1934) and the Spanish Civil War movie, *Blockade* (1938), was decidedly pro-Roosevelt; while fellow newspaper tycoon, producer and alleged script-writing contributor to the foreign diplomacy section of the movie, William Randolph Hearst, was much more sympathetic to the emergence of strong-willed leaders in Europe.[31] It was Hearst's film company, Cosmopolitan Pictures, that provided much of the finance to enable the completion of the movie and much of his will that allowed the film to overcome censorship and, at one point, to resist being shelved altogether.

The original release date for *Gabriel* was put back two months after the attempt on President-Elect Roosevelt's life in Miami in January, which uncannily resembled the assassination attempt on Hammond in the film which sees assistant 'Pendee' shot in the lobby of the White House itself. The Hays Office unsuccessfully urged for the scene to be cut, while Louis B. Mayer as head of MGM thought the picture would be nothing short of catastrophic for his company. In a bid to circumvent some of the criticism it thought the movie would inevitably receive, MGM had the original 1 hour 40 minute running time that was shown to preview audiences cut back to eighty-six minutes, omitting some of the exposition and a few of the more violent gangster scenes.

Nevertheless, as both Pitney and Christensen and Hass allude to, the studio need not have worried quite so much. In the end, the film was much talked about, yes; but considered incendiary, no. *The Nation*'s review of *Gabriel*, for example, which seemed to incline the film towards an unequivocal plan for dictatorship to solve the Depression, is, as Pitney intimates, one of the few that was overstated.[32] And as if to confirm the dilution of the message, the film proved to be one of the hits of the season for MGM with audiences who were probably not yet ready to tear up the theatre and have fascism imposed, but who nevertheless liked Hammond's style and Walter Huston's strong-willed portrayal of him. Wanger's guiding hand and his judgement of the movies led to him being given a further stab at political topics the following year, with the much more prototypical anti-fascist movie, *The President Vanishes*.

Against the background of a coalition of 'big businessmen, corrupt politicians, and fascist Grey Shirts plotting to drag the United States into a war in Europe', Wanger and director William Wellman adapted Rex Stout's novel about a president, Stanley Craig (Arthur Byron once more), who arranges his own abduction to sidestep the impending fascist takeover of his government because he will not accede to war.[33] With Edward Arnold playing the duplicitous Secretary of War and with support from Paul Kelly, as well as a very young Rosalind Russell, *The President Vanishes* still allows for romance and melodrama to occupy almost as much space as ideological contemplation, but Wanger at least was prepared to augment conventional storylines with a more assertive feel for contemporary political problems and debate. The Roosevelt renaissance was by now under way and Hollywood had not entirely missed the boat when it came to sorties associated with themes and ideas of the day. Producers like Wanger, writers such as Swerling, and directors like Wellman and La Cava had agendas that were more inquisitive and prepared to take more risks with political material than the era is sometimes associated with, and the political movie was creating a small but significant niche for itself among the film rosters.

A small but notable collection of political and social movies therefore engaged with, and presented to their audience, some of the most unprepossessing aspects of the Depression at the start of the 1930s. The industry's critical and commercial champion in this regard was only just getting started with some of these topics as *Washington Merry-Go-Round*, *Gabriel Over the White House* and the other pictures arrived. Yet his moment was at hand, and critically as well as commercially he was about to change the face of political subject matter and the way it was accepted in Hollywood forever.

SYMBOLISM, ICONOGRAPHY AND THE MOVIES OF FRANK CAPRA

The Washington Masquerade saw politics played out in terms of desire and duplicity as much as it was in terms of power and persuasion. In *Washington Merry-Go-Round*, B. G. Brown rallies and directs his disciples to rise up from their wasteland in the veterans' camp, and to reject their lot in life as well as the dictatorial hand of Edward Norton. In *Gabriel Over the White House*, Judson Hammond is redeemed by the ethereal presence of the Archangel Gabriel, who teaches him not just to confront his own mortality but also to practise a new kind of political statesmanship for a new kind of era. Directors like Brabin, Cruze and La Cava thus initiated the portrayal of a particular style of communal activity in their political movies, entreating the populace to become aware of their democracy, revere the documents that had created it, and actively seek to influence its processes. No director, however, melded these ideals together with his own technique, nor revisited the sites of iconic devotionalism as many times, or as acutely, as Frank Capra did.

Capra's track record as a chronicler of the American condition in the 1930s and 1940s is unparalleled, and all the more impressive for a man who often insisted that his art was about comedy and entertainment far more than social and political immersion in the issues of the day. But, as Bernard Dick puts it: 'Capra could expand [a] film's social dimensions beyond the parameters set by the script – the result was pure Capra: a movie in which romance, social differences, political conversion, and the triumph of goodness coalesced into a myth of America.'[34] It was these constituent elements, together with a keen instinct for the effects of the Depression, and what at first appears to be a sympathetic eye for the ideals of Roosevelt's New Deal, that suffuse the narratives of his best films in this period, from *American Madness* (1932) through *Mr. Deeds Goes to Town* (1936) to *Mr. Smith Goes to Washington* (1939) and *Meet John Doe* (1941). Even the movies that are not often associated with this collection – *Lady for a Day* (1933), *It Happened One Night* (1934), *Lost Horizon* (1937) and *You Can't Take it with You* (1938) – have social, cultural and political themes in abundance that say as much as any other films of the period about the kind of place America was, and about the hopes and fears of its populace.

Each of the films helped cement the notion of a populist ideology at play in his work – sometimes a by-word for what some scholars called 'Capracorn' – and each paved the way for the classic triumph of lone, crusading individuals battling forces bigger and more ruthless than they could ever contain, but over which they still ultimately triumph. Indeed, it is some tribute to the power and influence of his films that Brian Neve goes as far as linking Capra's series of movies in the 1930s and 1940s with the 'populist tradition' itself, dating back to the 1890s and recorded in such classic social and political histories as *The Age of Reform* by Richard Hofstadter.[35] The victory of 'democratic man', as Glenn Alan Phelps further describes it, was therefore the vanquishing of the forces of wealth, power and megalomania immersed in the era's populist thought that became the ideological cup from which Capra and his audience drank during the dark days of the Depression.[36]

Frank Capra, Hollywood's leading filmmaker of the 1930s

Capra's background and upbringing were, of course, perfect for this ideological trajectory. Born in Sicily, raised in southern California, and the embodiment of the rags-to-riches story that so invigorated the American ideal, Capra worked hard to get to college, plied his trade in run-of-the-mill businesses and sought a break in the fledgling movie business for which he initially had few credentials. But make it he did, and the tenacity, common sense and gratitude for his lot in life and luck in making it to America often found their way into his most enduring characters. It was this that stuck with audiences and critics; the political dimensions could be read and criticised a number of ways, but the commercial viability of his movies always lay in public affinity with his characters' reasoning and rationale for their actions in life. It is a strain of construction in political movies rarely replicated as neatly as it was with Capra's pictures.

Capra had been at Columbia, a 'poverty row studio' with few prospects when he joined, for over four years when he teamed up with the writer and production crew that were to change the force and focus of his filmmaking. Up until 1932 his movies had, on the whole, been either broad slapstick comedies or daring action adventures. The comedy routine came from his association with the great silent comic, Harry Langdon, with whom he made two classic interpretations of the genre: *The Strong Man* (1926) and *Long Pants* (1927). But Capra and Langdon parted on acrimonious terms and for a while the director who had been given his break by the great Mack Sennett struggled to find a job in Hollywood. Then up stepped Harry Cohn and his go-ahead Columbia outfit. Cohn had ambition and was outrageously dictatorial at times, qualities matched only by Capra's own desires and assuredness. But the two of them – at least in the early years – forged a relationship that, while undoubtedly based on competition rather than compromise, nevertheless recognised and appreciated each other's qualities at the same time. As Neal Gabler puts it, 'Both were iron-willed and uncompromising. And if they were often like two immoveable objects, it was this very obduracy that created a grudging mutual respect.'[37] Capra's early pictures for Columbia were churned out at a prodigious rate – he made eight in 1928 alone – but he was slowly finding a style and pulling Columbia out of its lowly status along the way. With his action films *Submarine* (1928), *Flight* (1929) and *Dirigible* (1931) especially, he achieved the impossible feat of putting adventure in the air or below the sea, making it tense and believable, and doing it on a shoestring budget that amounted to next to nothing even in Depression-era Hollywood. A first-rank 'A' picture at Columbia rarely had a budget that topped $150,000. Cohn's envious glances at MGM, the studio he had designs on rivalling, told him that they were spending as much as $1 million on their leading productions in comparison.[38]

Nevertheless Capra's stock had risen enough in three years for the last of these sky-born adventures, the South Pole-set *Dirigible* with Jack Holt, Ralph Graves and Fay Wray, to open at the prestigious Grauman's Chinese Theater on Hollywood Boulevard. Premieres at large movie houses gave studios traction, especially if you were a studio that did not own a chain as most of the 'majors' did; so Columbia and Capra were finally on their way. As Charles Maland confirms, 'All [this] suggested Capra's growing confidence with the film medium, and the thematic concerns and moral issues are considerably clearer.'[39] The last two of the pictures also saw Capra team up and establish a working relationship with writer Jo Swerling, who would go on to pen *Washington Merry-Go-Round* for Cruze only a year or two later.

Swerling helped Capra to expand his repertoire by concocting more melodramatic stories such as the religious drama, *The Miracle Woman* (1931), and the downbeat relationship tale, *Forbidden* (1932), both of them starring the incomparable Barbara Stanwyck. But it was also Swerling who introduced Capra to the screenwriter who would change the dimensions of his films still further. Soon after he arrived in Hollywood, New York-born writer Robert Riskin added some dialogue to Swerling's script for *Platinum Blonde* (1931), a film that became Capra's biggest hit for Columbia to that point with the emerging Jean Harlow in the lead role. But by selling his own original story, 'Faith', to the studio and then seeing that the director assigned to it, thanks to a number of fortuitous coincidences, was Columbia's finest, Riskin made *American Madness* with Capra a year later and their partnership was set fair. Telling the tale of a well-intentioned and principled banker (Walter Huston) might have seemed risky in the midst of financial chaos, but the message of resolve and steadfastness in the face of calamity struck a chord with audiences looking for reassurance from and hope in their institutions and financial leaders.

When Huston's character Tom Dickson is faced with financial ignominy as a run on his bank takes hold – thanks to rumours circulating about its solvency after a robbery – and then has to confront his wife, who he believes to have been unfaithful with one of his employees, Dickson's world appears almost as hopeless as it was for the patrons watching the movie, struggling to feed their family and hold down a job. But he is saved by the will and loyalty of his customers, who are entreated back into the bank to deposit money by his loyal associates, bank teller Matt (Pat O'Brien) and secretary Helen (Constance Cummings), who phone everyone who knows and has been given credit by Dickson in the past. Struggling through a mob scrambling to take its money out of the bank, these customers save Dickson from closure, stopping the takeover that his partners are trying to instigate against him; the banker is reunited with his wife after the non-existent affair, which proves to have been a ruse of Cyril Cluett (Gavin Gordon), the bank's no-good gadfly who was caught up in the robbery as the 'inside man'.

American Madness has plenty of authority figures in its midst but no politicians. Its *mise-en-scène*, the huge, studio-encompassed set for the bank, was its arena, and within this are played out the trials and tribulations of American hope and confidence at the time. But it did set up patterns that would be vital to Capra's more overt political pieces further on down the line, notably the director's positioning of the masses within his stories. In desperation at the bank run that initially seems to spell disaster for Dickson and their investment, the board of directors accuse him of not listening to them and forever acting on trust and faith (hence Riskin's original title) when it comes to his customers. Dickson replies that none of them is thinking out there and that 'you can't reason with a mob' in any case: an early indication of Capra's interest in the manipulation and brainwashing of the wider populace. Just like the Bonus marchers in *Washington Merry-Go-Round* and the army of the unemployed in *Gabriel*, Capra portrays the effects of what might happen should the public become so desperate as to heed the words of rumour and innuendo and then act as one. The masses come back to haunt his best films, therefore, not least the electors of Jeff's home state in *Mr. Smith* who believe machine boss Jim Taylor before they believe Jeff about the graft and deceit in Washington; and the mob who find out the truth about Long John Willoughby at the baseball stadium rally in *Meet John Doe*. Indeed, the bank run scenario and mob mentality were such a scorching metaphoric image for Capra that he repeated the trick almost intact for the run on the Bailey Building and Loan in his most enduring picture, *It's a Wonderful Life* (1946).

Following on the success of *American Madness*, *Lady for a Day* and the runaway Oscar-winning success of *It Happened One Night* followed in 1933 and 1934 respectively, the last winning Capra his first Academy Award for directing and Riskin the only Oscar of his career for writing. But it was after a brief hiatus caused by a mystery illness that afflicted Capra in 1935 that the two really planted the seeds of the social and political ideas they were to bring to some of the defining films of the era. Riskin's adaptation of Clarence Budington Kelland's short story, 'Opera Hat', told a seemingly heart-warming and, again, reassuring tale. But *Mr. Deeds Goes to Town* (1936), as it was renamed, was so much more than merely heart-warming; it really mapped out who and what America was and aspired to be in 1936. Its themes rang out through the ages, so much so that nearly half a century later Ronald Reagan would quote from the film as a representation of his own philosophy and principles.[40]

Capra and Riskin had two key elements working perfectly in tandem in their films by this point, as Maland explains: 'One reason for the success of *Mr. Deeds* is the engaging narrative pattern, but another reason, closely related, is the implicit value structure endorsed by the film through Deeds.'[41] That value structure was, for a long time, fundamentally associated with Roosevelt's own political philosophy. It was perceived to be about community, helping each other, working for and on behalf of the state for the betterment of the nation. But Capra was not the New Dealer Riskin was. Capra was not even a fan of FDR, despite a couple of brief meetings between the two in the coming years, including a lively press conference in the Summer of 1938 when Capra was in Washington scouting locations for *Mr. Smith*. In fact, he went out of his way to vote for Roosevelt's Republican opponents in four successive presidential elections.[42]

This revelation, therefore, slowly but surely attuned critics to the idea that a somewhat ingrained moderate conservatism was being played out in Capra's films from *Mr. Deeds* onwards, rather than some kind of progressive liberalism. Quoting the likes of Jeffrey Richards, Richard Griffith and Raymond Durgnat, who have discussed the Capra philosophy, Brian Neve further elaborates on this contention by stating that Capra's form of populism focused on that which backed individuals against the force of organisation; and in Capra's eyes there was no bigger force than the monolithic New Deal, which was creating a federal government behemoth the like of which America had never seen before.[43]

By this reading *Mr. Deeds* was not about a humble rural artisan (Longfellow Deeds, played by Gary Cooper), drawn to the big city by a family inheritance which he is suspicious of and does not really know what to do with. The importance therefore does not lie in the movie's pivotal moment when, after a dramatic confrontation with a poor farmer (John Wray) who invades Deeds's mansion with a gun and who is sick of Deeds's face appearing in the newspapers all the time because he keeps doing ridiculous stunts ('who feeds doughnuts to a horse when there are people starving out there?'), Longfellow proceeds to give away his fortune in what seems to be a redistribution scheme largely akin to certain New Deal alphabet agencies in Washington. No; the film by this interpretation becomes about individualism raging against the system. Deeds is pursued by 'shyster' lawyers each and every step of the way; he is detained in an asylum and condemned as unfit to make decisions; he is hounded by the press and duped by ace reporter Babe Bennett (Jean Arthur). All of this attacks his liberty and sanity, as though he is no longer fit to exist in a modern society where conformity is the norm and odd or exuberant behaviour is frowned upon. For Capra and Riskin, then, these were reflections of the modern world, a world that is a lifetime away from the traditions of the recent past, which still seem to be embedded in Deeds's home town of Mandrake Falls. Longfellow thus realistically represents, for Neve and the critics he cites, an embodiment of middle-class individualistic values that are disappearing fast from Roosevelt's America.

The film therefore not only established a more concerted attempt on behalf of Capra and Riskin to investigate the forces at work in modern American life; it also prompted thoughts that something more contentious and problematic was occupying the minds of its creators. That did not stop them reconciling Longfellow's common-sense decency with a triumphant conclusion to events, however. Despite facing the prospect of long-term detainment in a mental asylum as lawyer John Cedar (Douglass Dumbrille) attempts to wrest the $20 million fortune that Deeds has inherited out of his control by declaring the 'pixilated' simpleton insane, Longfellow wins the day in his court appearance where, agonising over his defence, he finally speaks up for the common 'fella' and wins the heart of Babe Bennett.

The triumph of innocence and common sense prevails and Capra and Riskin were energised still further by the reception of and acclaim for *Mr. Deeds* and the movie's perfectly judged narrative arc. Their 1937 adaptation of James Hilton's story *Lost Horizon* – the only time they attempted to put a full-scale novel on screen – was thus turned into the most ambitious project Columbia had ever undertaken. With lavish sets and daring action, the film cost $2 million to make and barely turned a profit in the end. But the duo's fascination with the mythical world of Shangri-La set deep in the Himalayas, and the essentialist philosophising that was included in much of the original cut of the movie (132 minutes, subsequently scaled back to 118 by Harry Cohn) only emphasised their intention of making thought-provoking as well as entertaining cinema in the second half of the 1930s. A year on, *You Can't Take It With You* (1938) won Capra his third Academy Award for Best Director, and the film, starring Jimmy Stewart and Jean Arthur, unlocked more variations on the battle of the classes and the haves and have-nots in society that had been such a massive impulse for both writer and director since *Platinum Blonde*.

In 1939 Capra undertook his next film without Riskin but resolved to pull under his wing the final member of the trio of writers at Columbia who were progressive, politically minded and, in the case of Sidney Buchman, somewhat sympathetic to communism. Buchman adapted another short story for Capra, 'The Gentleman from Montana' by Lewis R. Foster, which became the basis for *Mr. Smith Goes to Washington*.

Like many of its antecedents, the film, while remaining an enduring classic, is often loved if not revered for its wholesome attitude and aspiration. Jimmy Stewart's rural idealist, Jefferson Smith, is naïve yet hopeful, antiquated yet eternally optimistic. His battle against the forces of political power in his state, his exposure of the corrupt practices of his once admired friend and fellow senator, Joe Paine (Claude Raines), and his against-the-odds filibuster that climaxes the picture are often invoked as classic dimensions of the way political narratives work in Hollywood movies. Indeed, for Beverly Kelley the film summarises much of the populist philosophy that Neve and others have remarked on as running through Capra's canon. But Kelley is also somewhat suspicious of what this all means and whether it is as complimentary to Capra and the movement as it sounds. She reminds us that populism had plenty of reactionary elements, wrapped up for some in the murkier notions of financial and business conspiracies as well as anti-Semitism. Kelley actually ascribes a lot of anti-theories to Capra (intellectualism, media, government), some of which were associated with the populists, and which she only sees militated against by the patriotic symbolism that envelops *Mr. Smith*.[44]

If Kelley is right to highlight something of a duality at work in the

Jeff Smith pays his respects at the Lincoln Memorial in Capra's iconic political movie

movie, this further reflects the picture's troublesome passage though the halls of the PCA. Joseph Breen thought Foster's story too incendiary in 1938 when it was first submitted to the Administration, only to change his mind a year later after accusations of censorship and restrictions of trade were starting to be thrown at him and government more generally.[45] Breen may have been more worried about causing offence to members of the Senate than he was about the subtle ideological premises at play in the film. Even so, for Kelley the crucial patriotic iconography that resonated so widely with audiences at home and abroad, and which is established in particular by the famous early montage sequence designed by Soviet émigré, Slavko Vorkapich, is about as perfect a piece of propaganda imagery as one is able to imagine. The Washington Monument, Arlington National Cemetery, Mount Vernon: it is these recurrent images and the site of the Lincoln Memorial especially that are the cornerstones of Capra's political platform for the film. When Jeff concludes the trolleybus tour that has been cinematically woven into the montage, he climbs the steps of the memorial and listens to a young boy recite the words of the Second Inaugural Address carved on one wall. A black man follows Jeff and looks up at the statue of Lincoln with respect and reverence. Jeff observes each character in turn, and his belief in the words and deeds of Washington, Jefferson and Lincoln as foundational elements of his life is confirmed by the scene and by others' belief in the rhetoric encased therein. It is also the clearest link back to the ideological association drawn out by Swerling in *Washington Merry-Go-Round* seven years earlier. When political machine operative Kelleher argues for Brown's 'selection' as the party candidate in that film, he talks of him 'reciting Washington and Jefferson, he's got star-spangled underpants'. Likewise, one of Taylor's sidekicks, Chick McCann, complains that his head hurts after the train journey to the nation's capital because Jeff has not stopped talking politics and leaders and history.

In a way, then, while the iconography is the stabilising factor that resonates so profoundly with audiences wishing to believe in America's fundamental principles, the link to populism is more of a regressive act for some scholars: a reminder of a bygone era that is long past but is hopelessly reinvoked in characters like Deeds, Smith and subsequently Long John Willoughby, who really should know better about how the world works and what politics means by the fourth decade of the twentieth century. Quoting David Thomson's view of Jeff Smith, Phillip Gianos even goes so far as to label Capra's heroes as authoritarians, Thomson seeing Smith as a 'tyrant, a wicked, folksy idiot'.[46] Even if such a critical position is fair, however, what is often less remarked upon, about *Mr. Smith* especially, is how dark a film it actually is at times in comparison to Capra's earlier efforts.

Following on from *Mr. Deeds*, where Longfellow rejects modernist impulses like the mass media (which have exploited him) and psychiatry (which allegedly determines his madness during the court hearings), some of the sentiments about the late 1930s world in *Mr. Smith* are equally acute. Capra's disillusionment with the leadership of Franklin Roosevelt and the principles behind the New Deal – which Kelley admits go somewhat against the grain of those populists keeping the flame alive by this time – is not so much a desire to reclaim the past as a recognition of the regulated, mechanised and, in Capra's eyes, authoritarian society to come. As he himself said of the President, 'I voted against FDR all along, not because I didn't agree with all of his ideas, but because I thought he was getting too big for the country's boots. I am passionately against dictatorship in any form.'[47] It is a recognition of power and will that was to find its natural time and place at the very beginning of Capra's next picture – *Meet John Doe* in 1941 – when the more overt elements of this darkened frame of mind manifest themselves. At the start of that film, a takeover of a newspaper, *The Bulletin*, is occurring and the paper's motto is being removed from the frontispiece positioned at the building's entrance. The words 'A Free Press Means a Free People' are being replaced by the *New Bulletin*'s slogan illustrating the significant and ominous progression of the modern world, 'A Streamlined Newspaper for a Streamlined Era'.

So the argument here suggests that Capra's politics and vision are neither as wholesome nor as sentimental as some would have it. And that alternative outlook is revealed early on in *Mr. Smith*. On the train ride to Washington, Jeff and Joe reminisce about the past and the subject of Jeff's father, Clayton Smith, arises. Paine recalls how Clayton was murdered by forces looking to close down his crusading newspaper, a crime that the close-up of the Senator hints Paine knew something of, even if he was not complicit in the act, the two of them having previously been partners. In addition, when Jeff tries to make himself useful in Washington by designing a bill for a boy's camp in his state, Paine warns him off with dire consequences should he stand in the way of 'Big' Jim Taylor (Edward Arnold) and his political machine. 'You're a boy in a man's world, Jeff,' cries Paine, pleading with him to give up his plans. When Jeff's young supporters try to help and assert

Jeff's honesty by printing special editions of his *Boy's Stuff* newspaper to sell to the voters back home, Taylor's hoodlums not only shut the press down, but also physically attack the boys without sentiment or remorse. Jeff refers to 'Taylor's armies' marching on Washington in his filibuster speech as though force and coercion are never far away in the minds of the controlling elite. None of these examples smacks of an easy prophecy about the way politics and society interact in the 1930s and underlying forces hint at Capra's prior influences as well as his contemporary fears.

The film's debt to *Washington Merry-Go-Round*, for example, is ever clearer to see. Jeff Smith is nothing like as tough and streetwise as B. G. Brown and he arrives in a Washington that, by the end of the 1930s, is not in as much turmoil as the earlier narrative displays. Nevertheless, in allying himself with a woman who knows the 'wilds of Washington', Jeff forges a relationship with the sassy but somewhat cynical Clarissa Saunders (Jean Arthur teaming up with Stewart again for the second time in a year) in just the same way that Brown pursues Alice Wylie. Saunders knows how congressional politics operates and knows that she works for a crooked political machine under the orders of Taylor. Giving him the nickname Daniel Boone, as if to emphasise his not only rural but also antiquated outlook on modern politics, Saunders sees something in Jeff that she remembers in herself, and when Smith is inevitably threatened by the Taylor machine once his Boys Camp Bill is revealed, she comes to his rescue by helping him devise the filibuster that she hopes will buy enough time to unravel the whole plot and expose Taylor and Paine.

Just as Brown realises how rotten the political show is when presented with the Digger Bill, so Jeff uncovers bribery, corruption and unseen personal traits as he comes to understand the Willet Creek Dam affair; the very plot of land he wants to earmark for the camp is the one that Taylor and Paine have got their eyes on for money-making, graft and, ultimately, the means to propel themselves towards the White House. Taylor is not as cartoonish as Norton in his evil intent, and Paine is certainly not as resigned to his patrician lifestyle as Senator Wylie in *Merry-Go-Round*, but the similarities survive. Taylor orders the state's newspapers to denounce Jeff as a fraud when the news of corruption breaks, in a manner as easy and assured as Norton's use of troops in South America to protect his business interests. Wylie takes a paternal interest in Brown to such an extent in the earlier picture that they could be his lines being uttered when Paine says to Jeff, 'thirty years ago I had your ideals; I was you. But I had to make compromises.'

But just as in the preceding film, conclusions are also hard to draw. Jeff's filibuster is a masterful piece of oratory that spans more than twenty-four hours and encompasses history, philosophy and interpretations of the Constitution. But by its dramatic conclusion he seems broken by the effort, as Taylor manages the press like the army Jeff warns of, and fake telegrams are brought into the Senate chamber as 'proof' that Jeff does not have public opinion on his side. That opinion is, in fact, 'Taylor-made', as Diz Moore (Thomas Mitchell), a member of the press and lugubrious friend to Saunders and Jeff, sardonically remarks.

Jeff collapses on the floor of the Senate, exhausted by it all. But Paine, seeing the reaction and shaken by Smith's commitment and, presumably, the expense Taylor has had to go to in order to close off the threat of exposure of their plans, races from the chamber, only for gunshots to ring out a second or two later. A very brief shot shows a colleague presumably attempting to stop Paine from committing suicide, only for the Senator to rage back into the chamber, claiming Jeff's proclamations to be true. Unlikely as it seems, the day has been saved and Saunders's banshee-like howl into the chamber below just as the credits roll almost confirms the unbelievable triumph of the people over the forces of institutional control. The convenience of the finale masks all sorts of questions again, though. Is the Taylor machine truly defeated at the close? What is to stop Taylor carrying on as a force in his state, with Paine sacrificed as a 'rotten apple' interested in personal glory? Why would Jeff's intervention necessarily prompt the other Members of Congress, as well as cynics of the press like Diz Moore, towards a change of heart about politics? What is supposed to happen to Jeff, who, like Brown, is on the verge of expulsion from the institutional body politic?

Capra did have an answer of sorts. A final scene – included, interestingly enough, in the trailer for the movie – has Jeff and Joe return home to their state in triumph, with Paine presumably redeemed at Jeff's insistence and untangled from the Taylor machine in which he had mistakenly and naïvely got caught up. At least, that is what is potentially on offer. But the scene never appeared in the final cut and, in fact, the questions and ambiguity that persisted at the close of *Mr. Smith* gave a signal, as already indicated, of the encroaching darkness that resulted in the final pre-war political effort on which Capra and Riskin joined forces for just one more time. Adapting another magazine short story, originally from the 1920s and called 'A Reputation', Capra and Riskin teamed up with Gary Cooper to make *Meet John Doe* (1941).

With the director and Riskin reunited on their own terms now as part of Frank Capra Productions rather than as the face of Columbia – where Capra's relationship with Cohn had finally been torn apart – *Meet John Doe* is really the high watermark of the social and political aspirations for which the pair strove during a decade-long collaboration. The two of them negotiated a distribution deal through Warner, Capra having rejected an advance from David O. Selznick, who was prepared to pay up to $200,000 a picture to secure the director's services – an unprecedented amount in Hollywood at the time. These studio negotiations are important for two reasons. One is that the strength of Capra's (and to an extent Riskin's) name in the marketplace consolidated the appeal of films that had consistently strong ideological dimensions proving the commercial worth of their political movies at least. The second point is that Capra craved even more independence to put his own stamp on even more strident texts, and *Meet John Doe* handily falls into that category.

But there is another comparative facet that reveals why Capra's new position in 1940 showed how far political movies had made their mark and how much he wanted to carry it further. As Thomas Schatz recalls, Capra's successful push for independence was contrasted against his contemporary John Ford's greater restrictions. Ford's *Young Mr. Lincoln* and his adaptation of Steinbeck's *The Grapes of Wrath* (1940) were hugely successful, but the last at least was cut and edited in post-production by studio head Darryl Zanuck. Ford admitted that Zanuck was good, but he also confessed that he was required to acquiesce to Fox's head of production as part of his deal at the studio. Ford effectively did not see the end product until it was being shown to preview audiences. The contrast with Capra was marked, therefore, as Schatz concludes: 'While Ford's pre-war career carried him from a position of relative independence to a restrictive period as a studio-based unit filmmaker, Capra's career at the same time traced roughly the opposite trajectory.'[48]

Capra won his freedom to make *Meet John Doe* as he pleased and on the face of it the movie has all the usual elements pertinent to his narratives: an 'ordinary Joe' looking to get a break; a ballsy, smart, female protagonist; a couple of wise old heads looking out for the hero; and a villain set on takeover, exploitation and power. None of this should be too surprising, for what Riskin and Capra were working with was a stage-play version of the original story that had been written by Capra's former partner, Jo Swerling. Swerling's 'The World is an Eightball' only really differed in one key respect, as Charles Wolfe observes; its central protagonist, Ferdinand Katzmellenbogen, is more like the kind of goofy, off-beat character that director Preston Sturges would most likely employ.[49]

And in the name change and the less satirical reading of the situation of a potential hero wanting to die in protest at the world's ills lay the roots of a darker and more disturbing commentary for Capra and Riskin. Where this movie differs from its counterparts is in the more contemptuous human traits on offer in all the characters, initially at least. Journalist Ann Mitchell (Barbara Stanwyck) is at first portrayed as money-grabbing and single-minded. She works to keep her job and is to be handsomely paid for the columns she writes in evil tycoon D. B. Norton's (Edward Arnold) newspapers. Editor Henry Connell (James Gleason) is 'hard-boiled', as he himself admits: a tough, uncompromising newspaperman who does not mind sacking people and is not interested in hard-luck stories. The Colonel (Walter Brennan), Long John Willoughby's companion, is apolitical and, as far as anyone can tell, amoral too. He does not think much of people, society or politics, and talks only of the 'heelots' constantly on the make. The Governor (Vaughan Glaser) is a wilfully ineffective politician who cannot stand up to the business interests in his state and is more concerned about the bad publicity that might come from a disillusioned citizen jumping off City Hall roof. Even Willoughby is only initially interested in the plan to make him a hero to ordinary people around America because he wants to get his busted arm fixed so he can play baseball again.

The characters did not appear, therefore, to make for the kind of heart-warming constellation of players for which Capra and Riskin were renowned, and commentaries of the time picked up on this state of affairs. Writing an open letter to Capra in *New Masses*, Herbert Biberman appealed directly to the director to consider the new film's dilemma in contrast to *Mr. Deeds* and *Mr. Smith*.

> In the two earlier films you began with the people [he wrote]. In *Meet John Doe* you begin with the fascist [meaning Norton]. In the former the people act, in the latter they are acted upon. In the former, they are observed from life, in the latter concocted out of theoretical confectionary.[50]

Biberman writes indeed as if Capra were in the business of testing political principles and American democracy outright rather than film-making; and he questions the tactic of both asserting that politics is a 'mug's game', a view which several characters do ascribe to, and wanting the people simply to re-establish a *status quo* in society, as though it were the last word on America's prospects for progress and equality, which he thinks is being lost in the film.

Biberman's outspoken entreaty to Capra is born, he feels, out of necessity. 'We in Hollywood have a tremendous responsibility to American history,' he implores in conclusion, but this comment alone cements the importance of Capra's film to the time and context of its making, whether the characters are believable or otherwise.[51] Biberman in effect feels the darkness here is all-pervading; central protagonists do not seem to care about politics, the most rational character appears to be the fascist Norton, and the masses are more interested in not rocking the boat than they are in chasing rights and values. His criticisms are not without foundation but that is the point. The real question is why Capra and Riskin should be drawn so far down this road as to make *Meet John Doe* as gloomy as it is, not whether it might send the wrong message. The narrative, further indecision about the ending, and the context of politics at the time help explain some of that dilemma in part.

Ann Mitchell is a victim of cost-cutting at the *New Bulletin* and is sacked, but as a last hurrah she writes a fake letter from an anonymous John Doe who states that he intends to jump off City Hall roof on Christmas Eve in protest at the evils of the world. The letter appears in her final column and, when readers see it, the city goes mad and the public clamour to know who this person is reaches mammoth proportions. New editor Henry Connell is forced to start a search – for Mitchell herself initially – only for her to confess to it all being a scam. She keeps her job, however, by selling the idea of 'hiring' a John Doe to play the part, make some speeches, write more letters and increase the circulation of the newspaper that has managed to grip the city's readership.

Owner D. B. Norton is taken by the idea as much as he is by Ann's charm, but when the circulation goes through the roof as predicted and people start spontaneously creating their own John Doe Clubs, Norton sees a further opportunity for which he has been waiting. Taking the credit for and leading the direction of the clubs, Norton visualises a way to propel himself into politics and make a run for the presidency. Here he has no intention of obtaining power and exercising democratic rights benevolently, though; he is only using this free and fair election as a stepping-stone to his permanent and enduring rule. 'There have been too many concessions made in this country, gentlemen,' he remarks to the assembled backers at a dinner towards the conclusion of the film. 'What this country needs is an iron hand.'

As the stooge John Doe, former Bush League baseball player Long John Willoughby realises that the people are serious about their clubs and the need to feel part of a community again. But when he finds out the truth about Norton and Ann's place in the scheme, he tries to convince the people at a night-time rally that they are being duped, only to be shouted down and hounded out of town. Finally, on Christmas Eve, Ann, the Colonel, Norton and members of a club from Millville that Long John has previously visited converge on the City Hall in the belief that their man will turn up to carry out the only symbolic action left to him: to jump off the roof as promised in the first letter just as the bells ring out for Christmas Day.

In setting the scene for the final climactic moments of *Meet John Doe*, a further ideological contemplation at work in Capra's films emerges. Indeed, this additional conceptual element links Capra and Riskin back to the other 1930s political movies discussed here. For there exists in many of the films the notion of what Phelps, citing *Meet John Doe* as its apotheosis, describes as 'Christian political communalism'.[52] Borrowing a phrase from Capra himself, Charles Maland interprets the later 1930s films as ones that reflected the 'ecumenical church of humanism'.[53] And Jeffrey Richards goes even further in equating all of Capra's principal protagonists as 'Christ figures', taking up the kind of position and responsibility that befall earlier characters.[54] In other words, the Capra heroes, not unlike B. G. Brown or Judson Hammond particularly, but also like Jefferson Keane or Stanley Craig more generally, are central characters who carry the weight of political authority with them, and do so often with strong religious principles and messages. *Gabriel Over the White House* is an obvious reference point, but for Phelps, narrative plays its part also. Characters go through epiphanies 'in the process of "becoming"', as he would have it, and villains are often the anti-Christ, men who believe not in faith or transcendent reality, but in secular materialism. For Phelps, secular materialism is individualism run amok, with no responsibilities to anyone or anything, only the pursuit of greed, materialism and power. It is, in his eyes, played out in the venal character of D. B. Norton in *Meet John*

Long John Willoughby contemplates his fate at the climax of Capra's Meet John Doe

Doe and rejected, as far as is possible, in the amoral character of the Colonel.[55]

Christian communalism, on the other hand, endorses social respon-sibility and the value of community, but these values are often discov-ered only as the narrative runs its course; this is why Phelps is so keen

to promote this film – and Long John Willoughby – as the poster boy
for such a theory. Willoughby's early pragmatism – get some food, fix
his 'busted arm', play baseball again – is slowly replaced by values and
beliefs that lock him into a philosophy that changes his attitude to
society. And one can see how and why Phelps would be keen to apply
this transformation to Capra's other political movies. In *Mr. Smith*, Jeff
is in awe of Joe Paine and all that a man like that can do for the people
of his state, until he slowly starts to learn the reality of Washington
politics. In *Mr. Deeds*, Longfellow acts as if, but also partly believes
that, his simple, honest-to-goodness outlook is enough to get him by
in any company, until he begins to realise that the big city is not the
rural hamlet of Mandrake Falls and that perceptions, affectations and
beliefs can come across quite differently to 'city folk'.

All this explains why the epiphany needs to take place in the narratives, but not necessarily how. For Phelps the answer lies in a number
of stories that again link the secular with the sacred. That is, the
heroes' transformation is accredited to words, deeds and actions that
return from the grave, pitched almost as the word of God itself. Long
John finds inspiration in the speeches his aspiring love interest Ann
writes, but her words are in fact her dead father's, cobbled from letters
he wrote to her outlining his most basic tenets and principles for his
daughter to follow.[56] Jeff's inspiration to fight on against the Taylor
machine in *Mr. Smith* and against his 'hero' Joe Paine lies in the phrase
'fight for the lost causes', the ones you fight hardest for, 'like a man
we both knew, Mr. Paine', as states Jeff during the climatic Senate filibuster referring to his murdered father, Clayton Smith. B. G. Brown's
inspiration for revenge on Norton in *Washington Merry-Go-Round*
comes from the letter his friend Tilden writes before his suicide – 'the
words of a dead man', as Brown refers to them – which convinces him
of the rotten state of Washington politics.

It is not just ideologically but symbolically too that the idea gath-
ers momentum through the political movies of the 1930s. From B. G.
Brown's late-night pilgrimage to the Lincoln Memorial and Judson
Hammond's divinely inspired rescue plan in *Gabriel* to Jeff Smith's
Christ-like collapse and removal from the floor of the Senate, religious
iconography is invoked at every turn. But in *Meet John Doe*, it reaches
a critical moment. Ann finds Long John on the roof and prevents him
from jumping initially, but seeing that he is resolved to do it, she begs
him to remember why the bells are ringing out. 'You don't have to die
to keep the John Doe idea alive!' she exhorts. 'Somebody already died

for that once. The first John Doe! And he's kept that idea alive for two thousand years.'

Long John becomes a symbolic saviour just as the words he has spoken, those of Ann's deceased father, are spiritual and philosophical musings from beyond the grave and of higher insight. Even the title and the pressure brought to bear on Capra and Riskin as the film moved towards the end of its production schedule intimate how much was at stake in divine as well as democratic terms. The working title for the movie was *The Life and Death of John Doe*, and the treatment that Riskin worked on, inspired by Swerling's work and that of originator Richard Connell and partner Robert Presnell, contained many of the themes that Wolfe describes as 'Christian brotherhood . . . [with] a motif of religious and political martyrdom'.[57] The title stayed for a goodly period and was only finally replaced when Capra grew wary of the pressure emanating from the Catholic Church, which was unhappy about the thought of a Capra hero having the pre-ordained intention of taking his own life, as for a while the script still intended. In the end, Capra's rationale for the change of heart and change of title was summed up in one of his most famous quotes: 'You can't just kill Gary Cooper,' he said.[58]

So each of the films of the era appeared to need inspiration and derived narrative momentum from epiphanies that set the heroes on the road to enlightenment and redemption. Critically, in fact, this feature rather defines the way the political film genre evolved over eighty years, and not just how it appeared for a time in the 1930s and 1940s. If anything, the religious dimensions of many other films in this area are a crucial element that unites political films across sub-generic categories as well as ideological convictions. Without a certain religious dimension, without a heroic epiphany that convinces the hero to take action, political films tend to lack any kind of resonance with audiences. There are exceptions to this rule, of course, but as we will see when we return to the 1990s and 2000s, the concepts offered by Phelps and other Capra scholars in particular apply remarkably well to a series of movies that recondition the 1930s ideals and sub-texts for a more modern age.

Five different endings supposedly marked the dilemma in which Capra and Riskin found themselves with *Meet John Doe* during the Spring of 1941. It is not clear that five were ever contemplated and there is not even a record of the fabled suicide ending ever being filmed, but the choices underline the point that political movies had spent a decade growing more recalcitrant, daring and darker in their assessments of America's democratic system. John does not jump in the end and he carries Ann away in his arms with the threat of a new grass-roots John Doe movement hanging in the air. But unlike some alternatively scripted closures for the film, Norton does not find nor seek redemption. His authority and control are not rescinded by Willoughby's actions and the future for all as they exit the building is about as unsure and uncommitted as Capra and Riskin dared make it. Answers to the issues and problems posed by a picture like *Meet John Doe* are no easier to come by now than they were at the commencement of the Depression, but the social and political examinations had grown more strident, more ambivalent about the forces at work in American life, and less optimistic about what the future might bring.

Both Capra and Riskin moved on to wartime service at the conclusion of *Meet John Doe* and the entry of America into World War Two. Capra did manage to squeeze in the filming of the comedic *Arsenic and Old Lace* towards the close of the year and in early 1942, but the movie waited nearly two years for a release. In the meantime, Capra's work for the army making propaganda films (most notably his *Why We Fight* series) and Riskin's direction of the Overseas Bureau of the Office of War Information (OWI) confirmed them both as filmmakers who were by now comfortable with material that was educational, conditioning audiences' values and beliefs, and brilliantly conceived in its imagery and iconographic intent. Indeed, so taken was Capra when he first witnessed the work of German filmmaker, Leni Riefenstahl, and so uncanny was the resemblance borne by a number of the images he himself had created in his movies to her own style (in particular D. B. Norton's fascist leadership of his paramilitary unit in *John Doe*), that he made it his mission with *Why We Fight* to usurp and dispel her power.

Capra's resolution to fight Nazi ideology and propaganda at every turn made him a vital component of the military's arsenal. As Thomas Doherty asserts, 'As a wartime historian and director of post-war policy, Frank Capra was there at the creation.'[59] Riefenstahl became his driving force, a director who, as he states in his autobiography, created 'terrifying . . . and blood-chilling imagery', most especially in the first film Capra viewed when he was handed the job with the army in 1942, *Triumph of the Will*.[60] It was both the intensity of this competition, played out through *Why We Fight*, and his immersion into the horrors of documenting the war that gave Capra a harder edge when it was all finished, a rededication to spirituality and divinity for sure, but also a desire to escape the shackles and desperation of conflict.

After the war, talk in the press and among the film community was about what Capra and Riskin would do next as a team, how they might take their filmmaking still further and delve yet deeper into political topics and social considerations. But Capra's wartime experience had inured him to the relentless destruction and hopelessness of war and he rejected the tone and manner of some of the movies now appearing. His friend William Wyler's *The Best Years of Our Lives*, for example, was a big hit in 1946 but Capra dismissed the downbeat tone in favour of myth, the small town and, once more, spiritual rejuvenation and redemption. Upon its release, his first film after the war, *It's a Wonderful Life*, was not a huge success, critics thinking it an about-face and a return to his earlier, less socially inquisitive self. It was only in later years, with repeated viewing on television and its credit established through successive video and DVD releases, that the film entered the canon of his best. Meanwhile, despite rumour and assurances, he never worked with Robert Riskin again. Made during the four years the two men spent apart, Capra's *Why We Fight* and Riskin's series for the OWI, *Projections of America*, different as they were in conception and outlook, are in fact the reason why 'the two men's working relationship ended the year World War Two began for America.'[61]

In 1948, Capra went on to make his last important, if not great film, *State of the Union*. Like *It's a Wonderful Life*, this movie was also made under the banner of Capra's own Liberty Films company, conceived after the war as the true independent home he had been craving at Columbia for years. *State of the Union* does not really provide a climax for the various forces, darkened ideology and rhetoric that had been brooding in *Mr. Smith* and *Meet John Doe*. Indeed, there are times when it is hard to discern it as a Capra picture at all. It does have a vaguely idealistic central hero, it certainly contains a sassy, independent and political astute woman, and one could argue it aims for some foresight if not redemption in its final reel. But about there, all pretences to its similarity with Capra's pre-war output end.

Grant Matthews (Spencer Tracy) is an aircraft manufacturer from out west, a businessman with influence and interests in politics and corporate affairs. Kay Thorndyke (Angela Lansbury) is a newspaperwoman who inherits her father's empire, the Thorndyke Press, and sets out to make a name for it and herself by nominating and then backing a presidential candidate all the way into the White House. That candidate happens to be Matthews and it happens to be Matthews because she is having an affair with him, fully known and exposed during the film to Matthews's wife, Mary, played by Katherine Hepburn.

Right from the film's first scene Capra's more melodramatic intent is revealed and Thorndyke's relentless pursuit of power is exposed. She visits her dying father Sam for the last time, and both say goodbye in their own emotionally restrained way. But as Kay exits and prevents a nurse from entering the room, a shot rings out, signalling Sam's end to the pain he is enduring in his final moments. Thorndyke assumes control of the organisation and ropes in wisecracking ace reporter Spike McManus (Van Johnson) and political manager Jim Conover (Adolphe Menjou) to advise her and Grant on the commencement of a presidential run. Spike talks of the 'Tafts and Vannenburgs and Deweys' with an eye to the actual upcoming 1948 election and dismissing Conover's claims of coming from Missouri with the comment that, 'if you came from Missouri, you'd have a job in Washington.' These initial scenes unequivocally focus on setting and political party affiliation in a way Capra had never previously done before. Grant is a Republican, albeit with a social conscience, and the comments about Truman's Administration reflect a cynicism and ambivalence to the post-war political landscape that Capra would never have revealed quite so stridently in the past.

The film follows Matthews's slow crawl towards credibility and a chance of momentum when, in a climactic scene set in his house, he is to proclaim his candidacy formally amid hoop-la, announcers and, significantly, television cameras. But Mary breaks down amid the pressure and heartbreak of her failing marriage, Grant's affair and expectations about her endorsement of her husband on live radio and before cameras. Drinking too much with the wife of a Matthews supporter, she is 'half-cut' and Grant looks to make alternative arrangements. But at the last minute Mary pulls herself together and begins speaking, before Grant, ashamed at his behaviour, intervenes to stop her and declares he is no longer running but intent on shaping politics from the outside and 'opening doors in Washington'. The conclusion's about-face may be typical Capra and the ending somewhat ambivalent as to the characters' respective fates, but the allegorical play on media presentation and increasingly individual-minded candidacies is a revelation of the American political world coming true in the post-war years.

State of the Union thus offered real political dilemmas and post-war complexity, and showed that a long way had been travelled from the

Depression-era narratives of Capra's career with Riskin. Joe McBride rather feels the press reaction was lukewarm because the film's inspiration, the stage play written by Howard Lindsay and Russel Crouse, was much more acerbic, unafraid to name names and point fingers. '*Time* [magazine] blamed its timidity on the corporate nausea of Liberty and MGM over the prospect of filming the play as written,' confirms McBride. 'The satirical carnage involved might antagonise every major force in the nation's political life.'[62]

Even so, *State of the Union*'s respectable box-office returns ($3.5 million) made it a more than worthy successor to the collection of political movies that defined the genre for generations to come. Capra had consciously designed a template for political narratives that utilised imagery and symbolism as much as they did ideas and philosophy. He created a picture of heroic intervention that successive filmmakers have returned to again and again with their own protagonists and he influenced the hopes and fears of a watching audience wanting the state to survive the crises of the time. *State of the Union* may not have been as great or as influential a movie as *Mr. Smith* or even *Meet John Doe*, but melodrama, institutional change and electoral cycles were being explored here and setting out a liturgy of conceptions and ideas that the political film culture in Hollywood adopted as its own in the decades that followed.

NOTES

1. M. J. Heale, *Twentieth-Century America: Politics and Power in the United States, 1900–2000* (London: Arnold, 2004), p. 77.
2. Michael Parrish, *Anxious Decades: American in Prosperity and Depression, 1920–41* (London: Norton, 1994), p. 241.
3. Phil Melling, 'The Mind of the Mob: Hollywood and the Popular Culture of the 1930s', in *Cinema, Politics and Society*, ed. Brian Neve and Philip Davies (Manchester: Manchester University Press, 1981), p. 21.
4. Anthony J. Badger, *The New Deal* (Cambridge: Cambridge University Press, 1989), p. 7.
5. Carl N. Degler, *Out of Our Past: The Forces that Shaped Modern America* (New York: Harper, 1984), p. 450.
6. Ruth Inglis, 'Early Attempts at Control', in *Films of the 1920s*, ed. Richard Dyer McCann (Lanham, MD: Scarecrow, 1996), pp. 48–9. Phillip Gianos mentions the closing of New York's movie theatres for a time at the behest of Mayor George McClellan, who revoked the licences of the city's 550 cinemas. The creation of a National Board of Review foreshadowed

the *Mutual* case. See Phillip Gianos, *Politics and Politicians in American Film* (Westport, CT: Praeger, 1998), pp. 45–7.

7. Ruth Inglis, p. 49.
8. Richard Maltby, *Hollywood Cinema* (Oxford: Blackwell, 1995), p. 363.
9. Will Hays, 'The First Years in Hollywood', in *The Memoirs of Will Hays*, reproduced in Richard Dyer McCann, pp. 54–5.
10. Colin Shindler, *Hollywood in Crisis: Cinema and American Society, 1929–39* (London: Routledge, 1996), pp. 27–8.
11. Colin Shindler, p. 29.
12. Kevin Starr, *California: A History* (New York: Modern Library, 2007), p. 278.
13. Eric Smoodin, 'Compulsory Viewing for Every Citizen: *Mr. Smith* and the Rhetoric of Reception', *Cinema Journal*, vol. 35, no. 2, Winter 1996, pp. 2–23.
14. Eric Smoodin, *Regarding Frank Capra: Audience, Celebrity and American Film Studies, 1920–1960* (Durham, NC: Duke University Press, 2004), p. 120.
15. Eric Smoodin, *Regarding Frank Capra*, p. 121.
16. Bernard F. Dick, *The Merchant Prince of Poverty Row: Harry Cohn of Columbia Pictures* (Lexington: University Press of Kentucky, 1993), p. 94.
17. Russell Campbell, 'Warners, the Depression, and FDR, Wellman's *Heroes for Sale*', *The Velvet Light Trap*, no. 4, Spring 1979, pp. 34–9.
18. Beverly Merrill Kelley, 'Communism in *Our Daily Bread*', in *Reelpolitik: Political Ideologies in '30s and '40s Films*, ed. Beverly Merrill Kelly, John J. Pitney, Craig R. Smith and Herbert E. Gooch III (Westport, CT: Praeger, 1998), p. 123.
19. Peter Roffman and Jim Purdy, *The Hollywood Social Problem Film: Madness, Despair and Politics from the Depression to the Fifties* (Bloomington: Indiana University Press, 1981), p. 84.
20. John Dewey, 'The Public and its Problems', in *American Political Thought*, ed. Kenneth Dolbeare, 2nd edn (Chatham, NJ: Chatham House, 1989), pp. 482–500.
21. Richard Maltby, *Harmless Entertainment: Hollywood and the Ideology of Consensus* (London: Scarecrow, 1983), p. 149.
22. For a more detailed account of Upton Sinclair's famous EPIC campaign, see Greg Mitchell, *The Campaign of the Century: Upton Sinclair's Race for Governor and the Birth of Media Politics* (New York: Random House, 1992); also Fay M. Blake and H. Morton Newman, 'Upton Sinclair's EPIC Campaign', *California History*, Fall 1984, pp. 305–12.
23. The backlash was so severe that no less a figure than Irving Thalberg personally oversaw this series of fake newsreels – paid for by the Hearst Corporation – and distributed for free to a number of Californian movie

theatres. See Kevin Starr, *Endangered Dreams: The Great Depression in California* (New York: Oxford University Press, 1996), pp. 142–55.

24. Review of *Washington Merry-Go Round, Photoplay*, vol. 42, no. 6, 1932, p. 57.
25. The real Button Gwinett did indeed sign the Declaration on behalf of Georgia so we might speculate that this is the state whence Brown is travelling to the capital.
26. See reviews of the film in *Cinema Booking Guide Supplement*, January 1933, p. 18. Also *Photoplay*, vol. 42, no. 6, 1932, p. 57.
27. Review of *Gabriel Over the White House, Cinema Quarterly*, Summer 1933, pp. 241–2.
28. *Gabriel Over the White House*, in 'Pictures Reviewed by the Editor', *Hollywood Spectator*, 24 June 1933, p. 7.
29. Andrew Bergman, *We're in the Money: Depression America and its Films* (New York: Elephant, 1992), p. 15.
30. John J. Pitney, 'Fascism in *Gabriel over the White House*', in Beverly Merrill Kelly, John J. Pitney, Craig R. Smith and Herbert E. Gooch III (eds), p. 56.
31. Terry Christensen and Peter J. Hass, *Projecting Politics: Political Messages in American Films* (London: M. E. Sharpe, 2005), p. 78.
32. John J. Pitney, p. 45.
33. Terry Christensen and Peter J. Hass, p. 80.
34. Bernard Dick, p. 95.
35. Brian Neve, *Film and Politics in America: A Social Tradition* (London: Routledge, 1992), pp. 29–31.
36. Glenn Alan Phelps, 'The "Populist" Films of Frank Capra', *Journal of American Studies*, vol. 13, no. 3, 1979, p. 379.
37. Neal Gabler, *An Empire of Their Own: How the Jews Invented Hollywood* (London: Doubleday, 1988), p. 166.
38. Neal Gabler, p. 167.
39. Charles Maland, *Frank Capra* (New York: Twayne, 1995), p. 52.
40. Joseph McBride, *Frank Capra: The Catastrophe of Success* (London: Faber & Faber, 1992), p. 341.
41. Charles Maland, p. 96.
42. Capra met the President again during the war when he entered military service as a documentary maker. Back in 1938, he came away from the press conference that day commenting, 'What a voice! What a personality!' See Joseph McBride, pp. 408–9.
43. Brian Neve, p. 38.
44. Beverly Merrill Kelley, 'Populism in *Mr. Smith Goes to Washington*', in Beverly Merrill Kelly, John J. Pitney, Craig R. Smith and Herbert E. Gooch III (eds), pp. 13–16.
45. Richard Maltby, *Hollywood Cinema*, pp. 369–71.
46. Phillip Gianos, p. 102.

47. Joseph McBride, p. 257.
48. Thomas Schatz, *Boom and Bust: American Cinema in the 1940s* (London: University of California Press, 1999), p. 86.
49. Charles Wolfe, '*Meet John Doe*: Authors, Audiences and Endings', in Meet John Doe: *Frank Capra, Director*, ed. Charles Wolfe (London: Rutgers University Press, 1989), p. 5.
50. Herbert Biberman, 'New Masses', in Charles Wolfe (ed.), p. 233. Originally published as 'Frank Capra's Characters', in *New Masses*, 8 July 1941, pp. 26–7.
51. Herbert Biberman, p. 235.
52. Glenn Alan Phelps, 'Frank Capra and the Political Hero: A New Reading of "Meet John Doe"', *Film Criticism*, Winter 1981, p. 50.
53. Charles Maland, pp. 89–115.
54. Jeffrey Richards, *Visions of Yesterday* (London: Routledge, 1973), p. 234.
55. Glenn Alan Phelps, 'Frank Capra and the Political Hero', pp. 52–3.
56. Glenn Alan Phelps, 'Frank Capra and the Political Hero', pp. 54–5.
57. Charles Wolfe, p. 6.
58. Joseph McBride, p. 435.
59. Thomas Doherty, *Projections of War: Hollywood, American Culture, and World War Two* (New York: Columbia University Press, 1993), pp. 70–1.
60. Frank Capra, *The Name Above the Title* (New York: Macmillan, 1971), p. 328.
61. Ian Scott, '"Why We Fight" and "Projections of America": Frank Capra, Robert Riskin, and the Making of World War II Propaganda', *Why We Fought: America's Wars in Film and History*, ed. Peter C. Rollins and John E. O'Connor (Lexington: University Press of Kentucky, 2008), p. 254.
62. Joseph McBride, p. 547.

Chapter 3

HOLLYWOOD ON THE CAMPAIGN TRAIL

Vote for me and I will bring the values of the common man to bear in Washington DC.

Bob Roberts in *Bob Roberts* (1992)

One could be forgiven for thinking that the quotation from Tim Robbins's 1992 film aligns Hollywood election movies with many other types of political film. For the line would seem to suggest that campaign movies also seek conformity in the intricate and complex world of electioneering and ultimately political representation. Lone, crusading heroes often enter the stage with a battle cry to bring stability and justice to the system and to rid it of corrupt misanthropes who are perceived as tearing down the walls of American democracy through their tissue of lies and deceit. There is nothing radically different here, it would appear, from the heroes that adorn *Washington Merry-Go-Round*, *Mr. Smith Goes to Washington* or *Meet John Doe*, spoken of in the previous chapter. Bob Roberts is a political amateur who decides to enter the senatorial contest in Pennsylvania, looking to oust an aging and patriarchal figure supposedly out of touch with the electorate. We follow his populist campaign as he catches up with and overtakes the incumbent in the polls, using tricksy modern media imagery, music, pre-arranged photo-opportunities and all manner of other 'spin'. But tragedy nearly befalls our protagonist before final victory is secured. On the surface it all seems very familiar.

In fact, *Bob Roberts* was a watershed not only for election movies but also for political films more generally by the 1990s; and if one is truly to understand the way Hollywood has approached the subject broadly, as well as this sub-generic collection of movies more particularly, coming to terms with what is really the satiric, nay somewhat nihilistic outlook of Robbins's film is a crucial determinant along the way. Certainly, *Bob Roberts* sets out to expose the merely superficial acceptability of

Bob Roberts turns into the 'rebel conservative' in Tim Robbins's film

candidates as much as many other types of election movie have done
before and since. One might assert that, in doing so, it too stakes a
claim for the moral high ground that Hollywood has often coveted
with political films. The system can be redeemed, might be one lesson
the picture offers; fake or duplicitous candidates can be unveiled and
stripped of their pretences and frippery, is another possible reading.

And yet the spotlight Robbins is casting on the 'whole show' here
and the sordid and dispiriting nature of the political process in the
late twentieth century – the forsaking of principles and even your very
soul, for the sake of getting elected to office – constitute a message
from which it is hard to escape. Bare recollection of the plot as outlined
above does not allow for the fact that it is the central character that is
under the spotlight of inquiry, not his opponent, and it is the 'system'
that is ultimately trying and failing to prevent a renegade like Roberts
from assuming power. Bob Roberts is not the hero, in other words; but
barely is he an outright villain either, or certainly not in the manner by
which we have identified such figures so far. Roberts is an anti-hero,
for sure, Machiavellian certainly, but also a product of the conditions
and terms of reference under which elections and wider American
politics had come to operate by century's end.

Further to all this is the fact that *Bob Roberts* is arguably the funniest political film ever made, but this does not make the pill easier to
swallow, only harder to accept. There is a sycophancy running through
the movie that is often humorous (the TV news anchors addressing
each other in a series of euphemistic entendres) but still stands out as
a condemnatory treatise against Hollywood itself, as much as it is a
charge against the public's gullibility and culpability in the whole process. The film industry likes to moralise and make believe that everything is alright, it seems to say; but you know, it's not, and people with
less redemptive qualities than Satan are actually winning elections in
this country and you the audience are helping them, declares Robbins.
As Robert Sklar noted in his review of the picture at its time of release:

> *Bob Roberts* is an entertaining film that may not have much of a
> viewpoint at all. Its publicity describes the film as a satire, and the
> problem with satire as a form is that it is good at offering targets
> but less good at taking positions.[1]

Sklar is right, of course, and not just about the satire. Countless
political movies throughout history, as we have already seen, can be

mildly diverting, funny, even serious and gripping in their narratives, but finding satisfactory denouements is the hardest trick of all to pull off. Sklar might therefore be implying that *Bob Roberts* limps to an equally unedifying ending where answers to problems posed are not easy to come by. The eponymous 'hero' has survived a (fake!) assassination attempt, defeated the incumbent Brickley Paiste (a brilliantly nonplussed Gore Vidal) in his bid to win a Senate seat, and even survived the probing of British documentary-maker Terry Manchester (Brian Murray), whose mission it has been to get inside the head of Roberts. The audience view the narrative, such as it is, through the lens of Manchester's documentary, with the aid of Nigel, his unseen cameraman; hence the much-used term 'mockumentary' has been taken up as a description of *Bob Roberts* and its clever audience-observing-the-documentary-maker-observing-the-candidate set-up.

But in conclusion, with a crusading reporter (Bugs Raplin) apparently assassinated because he sought to expose Roberts, with campaign workers quitting the Roberts team and refusing to talk, and with Paiste archly speaking to camera (as though in interview for the documentary) and commenting on the 'whiff of sulphur' surrounding his opponent, Manchester is left to muse on his findings at the Jefferson Memorial in Washington DC, wondering whether the principles of the republic can ever be truly upheld in modern-day political dogfights such as this race. Robbins is boldly looking to avoid an easy way out that will bring the whole plot crashing in on Roberts, but it is nevertheless an uneasy ending, as Sklar implies, which leaves the viewer, having laughed riotously at certain moments, puzzled at the downbeat finale and lack of collective satisfaction.

And yet that is surely Robbins's point. He not only adopted the cinematic style of choice – the documentary, *cinéma vérité* construction – that a number of electoral movies had employed before him, but also inserted MTV music era parody (the 'Wall Street Rap' video's parody of Dylan's 'Subterranean Homesick Blues', especially), crusading journalistic cliché and progressive left-wing folk music traditions, all turned on their head. To quote Bob's further pastiche of Dylan, the times they are a-changing *back*. The film represents a conservative reactionism that Robbins sees as a pervasive force running through American life, and it makes for a very funny ride as the campaign proceeds, observant of the times – the first Gulf War and mentions of Iran-Contra, for instance, are never far away – and believable in a strange, mockingly pretend sort of way. Even more so than the host of political films that followed it during the decade, *Bob Roberts* was a garrulous piece of muck-raking whose 'scorched earth policy' may have left it with few outlets for redemption by its closure, but which none the less revealed many truisms about Hollywood, public reactions to candidates, and the whole political culture in general by the early 1990s.

Indeed, the film's 'mockumentary' approach to style and structure could be accused or applauded, depending on your position, for its no-holds-barred sentiment to such an extent that perceptibly there was nowhere left to go for the election movie in particular and political films more generally after this. If a political picture could come along that was this persuasive in its endeavour to convince an audience that the 'rebel conservative' could work as a concept and preach such extreme ideas and ideology so convincingly, what was left for Hollywood to say at all? And in fact, as we proceed to examine electoral movies that followed in its wake, it becomes clear that *Bob Roberts* never has been nor never could be repeated in quite the same manner. Through a closer examination of these types of political film, the reasons for this will be approached later in this chapter.

Critics might point out that *Bob Roberts* was not a box-office hit at the time of its release (it took $4.5 million in the US) and so therefore fell victim to the paucity of cinema-goers who were and are interested in this kind of subject material. How might we explain its importance and influence, then? Well, rather like its rock-music companion piece, *This is Spinal Tap* (1984), the film later became a cult phenomenon on video and then DVD, where its initial outlay was more than surpassed in rental and sell-through revenue. It could also claim to have inspired more than a few pictures that followed, including the mad-cap plotting of a film like Warren Beatty's *Bulworth* (1998) later in the decade: a movie that at once stole some of *Bob Roberts*'s stylistic clothes and exploited the role of powerful forces shaping the political culture in a not dissimilar manner.

Crucially, however, *Bob Roberts* really displayed how and why electoral movies work differently and should be treated separately from other political films. The movies we have examined so far subscribe to cinematic and ideological conventions that play on their re-affirmation of the political system. Certainly, in the 1930s and 1940s, as we have seen, political movies that set out to consolidate the strength and longevity of America's democratic experiment met with approval in a time of crisis and depression. Using iconographic symbolism as well as political themes and theory, notions of individualism and egalitarianism, as well the importance of religion and faith, were all readily apparent in political movies of this era, just as they have been subsequently.

Electoral movies are not radically different in this respect. Messianic figures are often invoked and proclaimed as saviours of the political system; religion, faith and spiritual belief still have vital roles to play in the campaign film; and some sort of moral or redemptive lesson is usually on hand to close such pieces. But electoral movies are different in many other ways, and not least for the broad impact and influence they have had on real campaign politics in the US, intentionally or otherwise. Hollywood films about elections have by definition equated image and personality increasingly with electoral viability and success, and so has real politics. By the time of *Bob Roberts* the investment in character, over and above ideology, party relations and career trajectory, had become fixed in Hollywood minds and superseded all else. And why wouldn't it, because that has long been the key to the successful arc of political narratives? There has to be a hero, a saviour, a leader, who will save the day in the last reel.

As early as Franklin Schaffner's *The Best Man* in 1964, the modern way of electoral politics was set in the public's mind and played out in a narrative that was adapted from Gore Vidal's stage play of the same name. Henry Fonda plays William Russell, the living embodiment of the high-minded and intellectual figures he quotes to reporters and supporters: Oliver Cromwell, Bertrand Russell and others. He is the leading candidate for his party's nomination for president but is in a raging battle with a younger, hungrier and more rabble-rousing opponent, Joe Cantwell (Cliff Robertson). In a twist that ultimately allows Russell to hand the nomination to a faceless Western governor, John Merwin (William R. Ebersol), he ruminates to his wife that the perception of personality is everything in politics and that Merwin, who is 'nobody', will soon become 'somebody' as the features are drawn in and people get used to the idea of him as the candidate. That is how modern-day politics works, surmises Russell.[2]

In a non-election movie, President Andrew Shepherd (Michael Douglas) in Rob Reiner's *The American President* (1995) speculates on the prospect of a modern-day candidate in a wheelchair (meaning Franklin Roosevelt) ever being elected president. Over thirty years or more, appearance and preconception became defining traits of what was acceptable for the public on screen; and much of that acceptability carried over into real political discourse and campaigning. Hollywood over the decades has reminded audiences of the times when they made such choices and determined the kind of characters and personalities who transformed the presidency, as Reiner's film demonstrates.

Character as politics has thus allowed Hollywood to regard election films as a perfect construction of the battles between good and evil: as a means to investigate, condemn or condone theories of state and national power that are acceptable or antithetical to the prevailing norms. In election movies, any discussions about ideology are almost always filtered through the prism of personality, flawed or otherwise. Unlike movies that are concerned with the more general aspects of Washington or national political culture, say, the institutions are not being held up to scrutiny here, and even the system rarely is – although in the 2000s that focus would change somewhat, as we will see.

And yet it is precisely for this reason, the very simplicity of their narrative and dynamic about campaigns, that Hollywood election films have had such an impact on the American system since World War Two. Before image and personality had become the mainstays of electioneering, there was Hollywood putting them centre-stage in movies that offset personalities against each other in dramatically binary terms, even amongst those supposedly of the same party. In other words, the history of campaigns in the US is matched, to a degree, by developments in Hollywood in a manner that few other sub-categories of political film can claim.

It was during Dwight Eisenhower's 1952 campaign for the presidency that television began to be a vital tool in the armoury of the candidate. In the 1950s, the three main networks – ABC, NBC and CBS – provided a cosy, somewhat relaxed atmosphere in which candidates could present their policies, and questions were polite if not reserved in their inquisitiveness. However, as Edwin Diamond and Stephen Bates comment, 1952 was not just about seeing the candidates' faces on screen consistently for the first time. 'The year 1952 transformed the way Americans elected their president,' they assert. 'A change directly related to the twin developments of television and the TV spot.'[3] The spot was the means by which candidates advertised their manifesto, but in reality it was more about advertising themselves. Using TV as blanket coverage and 30-second adverts, national candidates in particular could present themselves as the new future of their party and of the nation at large to wide sections of the public, some of whom had never even heard of them before they announced they would run for office, let alone could recognise their face on the street.

Dwight Eisenhower did not have this problem, of course. The

Supreme Commander of Allied Forces in Europe during World War Two was not short of name- or even face-recognition when he finally decided to run for the presidency. But what he was short of, and what TV and campaign advertising especially circumvented, was political experience or even, dare one say it, credibility as a political candidate. 'Ike' was courted by both parties as a possible runner for office, which today would automatically beg the question of what his political credentials and beliefs actually were. Back then, the series of slogan-dominated 'ads' made those questions an irrelevance and Eisenhower an irresistible figure for national unity.

Eisenhower's campaign team started a trend that quickly accelerated through the gears. John F. Kennedy's 1960 campaign, Ronald Reagan's use and courting of the media from the late 1960s all the way through his two terms in office in the 1980s, and the Clinton and Obama campaigns of recent times: each man has moved on the awareness, sophistication and deployment of the TV 'spot' and associated 'media platforms' – as we would describe it today – to present himself as the candidate who resonated with most sections of the population. The focus and attention given to advertising and promoting candidates in the media, but especially on television, has thus become the de facto expression of the modern campaign. In 2000, the political parties finally reached the point where they spent more on TV ads ($79.9 million) than they spent on the candidates ($67.1 million). Total spend on television advertising in all its forms that year came close to $1 billion as the new millennium dawned.[4] By 2008 and the election of Barack Obama, online strategies had begun to predominate and internet statistics dwarfed all else. Campaign social networking created 2 million profiles for the Obama camp alone; through automated software 70,000 people raised $30 million for his campaign; and overall, the internet was thought to be responsible for $500 million of online fundraising.[5]

Since the 1950s, therefore, those 'media platforms' have become a spider's web of associated and affiliated networks, print outlets and, increasingly, web-based sites of discussion, debate and dissemination, as the statistics demonstrate. The media have been subject to almost as much criticism as the politicians have, the most salient and recurrent accusation being that politics has been 'dumbed down'. 'Dumbing down' has taken many forms. For a while, it was the lack of penetrating inquiry by news networks, 'serious' interviewers who were for a long time the people with most direct access to candidates on an election trail, when it came to TV exposure at least. The 'spot' has been lambasted even more, as being a paid advertisement – funded increasingly by Political Action Committees (PACs), sometimes referred to as 'soft money' contributors – on behalf of candidates who, most of the time, do not even speak about their policies or their qualities, but rather their opponents' flaws and the scandals engulfing or about to engulf them. Some advertisements have, in their own right, become legendary (Lyndon Johnson's 1964 nuclear annihilation 'ad' was so scary that it was shown only once and immediately banned) and controversial (the George Bush Sr advertisement about the Willie Horton case in 1988 put paid to much of the momentum gained by Democratic candidate Michael Dukakis that year), so much so that the appearance of even one galvanising television ad of this kind during an election can define the tone and focus of the debate, and the character of those running for office.

It is not only the candidates and their organisations that have been perceived to be ignoring key and in-depth political debate in favour of personality contests, however; the electorate themselves have been accused of falling for the most basic of evidence presented to them in these forms as 'facts' that they accept wholesale as gospel truth. Gavin Esler reports that, during the concerted Republican congressional campaign of 1994, which led to prospective speaker of the House Newt Gingrich assuming the un-official leadership of the party, political strategist Frank Luntz helped exploit a campaign policy that played on the fears of a populace who were seemingly ignorant about fundamental political positions. Luntz discovered, and then had candidates and advertisements reiterate, misguided assumptions amongst the electorate, who believed, for example, that unemployment was running at New Deal levels of 25% when it was only 6%; that the budget deficit was rising when it was actually falling; and, most spectacular of all, that America already had a high-tech missile defence shield rather like the 'Star Wars' system Ronald Reagan had proposed in the 1980s, when it had already admitted the technology was not yet developed enough to deploy such a system.[6]

If this is the way that television and other media concentration on political campaigns has developed over more than half a century, then it is little wonder that Hollywood should be ascribed some influence over the process too. And one need not assert that Hollywood is the progenitor of the personality style, either, just to use that as convenient shorthand for the link that exists between the two. Theoretically, the source of personality- or candidate-based politics has a long enough heritage in its own right. Max Weber was writing about the 'authority of charisma' well before television arrived and Hollywood's heyday emerged, and yet his views on the ability of political figures to mould opinion and establish cognitive relations with diverse sections of the populace clearly remain relevant for modern media-fixated political systems and particularly for the US.[7] Timothy Luke elaborates on Weber's ideas when he states that 'Electronic media – and the complex codes of images they generate – have partially displaced large formal bureaucratic institutions as channels of personal identity, cultural communication, political administration and social organisation.'[8] Luke, writing before the widespread onset of the internet, may well not have realised how prophetic that statement was going to look by the arrival of the twenty-first century.

The other development that aided the emergence of a closer symbiotic relationship between Hollywood and campaign politics was the personnel crossover that occurred from the late 1960s onwards. Screenwriter Jeremy Larner, who worked with Michael Ritchie and Robert Redford on *The Candidate*, had been involved with Eugene McCarthy in 1968, while Ritchie had lent his support to the Democrats more generally. Marty Kaplan was engaged by Walter Mondale in 1984 to write speeches in that campaign before turning his hand to Hollywood and working with Jonathan Lynn on *The Distinguished Gentleman*. And Gary Ross, screenwriter for Ivan Reitman's *Dave* and then a director in his own right, had worked on speeches and policy for Gary Hart before he became a Hollywood insider in the 1990s.

Each brought their own experience and wisdom to bear on Hollywood campaign movies and such were the composite elements working in both arenas that it is hardly surprising the lines of reality and reconstruction have become blurred. A character's trustworthiness, reliability and honesty have become defining traits for electoral politics in America, but whether one could reliably say that this emerged out of the natural political culture or came about because of Hollywood influence is somewhat harder to discern.

Indeed, Hollywood set about articulating and re-aligning many of the presumptions about campaigns to such an extent that when it found itself playing catch-up to a set of notions and ideas that it had already articulated well, the resultant movies were far less assured and much less popular. Sidney Lumet's long-neglected 1986 film *Power*, for example, features Richard Gere as a manipulative spin doctor, Pete

St John, working on a New Mexico gubernatorial campaign. The tone of the film suggests that St John is a wizard of art and creation, making barely credible candidates look like John F. Kennedy most of the time. But the film's revelation about imagery and character being moulded from behind the scenes and within editing suites was, frankly, old hat by the mid-1980s. And while the narrative does turn towards a more conspiratorial and thriller mode in the second half, as St John discovers that he has been hired for darker and more dubious reasons, the object lesson about political campaigns as advertising slogans for voters too lazy to look at manifestos and read the newspapers had already been revealed in a slew of films over the previous thirty years or more.

In effect, *Power* was trying to examine the process of elections in and of themselves, but personality is too often the context around which such films must naturally revolve. In addition, each of the more successful and resonant movies in this sub-genre has not tried to engage with the mundane process of talking about job creation and balanced budgets, but opted for wider values to do with truth and principles. Indeed, the more interesting films have often been at pains to claim that personal appeal is a very dangerous practice with which to engage. As Richard Maltby has remarked in relation to *The Candidate*, 'The movie asserts that politics has no place for sincerity, but it relies on the sincerity of Redford's performance to convey its theme.'[9]

Maltby is, of course, right to highlight the discrepancy here. If Hollywood makes electoral movies that warn the public of the dangers of relying too much on charismatic personalities but then casts a 'star' like Robert Redford as its central example, one has to be wary of the image-conscious demands of the film industry and how this mixes the message for viewers who are entirely comfortable with celebrities representing them.

Nevertheless, in Ritchie, Larner and Redford's defence, one can identify a degree of irony in the star's personification of candidate Bill McKay. McKay is often aware in the movie that he is skirting the boundary between sincerity and falsehood, between exploiting his good looks and easy manner while adopting sound-bite phraseology and convenient photo-ops. This was one of the reasons why the three of them rejected the idea of making McKay a kind of Bobby Kennedy figure. 'If we had anyone in mind, it was someone like a Ralph Nader or Jerry Brown, the kind of guy who hates politics, then gets involved with it,' Ritchie said later.[10] So by this argument *The Candidate* concentrates on a false idealism and lack of honesty as a focus for all politics, and the anti-politics message of the film actually morphs into *the* message of electoral and political success from the early 1970s onwards. If you position yourself as the outsider demanding change, raging against the system and determined to help the disenfranchised, you will achieve electoral victory, the movie asserts, only to fall into the same trap as other candidates who came earlier and with similar idealism. *The Candidate*'s famous final line, McKay's anxious appeal to campaign manager Lucas, 'What do we do now?', underscores the point. The rules for knowing how to win campaigns bear virtually no relation to the skills required for representing and governing – this was the judgement by the early 1970s. If you lose that link, *The Candidate* appears to argue, you are left with a political system on the verge of meltdown.

HOLLYWOOD AND EARLY ELECTION CAMPAIGNS

In the previous chapter, we identified the way in which a movie like *State of the Union* signposted the way ahead for election films in 1948 by giving the audience a taste of the behind-the-scenes manœuvrings during a prospective campaign. Perhaps the best example of a film that captured some of the atmosphere of early twentieth-century electioneering even before Capra's piece, however, was Orson Welles's classic, *Citizen Kane* (1941). In a film that, as Joseph McBride comments, tries to examine notions of truth and objectivity, Kane's Declaration of Principles document, his mandate to obtain high office, perfectly encompasses later debates in the genre about the manipulation of ideals and principles.[11]

Inspired by Welles's portrait of a biographical rise and fall, Robert Rossen's award-winning adaptation of Robert Penn Warren's Pulitzer Prize book, *All the King's Men* (1949), followed a similar pattern. Broderick Crawford plays Willie Stark, a small-town lawyer with dreams of high office. This 'rags to political riches' movie trope was consistently invoked by some directors during the forties, not least Capra but also Preston Sturges, whose early career offerings, *The Great McGinty* (1940) and *Hail the Conquering Hero* (1944), both played upon the notion of publicly misguided adulation for heroic protagonists and demands for grassroots political leadership. Rossen's version of this fable was to prove more melodramatic and less comedic than Sturges's, and also took its inspiration from real-life events: those surrounding legendary Louisiana politician, Huey Long.

Willie Stark addresses the masses in All the King's Men

Just as with Kane, the story is dictated by documenting a public life through an active narrator. In Welles's film, the reporter Jerry Thompson (William Alland) is assigned to find out the significance of Kane's final word, rosebud, and it is he who carries the audience through the life of the newspaperman and failed politician in retrospect. In Rossen's movie, the idealist reporter Jack Burden (John Ireland) is narrator, a man who starts out as an active crusader for Willie only to become mired in controversy and disillusioned by his leader's increasingly dictatorial behaviour once he wins office.

Burden comes across Stark for the first time as Willie battles against graft in his small hometown of Kanoma. The reporter inadvertently sparks interest in the no-hope candidate just by writing about Willie's activism but his pro-Stark stance finally gets him into trouble at his paper because the editor takes his orders from the machine politicians who run the state and they will not back the underdog. Stark loses but learns many of the lessons needed on the stump, especially his tub-thumping delivery inspired by a weakness for alcohol. When Burden asks him what he learnt most, Willie replies, 'I learnt how to win.' Returning four years later, he is wiser and even more ebullient, and Burden begins working directly for his friend and candidate as he starts on an unstoppable journey towards the Governor's mansion. In the meantime Stark has pulled Burden's friends and family into the fold, especially Adam Stanton (Shepperd Strudwick), who accepts the post of head of a new hospital that Willie pledges to build during his campaign and puts into construction as soon as he enters office. The judge, Monte Stanton (Raymond Greenleaf), becomes Attorney General of the state and Burden's romance with Ann Stanton (Joanne Dru) sours when he learns that Willie has taken her on as his mistress. The rise, further rise and dramatic fall of Willie occur at an increasingly frantic pace as the film attempts to pack all of the issues contained in Warren's book into 110 minutes.

Indeed, Brian Neve reports that as much as an hour's material was cut out of the final version of the picture as Rossen tried to piece all of the fragments of the story together, forsaking some of the elemental backdrop of Warren's tale.[12] As Neve further points out, the movie still speaks to the notion of democratic authority and fires warning shots across the bows of recent New Deal central planning and control.[13] Willie's public works programme is highly acclaimed by the voters, but behind the scenes it is immersed in bribery and favours: an indication that state-sponsored authority cannot exist without graft and deceit. Willie's crusade to oust the elite and stand up for the 'hicks' in his state is successful but increasingly driven by the desire to accumulate power for its own sake. From the perspective of the time, therefore, the movie is nothing if not an examination of totalitarian will. Rossen utilises the symbols of recent fascist dictatorships by presenting night-time rallies with flaming torches and giant pictures of Stark adorning podiums where Willie stands high above his adoring audience. Stark's rhetoric becomes more vocal, more biblical, almost demonic, as he comes to trust less and fight more against the perceived enemies trying to bring him down.

Pointedly as well, at different moments in the film, the capable but ambitious Stantons all have reason to flea the Stark cause but cannot resist the temptations of power and money. The judge finally resigns, unable to stand it any more, and plots to have Willie brought down before his own position is compromised and he commits suicide. Even when Willie is finally investigated by the state's authorities, his control over the masses frees him from what his opponents increasingly perceive as oppression and he avoids their calls for justice, dismissing them as charges fabricated to evict him from office. Finally, subjected to control and humiliation that he can stand no longer, Adam Stanton enacts revenge as Willie emerges triumphant from the State House after the impeachment investigations clear him of bribery and he stands on the steps, claiming victory over those trying to end his governorship. Adam fatally shoots Willie at close range, only to die at the hands of Willie's enforcer, Tiny Duffy (Ralph Dumke).

Stark is, on one level, the human examination of power created and manipulated at local levels, which is seen as a metaphor for wider and prevalent controls on the populace by the end of the 1940s. In mirroring the career of Huey Long, the film lifts the lid on how rhetoric and personality can dominate collective thought and will. It was a salutary lesson for Rossen because, against the backdrop of the making of the film and as the anti-communist furore grew louder in Hollywood, he was about to become a victim of just the sort of political repression he was examining and condemning in Willie Stark. He reputedly wrote to studio head Harry Cohn, insisting he was not a member of the Communist Party, but when HUAC returned to Hollywood in 1951, Rossen was named and Columbia broke its contract with the director.[14]

All the King's Men brought drama and pathos, semi-autobiographical leanings and fictional reconstruction to a political movie that had electoral campaigns in it but was not strictly about electoral politics. Franklin Schaffner's *The Best Man* (1964), on the other hand, wrapped its narrative around nothing but campaigning, and its tight three-day narrative surrounding a convention held in Los Angeles is reflective of the stage play from which it originated, written by Gore Vidal.

William Russell (Fonda) and Joe Cantwell (Robertson) are the principal contenders in a convention battle in Los Angeles. Russell is popular, easy-going and fiercely intellectual, but nevertheless the progressive and, it seems, natural leader of his party. Both he and the more gung-ho Cantwell believe that the endorsement of former President and now aging (indeed, dying) patrician of the party, Art Hockstadter (Lee Tracy), will seal the deal when it comes to floor votes being counted. It is an interesting conceit that, by 1964, the film is still dealing in 'locked' conventions where no clear winner is emerging, a situation that the expanding Primary system was largely condemning to history by this point. Nevertheless, when both find damaging and salacious material that they believe will knock the other out of the race, it is left up to Russell's conscience to do the right thing and make a judgement call. His old friend Hockstadter, taking his last breath, dismisses Russell for being so principled about such dirty tricks when, he says, politics is full of this business.

Hockstadter urges Russell to use the damning evidence against Cantwell but in any case subsequently passes away before he can announce his endorsement. Cantwell seemingly proves that the scandal about military tribunals and court martials that engulfs him is a fabrication – though his rebuttal and evidence are themselves presented as possibly a bluff – and so Russell ultimately decides to sacrifice himself so Cantwell can have no chance of the nomination; he instructs his delegates to vote for the vacuous Governor John Merwin, who then takes the prize in the final reel.

Richard Maltby contends that there are competing forces at work in the film, which, on the one hand, are trying to project modern political notions of 'spectacle and message' while, on the other, attempting to deal with Hollywood concerns about 'content and neutrality'.[15] A familiar refrain in many political movies up to this point is the fact that the political party is never named, though Vidal's sympathies and the fact that they held their 1960 convention in LA would point us towards the Democrats as inspiration. Marion Rosenberg confirmed as much when she credited fellow producer Larry Turman with a lot of the inspiration for how they wanted the film to look and some of that imagery was the product of watching Kennedy, of whom Turman was a big fan. Indeed, the film's schedule was delayed and the release put back until the Spring of 1964 because of Kennedy's assassination, an event that hit the crew, and Fonda especially, particularly hard.[16]

Nevertheless, Maltby's inference is right; the battle between East

Coast intellectual Russell and rabble-rousing McCarthyite Cantwell seems to cover a political spectrum that is as extreme as it is unlikely. But it is the way in which to offset competing political and personal forces in the film, to show how the two can intermingle but also be unbalanced by character, the subtle casting of which helps this along. Fonda had played Abraham Lincoln earlier in his career, of course, and Robertson came straight to this movie off the back of playing J. F. K. in the wartime autobiographical *PT109*, so the positions of the protagonists cleverly arranges and disassembles conventional takes on character and personality. Fonda, whom we might presume to be upstanding and righteous, is in fact the politician having affairs outside his marriage, while Robertson, who should be personable and charismatic, is edgy, lacking in oratory (as Russell proves at one point) and reactionary.

Maltby, however, is still not taken by an ending where Russell admits the whole process is about the creation of spectacle and image, when he has spent so much of his time rejecting smear campaigns and cheap publicity while wanting to talk about principles and policies. But arguably this is the film's most important if contentious message.[17] Moving the campaign film on a step by 1964, Vidal arguably asserts the premise that even the most capable of politicians cannot escape the allure of the image in this modernising era. Rather like *Bob Roberts* thirty years later, Vidal and Schaffner are smart enough here to make demagoguery handsome and debonair in the appearance of Cantwell, not hangdog and menacing as with McCarthy. Political substance is forsaken but politics was already moving this way and who is not to say that movies like *The Best Man* were not already having their say in the changing nature of electoral politics in America?

Schaffner's picture is also noteworthy for two further reasons. One is a minor issue but no less important for the recognition and reception of political films. *The Best Man* demonstrates how recurring actors provide something of a refresher for audiences looking to associate the political intent of a movie with previous Hollywood outings. The use of Fonda, Robertson, and also Lee Tracy (from *Washington Merry-Go-Round* thirty-two years earlier) as aging ex-President Hockstadter, acts as a staging post for political recognition and intent across Hollywood eras and movies in an important manner.

The second more crucial determinant that marks *The Best Man* as an integral part of electoral movie development is that, as already hinted at, it evokes a recent campaign and not-so-distant events in its settings and characters. But the occasional use of stock footage and hand-held cameras on the convention floor hopes to give an authenticity to the piece too, conceivably taking its cue from *Primary* (1960), Robert Drew and D. A. Pennebaker's landmark documentary of the time, which first utilised a *cinéma vérité* approach to follow Kennedy and opponent Hubert Humphrey round on the Primary campaign trail in Wisconsin.

The contrast in the style and performance of the two characters in their film was something that Pennebaker admitted was not deliberate but evolved naturally. More than that, like a later subject – Bob Dylan in his legendary music documentary *Don't Look Back* (1965) – Pennebaker commented that Kennedy was a bit like the rock stars of the coming era. He always seemed to know where the camera was, he said; like Dylan he always had an eye for a shot, a look to camera or away from it.[18] It was at these developing shoots growing up through the electoral landscape of the 1960s, of a new campaign style using television, spectacle and image, that *The Best Man* hinted. In the films that followed, documentary motifs and off-the-cuff dialogue would become mainstays of the election movie.

THE BOYS ON THE BUS

The Best Man painted its electoral politics on a relatively small canvas over a discrete period of time. A decade on, Hollywood movies began to expand on the behind-the-scenes brokerage by widening the picture and examining the way campaigns were played out in front of TV viewers and the broader electorate. As Charles Champlin indicates in his analysis of the movie for *Film Facts* at the time of its release, what a film like *The Candidate* (1972) is about is 'process': not the 'embattled idealist fighting the powers of darkness', as Champlin describes it, but the process of 'campaigning in the age of jets and pit stops rather than whistle stops, especially in the age of television'.[19] All of these things, he feels, made the film credible because it showed the equal reduction of candidates down to mere suggestions of their political creed. They shake hands, wave at crowds, smile at people, and simplify their message to a level that is almost interchangeable whether one is a young idealist or an aging patrician candidate, as is the choice presented in Michael Ritchie's movie.

Over the years, Ritchie and Redford's story of a go-ahead liberal lawyer in California, tempted into running for one of the vacant Senate seats against an experienced but vulnerable incumbent, has attracted

Bill McKay on the campaign trail in The Candidate

praise and criticism in equal measure. For some, the convenience of the message – Redford's Bill McKay falls into the same kind of campaign sloganeering and desperation to win as his opponent does and thus imitates that which he is trying to replace – is obvious and clichéd, even for the early 1970s, and a not dissimilar political transformation from that which struck Willie Stark thirty-three years earlier. For others, though, certain scenes and some of the reactions of particular characters ring very true with the way elections were and are run and what politicians really aspire to in the modern political age. Champlin himself had covered a number of local and national campaigns, so when he says that Redford's performance is 'so right and natural' that you could be forgiven for taking it for granted, you know this is an observer who has seen idealists like McKay come and go in the real, murky world of politics before.

   Champlin further questions the role of the media in the film, not in this instance because there is something accurate about the characters inherited by Peter Boyle and Allen Garfield (as campaign manager and advertising/media spin doctor respectively), but because the picture leaves uncomfortable silences with regard to the media's wider manipulation of the electorate and conditioning of what they think voters want to hear from the candidates, as well as what they fear hearing.[20]

Champlin, anticipating the moves towards electoral politics over the following forty years, senses that what the film does best is prophesy the inevitability of contrived, generic, standardised campaigns driven by press and media sanction and coverage.

Peter Buckley's later re-assessment in *Sight and Sound* focused even more heavily, and with some greater distance, on the consumerist angle of buying and selling candidates. Buckley describes Ritchie's picture as a 'cold slick film' and he means that as a compliment.

> In a consumer society, even a politician is there to be consumed [he suggests]. But first you've got to package him. Sex, charm, charisma: wrap it up with a snappy slogan, put it in a perfect can, and you've got a winner.[21]

Buckley asks who and what is left to represent people when all this packaging and construction is done; and, indeed, if you want to keep running for office, how do you find the time to represent constituents in a modern age that requires ever more campaigning? This worrying premise not only came true over the following years in American politics, but also is once again the key message in the final moments of *The Candidate*, when McKay utters to Lucas (Boyle) those immortal words, 'What do we do now?' Having spent so much time electioneering and slogan-building ('vote McKay for a better way') without ever contemplating the prospect of winning, McKay is suddenly a part of the political establishment and he does not know what to do with it.

As reviewers were quick to notice, *The Candidate* shied away from the 'big politics' and presidential campaigning of *The Best Man* in the 1960s in favour of the localised nuts and bolts of running for a California Senate seat. Extending some of Schaffner's desire to encompass reality and documentary imagery, Ritchie and Redford (who also acted as producer) create a mock electoral film that has all the look of a pseudo-campaign documentary, again in the vein of *Primary* and with some of the daring wit that inspired *Bob Roberts* twenty years later.

Marvin Lucas is a campaign manager coming off the back of an unsuccessful election night. We see him fly away from his losing candidate as soon as the results are declared and head for California, where he seeks out civil rights lawyer Bill McKay, fighting cases of union infringement and workers' rights. Lucas's 'angle' is to persuade McKay to take that zealous activism into a state-wide campaign and combine it with the one other element he also has in his favour: the fact that he is the son of 'legendary' former governor, John J. McKay (a brilliantly spirited performance from veteran Melvin Douglas). Lucas tempts McKay with the idea that he can say anything he likes in the campaign because he is bound to lose to popular incumbent Crocker Jarmon (Don Porter). And yet through a combination of circumstances McKay gets a taste for the campaign, the media focus, and the public adulation that preys on his ego (including the acquisition of a political groupie and hanging out with Natalie Wood, who plays herself sup-posedly supporting Redford as McKay as a candidate), and before long he is making platitudinous speeches, telling jokes and looking glamor-ous on TV. The transformation from idealist activist to political clone is the film's central conceit but arguably its biggest problem, for McKay displays a naïvety that at times strains credibility. He insists to Lucas, for instance, that his father is not to be involved in the campaign, and we take this excommunication as McKay's determination early in life to avoid politics after growing up as part of a political dynasty. And yet this does not mean he has not learnt the ways or observed the tricks involved in the manner in which campaigns are run and how politics works. Often, however, he displays a little too much innocence, espe-cially around Lucas and later Klein (Allan Garfield), when he must already be familiar with some of the tactics of on-the-stump cam-paigning and political advertising that they are trying to instil in him.

McKay's submersion into the process could, of course, be couched in a biographical rise and fall that mimics other political narratives. But, apart from the basic premise, Ritchie and Redford largely eschew story and climax – the election result is never really in doubt by the close – in favour of episodic engagements as the campaign deepens, questioning both McKay's motivations and the audience's sympathy for him. As Robert Sklar notes in his own commentary on the film, Ritchie copied the style of *Primary* by filming hours and hours of foot-age with real people, sometimes with the candidates inserted, at other times as talking heads asked to say something to endorse or oppose one or the other of the protagonists.[22] Director of photography Victor Kemper took advantage of as many 'public' events as he could in a bid to immerse Redford in particular crowds and situations. The ticker-tape motorcade in downtown San Francisco, for instance, actually took place on New Year's Eve 1971, as employees from the city's financial district indulged in the tradition of tearing up and throwing out their old year calendars and directories on to the streets below. And long shots that periodically feature a TV news team amidst the hubbub surrounding the candidate were, in fact, the camera crew working at close quarters, often with hand-held equipment.

> The film was shot entirely on location [commented Kemper]. We used no sound stage at all. When we had a motel scene, we rented a room and shot it there. While we occasionally surrounded him with extras, Redford's presence itself usually generated an excitement in crowds that closely simulated that of campaigning.[23]

Redford/McKay spends time waiting outside the Long Beach shipyards as workers emerge off their nightshift, and walks among crowds in Watts in an effort to court the African-American vote. Most of all, the backroom dealing with union bosses, the campaign workers who are more interested in lunch than what the itinerary is for the day, and McKay's increasingly strange and – it has to be said – thoroughly bizarre relationship with his wife, all smack of the *cinéma vérité* aesthetic for which Ritchie, together with screenwriter Jeremy Larner, was searching. Having worked for political candidates like McCarthy in 1968, Larner knew the necessity of opening Redford's character to public disclosure, as well as being familiar with the private intimations and acute observations that make political life so interesting. When McKay backs down and his father is finally called into the campaign to endorse his son and drive the team to victory, the older man sits next to Bill and says, simply but devastatingly, 'Son, you're a politician now,' with all the mischievous insinuation that lies behind the comment.

Win Sharples's assertion that McKay can be championed for refusing to compromise his principles and beliefs and not turning away from the insistence that idealism can be brought to Washington seems a little generous in summation.[24] As the campaign and film draw to a close, with the result inevitable and no third act disaster to avert, McKay is almost literally driven to distraction. In the back of a car on his way to another engagement, he juxtaposes and mixes his sound bites – 'we cannot house our homeless, we cannot feed our feedless!' – and breaks down in a fit of the giggles in the TV studio trying to do a to-camera pitch for his candidacy. But all of this is the sign of madness and manipulation that Ritchie, Redford and Larner are driving for, and the film's downbeat finale matches much of the restless agitation at the heart of other 1970s movies in other areas of political movie-making.

Penelope Houston's contention that Redford manages to avoid too much sycophancy and allusion to Kennedy seems closer to the mark in this instance, and a further endorsement of a film that is reticent about simply encouraging in its audience a return to the 'Camelot' legacy that, after all, had been crippled only a decade beforehand.[25] McKay is 'handled' and shaped by the experience as much as he can be ascribed heroic status, and in this regard, as the next chapter demonstrates, star personas such as Warren Beatty, Gene Hackman and Redford himself again would appear as central protagonists in the following decade, in another category of political movies that were as conscious of the collapsing consensus and political intransigence as they were of the restrictive capacity of the hero to resolve the crisis at hand.

In the Summer of 1972, as the President's re-election campaign was beginning, the Nixon White House was clearly intrigued enough by *The Candidate* to try to have the film banned for its perceived left-wing bias.[26] That they failed and that *The Candidate* went on to become such an important piece of political cinema says much for the scope and ambition of the director, writer and star. The decade's companion piece, Alan Alda's personal project, *The Seduction of Joe Tynan* (1979), revealed the difficulties of making the political environment as real on film as *The Candidate* did. While a director like Robert Altman opted for background electoral politics, smothered by a music festival and concerned with an ensemble cast that weaves intricate narratives together, making his *Nashville* (1975) a film very much in tune with later texts such as *The Player* and *Short Cuts*, Alda attempted to play it straight with a level-headed Washington fable that, as he himself said, was about the seduction of money, sex and power.[27]

Directed by Jeffrey Schatzberg and written and produced by Alda, *The Seduction of Joe Tynan* uses only a prospective election as a backdrop from which to examine wheeler-dealing in Washington. The eponymous central character is a first-term Senator trying to make a career in national politics. But gullibility and naïvety get in the way when Tynan, flushed with success from pushing through a Works Bill on the floor of the Senate, is called on for a favour by Southern conservative elder, Senator Birney (another marvellous cameo from Melvyn Douglas). Birney wants Tynan to vote for the confirmation of a Supreme Court Justice from Birney's state, who has been endorsed by the President but who is, in fact, racist and even more conservative than Birney himself. However, the aging Louisiana man is really rounding up backers to put the Justice on the bench, thus removing him as a rival from Birney's own future re-election race.

The premise is potentially neat and the insider trading that is exposed rings true for the most part. But Tynan's deliberations over the nomination, and his rising status in the party, are compromised by his starting an affair with Karen Traynor (Meryl Streep), a labour lawyer who is opposed to the nomination and who may or may not be engaged with Tynan for the business of changing his mind. Like *The Washington Masquerade* over forty years before, the politics gets lost in the affair, and the impact of the conflicts and compromises is diluted for the sake of melodrama in conclusion. Tynan does contribute to the Justice's downfall in a high-profile investigation that brings him public attention and adulation, and suddenly his quick-fire success provides a potential springboard not just to a high ranking in the Senate but also possibly to a shot at the White House itself. But while Christensen and Hass praise the film's intent, ambiguity and feminist stance toward the era's political culture – though Traynor's rather convenient seduction is more than redolent of other late 1970s attitudes towards sex too – the repercussions and ramifications of the characters' actions are not always borne out and the film, while interesting and unfairly ignored with the passing of the years, does not quite strive for the lively ambition of Redford and Ritchie's effort.[28]

CONTEMPORARY ELECTION MOVIES

If *Bob Roberts* made the electoral movie a tough sub-genre to leap into in the early 1990s, it did not deflect the attention of Mike Nichols, who, with *Primary Colors* (1998), introduced the viewing public to modern imitations of real campaigns, or Warren Beatty, who, with *Bulworth* (1998), put paid to virtually any other serious documentary-like commentary on the process of elections altogether. Towards the close of Robbins's movie, Bugs Raplin (Giancarlo Esposito), the crusading journalist and editor of his own paper, *Troubled Times*, is interviewed by mock-documentary-maker Terry Manchester about the strange turn of events in Roberts's campaign. As the film grows darker, and the eponymous character's manipulation of the media and inconsistencies about his policies and past come to light, Manchester is becoming more wary, on the audience's behalf, of the phenomenon that is Bob Roberts. Raplin sums up the mood, conjoining the idealised Hollywood representation of what voters wistfully hanker after in their politicians and the harsh realities of modern campaigns. 'There are no more Mr. Smiths in Washington,' he dismissively asserts, prior to his own assassination after he is accused of trying to kill Bob, who is now confined to a wheelchair – even though his shattered legs manage to keep the beat during his songs. In a finale where the Roberts campaign is seen as suspiciously culpable of the death of a reporter and Bob has won the Pennsylvania Senate race by smearing a perfectly honourable incumbent, the deadpan ending at the Jefferson Memorial and the seeming acceptance of these inexcusable actions would appear to make any attempt to revive and re-assess the electoral movie a thankless task. Nevertheless, Nichols and Beatty took aim later in the decade with mixed success.

Drawing upon the best-selling anonymous novel of the time that was later revealed to have been written by *Newsweek* columnist Joe Klein, *Primary Colors* features Jack Stanton (John Travolta) broadly imitating Bill Clinton on the campaign trail in 1992. In fact, reports suggest that the imitation was even more uncanny than the final cut of the movie showed, with parts of Klein's book ending up on the cutting-room floor at the insistence of distributors Universal.[29] Released right in the midst of the Lewinsky inquiry in the Autumn of 1998, the film can surely be read as a concurrent document of the politics of the age. Jack Stanton and his wife Susan (Emma Thompson) are rather desperate politicos, out to impress and anxious to win the White House but with a devious streak that results in them resorting to snide gutter politics in order to win. Stanton's conscience through the whole exercise is Henry Burton (Adrian Lester), son of a famous civil rights activist, whom Stanton wants on his team for effect as much as for Henry's smart knowledge of politics.

While we follow Stanton's pursuit of the biggest prize, Nichols does not allow any judgemental scenes to intrude on the narrative. The Gennifer Flowers moment in the campaign, reworked here as the accusations of a hairdresser, Cashmere McCloud (Cia Carides), mimics the press conference and subsequent appearance of the Clintons on *60 Minutes* to deny the accusations of a 'twelve-year relationship' between the candidate and Gennifer/Cashmere. In one of the best scenes in the film, Henry watches the TV appearance in a diner while in constant contact with fellow campaign worker Daisy (Maura Tierney) at the studio. The public in the restaurant are more concerned with Stanton's sexual proclivity than his policies, and in conclusion Henry surmises that the most he has learned is that they like Susan's hair that way. The overall extent of Stanton's infidelity is never really brought up, though his seduction of a schoolteacher (played by Alison Janney) early in the film is clear enough. For Eric Pooley, 'the unresolved questions and muddied waters are hallmarks of the Clinton presidency; glossing over the indiscretions feels just right.'[30]

As Stanton's campaign survives scandal and passes tests of credibility, it becomes apparent that the challenge to him is emerging from an unlikely source: the late entry into the race of Governor Fred Picker (Larry Hagman). Picker's personal life, his sexuality and drug-taking, is more raucous than Stanton's and Henry has to accompany Stanton's investigator, Libby Holden (Kathy Bates), on a probe of Picker's past to uncover dirt and deceit. They duly find their evidence and even Picker knows it was only a matter of time. But Libby's strict code of rebuffing attacks on her man, but never throwing the mud first, is about to be rejected; in her disgust and against the backdrop of previous mental health problems, she takes her life and dampens Henry's enthusiasm for the whole exercise which he intends to quit.

In this moment of final crisis for the campaign, Stanton entreats Henry to remember that even Lincoln had flaws and made compromises so he could do better and more important work once in office. The final scene is the inauguration ball and the new President's hand is tracked by the camera until it shakes Henry's and the pact has been established. Does Travolta impersonate Clinton better than Clinton himself? Was Hollywood playing with or even usurping reality with a story that had contemporary allegiances to a sitting president? The film's obliqueness lies not only in its vagueness about the nature of the deals brokered but also in the way that Hollywood and Washington finally colluded in the making and maintaining of a political character tracking the history and actions of a current incumbent. *Primary Colors* suggested what was blatantly apparent by now: that political campaigns were not won and lost in the detail of policy and promises, but in the brokering behind the scenes and in front of the camera, in the use of 'spin', and indeed in the manipulation of 'spin' to create the right effect or tone, to create the right result perceptibly.

The film is a 'morality tale' just as much as it is about image-making and breaking though, as Myron Levine asserts. Henry is a throwback for the other characters as well as the watching audience. What was it like before elections become 'professional', back when candidates said things in which they actually believed?[31] Rather like Raplin's comment at the end of *Bob Roberts*, the 1990s campaign movie had a nostalgic reverence built in that somehow imagined an era without brokering, manipulation and scheming. Hollywood itself proved that was illusory, even in the era of Mr Smith.

Warren Beatty's *Bulworth*, of which he is both director and star, is in fact an attack on the very obliqueness *Primary Colors* introduces, on rhetorical vagaries, and on the covert relationships that cosily tie up the representatives, the media and the business people of America. If Beatty's aim in his side-swipe at politicians, Hollywood, multinational corporations and the like was to unveil a new kind of electoral movie, the film is still not entirely devoid of the kinds of structure that pre-ceded it in previous pictures. Beatty's concerns about electoral fund-ing, Hollywood endorsements and especially race as a cleavage within American politics may not have been tackled quite so ferociously or satirically as here, but the action is still based around a pseudo-documentary set-up whereby Jay Billington Bulworth's return to his home state of California in the run-up to his Primary re-election is to be recorded by a news crew from C-Span, the political TV network.

Bulworth is an incumbent US Senator who is good-looking and popular, but who is in the pocket of the insurance companies who fund his campaigns and make him sponsor and follow their whims on Capitol Hill. In the first scene of the film the camera pans around the Senator's office, resting on pictures of Bulworth's (in fact, Beatty's) early career as an idealistic politician hanging out with Angela Davies and Bobby Kennedy; images of Martin Luther King and Malcolm X also adorn the walls. In the background, campaign ads regurgitate the meaningless phrase 'we stand on the doorstep of a new millennium' over and over. Bulworth, in a pit of despair and threatened by the cor-porations backing him, arranges for an assassin to take his life while he is on the California trip, and he takes off fully believing he is about to die.

When he comes across Halle Berry's Nina in LA, however (who happens to be the contract killer assigned to take him out), Bulworth becomes immersed in an alternative culture. His first night home sees him on an odyssey that takes him from a neighbourhood black church, to a Beverly Hills film producer's home, and finally back to the heart of a South Central nightclub; his epiphany is to see how adopting totally different language, dress and mores can help him get back to base principles. Bulworth starts to speak bluntly and then in rhyme about the media, as well as the African-American and Hollywood communi-ties. Suddenly he has a change of heart about his own assassination.

Liberated so far as to call off the hit – which fails – he then begins to dress in 'street garb', as though he is some white, middle-class rap star.

Perhaps, even allowing for the C-Span reference, wholly constructing the narrative around a *cinéma vérité* format was an improbable conceit, given this scenario; instead, Beatty and his award-winning cinematographer, Vittorio Storaro, opt for a far more glossy and urbane presentation. Beatty has Bulworth positioned against the backdrop of textured interiors and unitary lighting collages both inside (especially in the TV debate scene, which is set against a very stark background of the Stars and Stripes) and outside (the scenes in South Central LA take on a darker hue contrasted against the golds and greens of the uplands of Beverly Hills). Rather than revert to choppy, on-the-stump filming, then, Beatty and Storaro give the picture an increasingly surreal atmosphere, almost as though it is happening in another world detached from reality.

Compared to earlier electoral movies where the central protagonist is often at the start of a career, Beatty does a good job of conveying a tired and weary politician brow-beaten by the monotony and degradation of years of representative politics. In a Chomskian stance, Bulworth proceeds to rail at the capitalist ethos and its social stranglehold, although, as Linda Holt notes, this is hardly a revelatory position.[32] Communication is identified as the central tool of the political operative and Bulworth comes to see black culture, and especially rap music, as his way out of the restrictive persona constructed around him in Washington. Merging rather dull and conformist middle-class culture with the perception of confrontational rap music as a way to jumble and confuse the media and the public seems to work. Bulworth wins the Primary by a huge margin, despite doing no campaigning in the final two days, and even gets a slice of the vote as a write-in candidate for president.

At the close the Senator wakes up from his long two-day sleep and is transformed back into his regular attire, something of a nuisance for his Chief of Staff Dennis (Oliver Platt), who has seen 'the numbers' on the new character and believes this is now the key to success. But the cynicism runs deep here. Don Cheadle's neighbourhood kingpin L. D. resolves to reform himself and ropes in Nina's brother, Darnell (Isaiah Washington), as though the African-American community has somehow seen the light thanks solely to Bulworth's antics. And his re-emergence at the end as something close to the old Bulworth in suit and tie questions for a second whether the whole ploy is a stunt. The inevitable shooting to follow leaves questions unanswered too, not least of which is whether the Senator really dies. Poet, soothsayer and moral conscience of the story, Amiri Baraka re-appears at the end of the movie outside the Mount Sinai hospital, suggesting that Bulworth is fighting for his life and may yet recover.

Bulworth takes aim at so many objects, it is a wonder that it hits any of its targets. The film is at times deeply sceptical as much as it is deeply funny. Mentioning the word socialism is contentious enough, but admiration for Black Panther Huey Newton, accusations of Jewish bias in Hollywood, and African-American support for O. J. Simpson all touch a raw nerve here, even if Beatty is arguably having his cake and eating it. Critic Angie Errigo suggested that at least the film accepted the collapse of party politics and the charge towards personal campaigns as a given, and the message of the people helping themselves because it was unlikely politicians were going to do it for them was also something of a call to arms, played out in Nina's backseat-of-the-car polemic to Bulworth about the collapse of the black manufacturing base and social inertia. But *Bulworth* also brought electoral movies to something of an ideological full-stop at the end of the decade and century. With little left to satire or slander and with a 2000 presidential contest just around the corner that made some of the movies on offer here seem like dull documentary fare, the abeyance of the electoral movie was predictable in many ways.

In the new millennium, however, once the biting satirical flames had died down after *Bob Roberts* and *Bulworth*, the election film did, in fact, find a way to spin the debate about politics in a slightly new fashion – but a fashion that wholly took its impetus from the real electoral events of the 2000s and was thus far more focused and reactive towards the system than it had been in the past.

Both *Man of the Year* (2006) and *Swing Vote* (2008) were moderately successful, fairly well-received election movies for the 2000s that shied away from the strategies of old. Neither of these films had particularly arch or scheming figures looking to disrupt or uncouple the system. Neither features key nomination conventions or TV debates as their set-piece ideological moment of change or confrontation, though both have the latter in them. The main protagonists are non-political beasts, at least in the active sense. One is a talk-show host who is more than a little sceptical about the politics he sees and the characters he sometimes interviews. The second is another 'ordinary Joe', but unlike a Jeff Smith, B. G. Brown or Bill McKay, this character has few redeeming

Tom Dobbs entertains the voters in Man of the Year

qualities and is not only reluctant to become a pawn in the political and electoral system but openly hostile to the idea.

Both are different, then, because while character is still to the fore – a personable talk-show host whom everyone likes, who is cajoled into becoming a candidate, and a down-on-his-luck blue-collar worker shown a chance to make a difference to the world – the electoral system is the real target here. More than this, these two films are in effect re-runs of that momentous 2000 Bush/Gore election; they are in essence heightened imaginings of the closest, most disputed and most controversial race in history. Both stories come down to dispute and error over the workings of the electoral count. In the former case, a company which makes and installs electronic voting machines miscounts the voting slips, and in the latter, Kevin Costner's disengaged voter becomes the crucial determinant in the state-wide count for president which in turn will determine the occupant of the White House itself.

Man of the Year features Robin Williams as TV chat-show personality Tom Dobbs, a shorthand impersonation of Larry King and Jon Stewart rolled into one character. Dobbs enjoys high ratings for his show, a mixture of satirical chat and love-in interviews that, as the election season draws near, becomes a mouthpiece for Dobbs's increasing frustrations about the system and the people operating in it. His manager Jack Menken (Christopher Walken) regales the whole story in retrospect, from an innocent question about running for president in a warm-up for Dobbs's show, to e-mails and write-ins, and finally to Dobbs declaring on air that he is officially running for office. Having progressed further in his run than he himself thought possible, Dobbs quickly falls into the classic dilemma of talking about the issues and forgetting his original personality; for a while he forgets the wisecracking truisms that made him so popular in the first place and which he has to reclaim.

Barry Levinson's film has a similar trope and style at work to his earlier *Wag the Dog*. The ensemble cast, which includes stand-up comedian Lewis Black playing Dobbs's producer/writer, Eddie Langston, has an edgy feel that allows Black and Williams to indulge in their comedic routine periodically; part of the action is also set in the documentary road-trip scenario so characteristic of earlier election movies. The other segment of the plot, however, where Laura Linney's computer technician uncovers a problem with the state-of-the-art polling machines being wheeled out by Delacroy, a company about to make huge amounts of money from their government contract, conforms to more melodramatic elements. Here the film becomes more of a conspiracy thriller that only catches up with Dobbs when election day is over and only periodically works.

The early TV debate establishes Dobbs's credibility when he hijacks the live TV event and then gets support from the likes of 'real' political pundits such as James Carville, who is being interviewed on screens as the action plays out around Dobbs. But Dobbs lives with a guilt complex that all he is doing is making a cheap statement because he understands how television works and his opponents are not as brave or smart in their self-deprecating and humorous manner. When Menken's emphysema lands him in the hospital through too much smoking, Dobbs has an epiphany somewhat akin to Bulworth's, but in his case just being different and entertaining is not enough. He resolves to tell the truth, admits to smoking marijuana and liking sex; he goes on the road to deliver a 'show' to his supporters but does it with spiky political material and attitude.

Dobbs's unlikely victory, confounding the opinion polls, is undone by the Delacroy machines, which have recorded the votes wrongly and overwhelmingly in his favour. Ultimately, the error is uncovered when Linney's character, Eleanor Green, breaks her silence, locates Dobbs and forces him to make a hard decision. Levinson's film squares technology off against democracy, entertainment against political debate, and finds the system and people wanting. As the TV anchors announcing the results reiterate, 'comedian' Tom Dobbs becomes president and the description is pointed and accusatory as much as it is funny and satirical.

In *Swing Vote*, Kevin Costner plays against type as Bud Johnson, a single father in a lowly job, whose only interests seem to be country music and Nascar. He lives in a glorified trailer with a young daughter, Molly (brilliantly played by Madeline Carroll), who not only cares about him and his ways, but is deeply passionate about politics. She encourages him to vote but when he predictably fails to turn up at the polling station because he is drinking in a bar, she covertly attempts to cast his vote in absentia. But as she is about to do the deed, the power goes off; Johnson's attendance at the polling booth has been recorded but his vote has not. The authorities track this down while investigating the problem and discover not only that Johnson is entitled to his vote but also that his home state of New Mexico becomes the deciding factor in the whole presidential contest. As a result, a kind of run-off takes place that sees the principled Republican President Andrew Boone (Kelsey Grammer) and his opponent, environmentally friendly Democrat Donald Greenleaf (Dennis Hopper), converge on the small New Mexico town of Texico and devote time, money, advertising and a final rally on canvassing for Johnson's vote.

Johnson, of course, discovers why politics is important, what he dislikes about the modern system of campaigning and about promises gone awry and hopes evaporated, and why responsibility, trust and faith in the people are crucial. Boone and Greenleaf bestow gifts and incentives upon Johnson and even his friends are taken in by the fame and attention. Eventually the candidates both run (very funny) ads aimed at Bud that completely undermine their political principles; oil drilling in protected environments fills Greenleaf's campaign and pro-choice sentiment is awash in Boone's.

In many ways, both films are re-affirmations of the spirit and plausibility of American electoral campaigns lost in Hollywood productions of the previous forty years. From the principled stance of William Russell in *The Best Man*, through the lost ideals of Bill McKay to the calculating duplicity of Bob Roberts and the zany disengagement of Jay Bulworth, Barry Levinson and Joshua Michael Stern's pictures ask despairingly, if the polling technology does not work, what is left on which we can rely? But at the same time they also breathe some hope and aspiration into electoral politics, along with a feeling that the examples of 2000, 2004 and subsequently 2008 have offered redemptive and valuable lessons for the health of American democracy. The electoral movie still has weight and import, then, and Hollywood's projection of its imagery and content remains as vital and pertinent as ever for our understanding of the way Hollywood and Washington work and interact.

NOTES

1. Robert Sklar, 'Bob Roberts', *Cineaste*, March 1993, p. 78.
2. One of the producers of the film, Marion Rosenberg, commented that they really did want an 'unrecognisable' figure to impersonate Merwin, and so used Ebersol, who was in real life the manager of LA's fabled Ambassador Hotel. Interview with Marion Rosenberg in Los Angeles, 5 December 2007.
3. Edwin Diamond and Stephen Bates, *The Spot* (Cambridge, MA: MIT Press, 1992), p. 37.
4. Stephen J. Wayne, *Is This Any Way to Run a Democratic Election?* (Boston: Houghton Mifflin, 2003), pp. 184–5.
5. Jonathan Parker, 'The Media', *Developments in American Politics 6*, ed. Gillian Peele, Christopher J. Bailey, Bruce Cain and B. Guy Peters (Basingstoke: Palgrave Macmillan, 2010), p. 97.
6. Gavin Esler, *The United States of Anger* (London: Penguin, 1998), pp. 249–53.
7. Max Weber, 'The Nature of Charismatic Domination', in *Weber: Selections in Translation*, ed. W. G. Runciman (Cambridge: Cambridge University Press, 1978) pp. 226–50.
8. Timothy W. Luke, *Screens of Power: Ideology, Domination, and Resistance in Informational Society* (Urbana: University of Illinois Press, 1989), p. 130.
9. Richard Maltby, *Hollywood Cinema* (Oxford: Blackwell, 1995), p. 380.
10. James Spada, *The Films of Robert Redford* (New York: Gilded, 1977), p. 157.
11. Joseph McBride, *Orson Welles* (New York: De Capo, 1996), p. 40.
12. Brian Neve, *Film and Politics in America: A Social Tradition* (London: Routledge, 1992), p. 142.
13. Brian Neve, pp. 142–4.
14. Brian Neve, p. 144.
15. Richard Maltby, p. 379.
16. Rosenberg suggested that the cast and crew felt an obligation to the murdered President to put as good a piece of political drama on screen as they

could. Interview with Marion Rosenberg in Los Angeles, 5 December 2007.
17. Richard Maltby, p. 380.
18. Pennebaker's comments are from a lecture followed by a question and answer session with the author and participants at the 2006 Film and History League Conference, Dallas, Texas, 3–6 November 2006.
19. Charles Champlin, Review of 'The Candidate', *Film Facts*, vol. XV, no. 9, 1972, p. 191.
20. Charles Champlin, p. 192.
21. Peter Buckley, Review of 'The Candidate', *Sight and Sound*, vol. 44, 1975, p. 48.
22. Robert Sklar, p. 77.
23. Rand Layton, 'Filming "The Candidate" on Location Calls for some Fast "Natural Habitat" Decisions', *American Cinematographer*, September 1972, p. 1022.
24. Win Sharples, 'Depth of Field: Michael Ritchie's *The Candidate*', *Filmmakers' Newsletter*, vol. 6, no. 2, December 1972, p. 55.
25. Penelope Houston, Review of 'The Candidate', *Sight and Sound*, vol. 42, no. 1, Winter 1972, p. 49.
26. The film makes very little of its party affiliations, though it is hard to envisage McKay as anything other than a Democrat. Inspirations for his character, such as real-life Californian representative John Tunney, suggest that. In addition, as the results pour in, one can just see the Democrat and Republican affiliations quickly marked out on TV screens next to the names of the candidates.
27. Alan Alda, *Things I Overheard While Talking to Myself* (London: Arrow, 2007), p. 116.
28. Terry Christensen and Peter J. Hass, *Projecting Politics: Political Messages in American Films* (London: M. E. Sharpe, 2005), pp. 149–50.
29. While filming, Travolta had claimed that he thought the President would be pleased with the end product because it 'flattered him'. Reports from the Clinton aides over the years have suggested that this was not quite the reaction garnered at the time. See Travolta's interview in Tony Allen-Mills, 'United Colors of Clinton', *The Sunday Times*, News Review, 1 March 1998, p. 9.
30. Eric Pooley, 'Tale of Two Bills', *Time Magazine*, 16 March 1998, p. 34.
31. Myron Levine, 'Myth and Reality in the Hollywood Campaign Film', in *Hollywood's White House: The American Presidency in Film and History*, ed. Peter C. Rollins and John E. O'Connor (Lexington: University Press of Kentucky, 2004), p. 292.
32. Linda Holt, 'Is This How White People Rap?', *The Times Literary Supplement*, 29 January 1999, p. 23.

Chapter 4

ACTION, CONSPIRACY AND PARANOIA IN HOLLYWOOD POLITICAL FILMS

Post-Cold War Hollywood produced an intriguing raft of films in the 1990s that partly harked back to the genre of spy and paranoia thrillers from the 1960s and 1970s, and partly predicted future incipient forms of surveillance culture and institutional power at work in American society during the 2000s. The revived phenomenon, critical though it was to perceptions of Hollywood political discourse, did not start on film, however, during the decade, but in television. The rise and rise of the at first cult and then all-conquering Fox TV hit, *The X-Files* (1993–2002), paved the way for a slew of copycat series and movies that tried to tap into at least a part of creator Chris Carter's mix of alien abduction, sci-fi adventure, random mystery and, most pertinent here, government conspiracy and cover-up. From *Independence Day* to *Dark Skies* via the comic *Men in Black* and serious-minded *Signs*, *The X-Files* was the prototype for a mixture of what we might term 'political sci-fi' texts that took hold in the era. Over nine series it is fair to say that the programme became so pervasive in Western TV culture as to build up a loyal audience/fan base that made the show one of the most watched, written and talked about in generations.

The secret to the on-going success lay not in the will-they-won't-they, on-off relationship between the lead characters, FBI agents Dana Scully (Gillian Anderson) and Fox Mulder (David Duchovny), nor in the occasionally oddball yet brilliant episodes that saw the two landed in out-of-the-way towns tracking down goofy paranormal-related mysteries in a melange of styles that partly resembled Agatha Christie meets Stephen King. The real foundations of the franchise's success were in fact built upon government – specifically the FBI with a few unaccountable agencies thrown in – oversight of everything from alien spacecraft through environmental controls to technological breakthroughs and the use of personnel and equipment to which the population were entirely oblivious. Blending the often disparate and sometimes confusing plotlines together were characters and reference points which not only were borrowed from other influential pieces, but which also of themselves set the agenda for the next generation of television series to follow that owed a debt to *The X-Files*, from *Lost* and *Heroes* to *The Mentalist* and *Cold Case*. There was, for example, the constantly exasperated boss of our two protagonists, Walter Skinner (Mitch Pileggi), who over time comes to reveal more of what they and he suspect is known about the government's secret 'work'. Then there was the series' 'Deep Throat': the 'cigarette-smoking man' (William B. Davies), who appeared at key moments as if by magic, acting on whose authority it was never clear. And finally there was Mr 'X' (Steven Williams), among a number of others who could pass for virtually any paranoid individual from any Oliver Stone (the name itself!) or Alan J. Pakula film you care to name. Each episode carefully repackaged past references with contemporary intrigue and plots that made the series a runaway success.

Hot on its heels and just as the show was moving on to the big screen in 1998, Hollywood revived the conspiracy/paranoia thriller in a series of features with decidedly mixed fortunes. *Shadow Conspiracy* and *Murder at 1600* (both 1997) were more specifically White House-related mysteries to do with sex and deceit. *Conspiracy Theory* and *Absolute Power* (both 1997) were better but similarly conceived plots about rogue figures in government (including the President in the latter's case) involved in shady duplicity. Closer in tone and style to *The X-Files*, taking up the fascination for *noir*-like pictures that saw *L.A. Confidential* (1997), *The Usual Suspects* (1995) and *Fargo* (1996) become major hits at the time too, and adopting a similar kind of homage agenda to past stories and characters within its own construction, Tony Scott's *Enemy of the State* (1998) was perhaps the best and commercially most successful of all these pictures as the 1990s drew to a close.[1] Although it might now be perceived as somewhat dated, at the time the technological and cinematic wizardry that the film employed as part of the plot once again provided an impetus to like-minded texts on TV and film in the following decade who wanted to use the same dizzying array of filmic styles – from *24* and *Numb3rs* (an episode of which Scott directed) to the *CSI:* franchise, as well as Scott's own directorial efforts such as *Spy Game* (2001) and *Deja Vu* (2006).

The tagline 'it's not paranoia if they're really after you' played upon the precepts of the genre established in the 1970s by the likes of Sidney Pollack, Francis Ford Coppola and especially Alan J. Pakula. Indeed, the clever casting in the film extends to having an aging surveillance expert called 'Brill', played by Gene Hackman, effectively serve as an updated version of Hackman's classic character, Harry Caul, from Coppola's definitive surveillance movie, *The Conversation* (1974). *Enemy of the State* therefore inserted film history reference points and brought all the trademark auteurist instincts of Scott's visual style to bear on a plot that prophetically revolves around a shady CIA/National Security Agency (NSA) sub-group within the corridors of power wishing to railroad through Congress a piece of legislation that would enable less government accountability when tracking down illegal and dubious characters. In other words, the political face of the attempts to circumvent government oversight led by Congressman Sam Albert (Stuart Wilson) in the film and endorsed by NSA director Thomas Reynolds (Jon Voight), allows for surveillance by any means, including wire-tapping, obtaining bank records, bugging homes and offices, and generally invading privacy laws in every conceivable manner. Of course, it also smacks of the kind of public non-debate and legislation that three years later would result in the Patriot Act and all the implications that went with it in post-9/11, Bush-era America.

But, for all this prophetic quality, and attractive and entertaining as *Enemy of the State* was, Scott's picture and the other movies that accompanied it towards the end of the Clinton era were accused of playing around with paranoia and activating it as merely a genre device that mimicked their 1960s and 1970s counterparts but elusively failed to challenge any contemporary suggestion of why and to what end government was supposedly subversive, paranoid or monolithic. When the events of 11 September 2001 occurred (ironically producing their own raft of conspiracy ideas), marking the beginning of the Bush Administration's 'War on Terror' and having ramifications that entailed a global assault on the enemies of America, Hollywood quickly reversed away from even parodic political thrillers and camouflaged anything that might resemble an institutional attack on the pillars of American democracy in genres, plots and escapism somewhat removed from the realities of the new century, even if they were allegorical to some of the events taking place.

As the years after 9/11 progressed, however, the initial shock and resistance to confronting government activity and actions in the aftermath of the attacks on New York and Washington slowly resolved themselves into a concerted Hollywood attempt to address a new era of paranoia and government force that was born out of unexpected consequences and was, as a result, much closer in tone and style to 1970s counterparts than to 1990s ones. The unforeseen (in the Bush White House, at any rate) direction of the war in Iraq and then later Afghanistan after the toppling of Saddam Hussein; the controversies surrounding non-combatant detainment; extraordinary rendition; and last but by no means least, government relations with prominent corporate interests that resulted in revelations and crises at home and abroad – all provided an impetus in the second half of the 2000s for a further strand of what has commonly been termed the conspiratorial paranoid style in Hollywood movies. In other words, the collection of films and in particular documentaries that resulted from addressing these concerns during the decade resembled nothing so much as the reactions of the film industry to Vietnam and Watergate in the late 1960s and early 1970s, and bred equally politicised cohorts in American cinema intent on exposing government malfeasance, the foreign policy arm of which is documented in Chapter 6.

As well as the TV series already mentioned, then, including Fox's newest hit series of the era, *24*, starring Kiefer Sutherland as counter-terrorist agent Jack Bauer, movies such as *In the Valley of Elah*, *Rendition* and in particular *State of Play* and *Edge of Darkness* were decidedly darker, more disturbing, almost nihilistic representations of corporations, government, lone gunmen and unapologetic capitalist, economic ideology. The hopelessness of singular, crusading individuals in the Hollywood tradition, striving to break the will of powerful, interlinked institutions, was more pervasive in these pictures and more resonant of an early twenty-first century order that suspected the rules of engagement, and the uncovering of power and authority was even less transparent than it had been in the paranoia collection of films from forty years before. Portraying nothing as mundane as the fabricated intrigue and deceit on offer in the 1990s, ideologically, cinematically and culturally the political thriller as conspiratorial and socially engaged treatise thus discovered new leases of life in the 2000s in ways that could never have been envisaged before the events of 9/11.

But for all their contemporary allegiances to and portrayals of pertinent issues of the moment, these movies and TV shows of early twenty-first century vintage did continue to display their lineage and the debt they owed to pictures from past Hollywood. Indeed, the setting and timeframe of prominent films such as *Munich* and *The Assassination of Richard Nixon* displayed a causal and definitive link between the concerns and political outlook of the 1970s, for example, and those of the

2000s. Both Stephen Spielberg's and Niels Mueller's movies offered up real stories set in the classic paranoid era that played as allegories upon contemporary fears of the spread of things like state-sponsored terrorism and disturbed individuals losing their way in society and reacting in violently redemptive manners.

But why should this sub-genre of political movie arise periodically in Hollywood's canon of production? What does it say about the film industry's relationship to wider institutions? And what kind of comparison does each era offer in terms of style, persuasion and political substance? Both Jonathan Romney and Adam Barker wrote in the 1990s of a discernible new era for the paranoid, conspiracy thriller. Romney admitted that the trend of the time appeared 'rather abstract, less about real-world skulduggery than about the power of media imagery and, ultimately, about film itself'.[2] His examples, from Peter Weir's *The Truman Show*, through David Mamet's *The Spanish Prisoner* (both 1998), to *L.A. Confidential* and David Fincher's *The Game* (1997), as well as, one might add, *Pleasantville* (1998), directed by Gary Ross, certainly assembled an amorphous set of styles and pastiches that were partly about nostalgia and recollection, technology and the manipulation of the watching public. But they were far less about political paranoia and conspiracy as we are attempting to define it here. These films had a certain postmodern irony about them and directed their attentions knowingly to their audience watching a film about movies, TV and surveillance in various forms, and examined how that experience could itself be manipulated and reconfigured.

Barker, meanwhile, did focus his attention on the political thriller, primarily the myriad reactions to Oliver Stone's *JFK* that had emerged during the decade and the inspiration a number of filmmakers had taken from Stone's bold conspiracy agenda. So offerings like Richard Donner's *Conspiracy Theory* and Clint Eastwood's *Absolute Power* (both 1997) fell neatly into Barker's theory of a 'heroic quest' model of political thriller whereby a central protagonist is the audience's focal point for the unlocking of secrets, deceit and cover-up.[3] In such a model the hero can never be diverted by doubt or the possibility of conversion to the conspiracists' cause, no matter how hard the bad guys try and how desperate the hero's situation becomes.

Barker cites Jim Garrison in Stone's film as the modern archetype for this kind of pivotal character, and it arguably explains the success of *The X-Files* as a series too, he thinks, that the heroes are often tempted and encouraged to fall in with the plotters and forsake their principles and beliefs. But for Barker this kind of narrative progression and the dilemmas and diversions that are thrown in front of the heroic protagonist also provided a link back to 1970s figures like Hackman's Harry Caul in *The Conversation*, Robert Redford's Joe Turner in *Three Days of the Condor*, and Warren Beatty's Joe Frady in *The Parallax View*. For Barker, therefore, the politics of the 1990s might not have been the same, but the cinematic construction, on the whole, was.

Going back still further, Michael Ryan and Douglas Kellner believe that the 1970s movies were in fact domestic extensions of Cold War paranoia and the kind of ideological battleground that had been mapped out by cultural historians like Richard Hofstadter in the 1960s. They were historical staging posts in America's battle with freedom and individualism, in other words: a society at once multifarious and tolerant that nevertheless looks to purge its undesirables of their dubious beliefs periodically and to re-assess the state of the nation's health. But the 1970s was the beginning of a suspicious relationship with institutions and the state, they affirm. Indeed, the crisis of liberalism at the heart of American political culture is mapped out for Ryan and Kellner in a series of 'liberal cause' movies that tacked on to the social, economic and political conspiracies at the end of the decade: notably, *Network* (1976), *Coma* (1977) and *The China Syndrome* (1979). 'Liberalism's philosophical commitment permitted the state to be threatening and impersonal,' they add, as these films conditioned audiences to believe all was not right in institutional establishments like the media, science and nuclear power.[4]

In the modern twenty-first-century context Ray Pratt links political and cultural paranoia together: an amalgam of the historical developments cited above allied to an increasingly '"false" sense of the world' in the new millennium, as he describes it. Surveillance is everywhere, and when that surveillance cannot explain assassination, missing planes, and people disappearing into thin air, it plays upon collective anxieties, he believes, and anxieties that tempt us to see history as 'conspiratorial' rather than 'anecdotal', contestable rather than confirming.[5]

So the crop of new twenty-first-century signature paranoia films defined their trademark stance and took their look from eras long before the break-up of the Cold War and the War on Terror had ever been conceived of, but how and why that recurring pattern of spectacle and issue should be played out within a similar cinematic framework in this sub-genre of political movie is a question that is more difficult to answer. Only with a historical analysis of the evolution of the political thriller do we start to see patterns and prescriptions that have been fermenting in Hollywood for a long period of time. These patterns, ably presented by Romney, Barker, Ryan, Kellner and Pratt, have coalesced into a catechism of doctrines that explains why the sub-genre remains pertinent and popular in America every time political crisis and change looms large.

THE PRE-COLD WAR THRILLER FILMS

Although the hardest thing to do with the collection of films on offer here might be to add a nomenclature accurately to each and every one of the texts being described (some are Cold War movies, some paranoia films, and a few more conspiracy thrillers), the roots of their development and standing within Hollywood film culture are clear enough. The Cold War film genre, as it transpired from the late 1940s, obviously drew its inspiration from the battles for dominance between America and the Soviet Union, most often identified in movies deriving their influence out of the legacy of World War Two fictional *and* documentary features. But the history to that point shows developments and influences that wind their way even further back into Hollywood's past. Indeed, as Tony Shaw's excellent analysis remarks:

> The American film industry had effectively been at war with communism for three decades prior to Joseph McCarthy. Not only was this thirty years before the appearance of William Wellman's *The Iron Curtain* (1948), often called Hollywood's first Cold War movie, it was also, significantly, thirty years before most scholars indicate the 'cultural Cold War' started.[6]

Shaw is referring to a long-standing ideological battle, the later cultural result of which was a fight for supremacy in other areas of society: notably, literature, art and space, as well as film in the post-war era. Our concern is to identify the reflexive style and nuance that a lot of these films employed, as much as it is to assess their contribution to the Cold War battleground; the key here is the intertwining of domestic political concerns with bleaker, modernist forms and stylistic flourishes that influenced cinematic presentation as much as it did ideological conviction further on down the line.

In the emerging gangster genre of the 1930s, as we have seen, movies like *Little Caesar, The Public Enemy* (both 1931), *Scarface* (1932) and *Angels with Dirty Faces* (1938), for instance, incorporated the scandal surrounding public officials and the pervasive force of institutional corruption into their narrative sweep as backdrops to the rise and fall of ambitious and cocky anti-heroes. Directors like Mervyn LeRoy and the aforementioned Wellman were well versed in the artistic pretensions that cinema could bring to social analysis and they attempted to segue stories of small-time hoodlums and hard-pressed law enforcers into tales of rising underworld kingpins, set against a backdrop of institutional failure and inertia.

But the early 1930s also mixed the glamorous with the grimy. Hollywood's interest in 'social problem' films has been outlined in Chapter 2 and here their influence on and attachment to the embryonic political thriller are accentuated by their relation to the legalistic and courtroom dramas that were proving all the rage too. At socially progressive Warner Bros, one of the most famous and interesting movies was *The Mouthpiece* (1931). A loosely based interpretation of the life of attorney William J. Fallon, the film reflected the rough, tough amalgam of criminals, crooked businessmen and shady politicians who lurked in the halls of public institutions. The film's success significantly paved the way for other like-minded features such as *Public Defender* (1931) and *State's Attorney* (1932).

And as we saw with more overt political films like *Washington Merry-Go-Round* and *Gabriel Over the White House*, Hollywood narratives made use of the gangster epithet and one-man vigilante crusade to give a contemporary authenticity to stories of political and institutional strife. In the latter film, bootleg gangster Nick Diamond is hunted down by the authorities and violent justice is imposed, mirroring the eye-for-an-eye redemptive ending of the Jimmy Cagney, Paul Muni and George Raft series of movies that launched a fascination with the genre. As Muni further displayed in LeRoy's *I am a Fugitive from a Chain Gang*, and as films like *Heroes for Sale* and *Our Daily Bread* confirmed in the nascent New Deal period, the 'social problem' film had no problem in examining the state of America and some of its institutions during the Depression, but it was less easy to identify narratives that dealt in the thrills and spills of political intrigue and spying.

In Britain, however, Alfred Hitchcock's burgeoning reputation of the time as a purveyor of mystery and underworld deception was being brought to bear on a series of classic British takes on the new thriller style. Both *The Man Who Knew Too Much* (1934) and his adaptation of

Conrad's *The Secret Agent* (retitled *Sabotage* (1936)) were huge successes and Hitchcock set the tone by having layered and confused narratives that were occupied by morally vacant anarchists and predatory assassins wandering the streets of London. Fritz Lang's career in Germany had concocted a similar outline within the artistic realms of expressionism, and was brilliantly realised in his famous series of *Dr. Mabuse* films. Both directors then went on to bring their taste for politically charged spy narratives to the Hollywood backlots by the end of the 1930s and their arrival really explained how the film industry helped to import an almost exclusively European sub-genre into America. Lang's first few American films, *Fury* (1936), *You Only Live Once* (1937) and the somewhat ill-judged heist caper, *You and Me* (1938), all show a director intent on bringing murder, deceit, intrigue and blackmail to an American film colony, if not wider society in general, mired – as he saw it – in all sorts of uninteresting feelings like optimism, romance and tidy cinematic resolutions. Lang was not really interested in any of these aspects so much as he was in human frailties, addictions and obsessions, though he was forced to use some of the softer American characteristics to placate the Hollywood firmament at times. Hitchcock felt the same but ploughed his own furrow in any case and almost single-handedly invented the World War Two espionage thriller with *Foreign Correspondent* (1940) and *Saboteur* (1942). Lang, hot on his heels, produced a response with *Man Hunt* (1941) and the later *Ministry of Fear* (1944).

Hitchcock and Lang's tactics highlighted a divide that existed between American and European film styles and a schism in cultural politics too. The tension between the two helped accentuate the ideological questions and problems that certain filmmakers were willing to explore. As already stated, Tony Shaw's investigation is more concerned with the push and pull between communism and capitalism, as outlined in the Cold War movies of the 1940s onwards; but in contrast to the two directors mentioned above, Ernst Lubitsch's *Ninotchka* (1939), arriving at roughly the same time as the initial Hollywood-produced Hitchcock and Lang films, immediately delineates for Shaw the series of binary oppositions that weaved European and American sensibilities together but which also helped define the Cold War movie for nearly half a century. 'Freedom versus oppression, materialism versus poverty, beauty versus ugliness, romance versus asexual androgyny would act as models for numerous later movies,' he asserts.[7]

As a bookend to exemplify these continuing dichotomies through the period, Shaw equates the Lubitsch film with Taylor Hackford's *White Nights* (1985), a feature made forty-five years later that landed dead-centre in the middle of the Reagan era and which confirmed all those 1980s traits for male bonding, ideological awakening and the realisation of what Shaw calls Soviet 'stultification'.[8] Telling the tale of two dancers (one a Russian defector whose plane is forced to land back in the country, the other an American living there), who both resolve to escape the disintegrating society of old-style communism, with art imitating life in the form of real-life defectee, Mikhail Baryshnikov, *White Nights* and movies around it such as *No Way Out* (1987) and even *Rambo: First Blood Pt II* (1985) might be complimented for predicting the immediate collapse of the Soviet experiment. But for Shaw they really replicated the same kinds of concerns and predisposition Hollywood had been engaged with around communism since the end of World War One, let alone Two.

Ideologically, then, it was easy to see why American society was uneasy about communism – and fascism – as the 1930s progressed and why Hollywood might make such a big deal about highlighting and then repelling it as best it could. Political theorist Michael Foley notes the impact of a writer like Herbert Croly, for example, in the early part of the century.[9] Profoundly influencing progressive leaders like Theodore Roosevelt and Woodrow Wilson, Croly's *The Promise of American Life* (1909) promoted a philosophical idealism reminiscent of Hegel – that is, national citizenship should act as a communal obligation on the population; this was precisely the sort of idealistic communitarianism that smacked of distasteful European 'systems' for Americans in general and Hollywood in particular, who baulked at this option as the 1930s slowly sank into conflict and destruction abroad.

When Hollywood did begin to look outward and embrace other national societies, it was done under the guise of World War Two propaganda and necessity. Most famously in a series of pro-Soviet narratives, some of which were inspired by real accounts and memorials, *North Star* (1943), *Song of Russia* (1944) and most especially Michael Curtiz's *Mission to Moscow* (1943) paraded Russian endeavour and sacrifice in the face of Nazi aggression and megalomania. Never mind that Joseph Stalin had a touch of the megalomaniacal about him too, that the purges of the late 1930s had been but a trifling incident, or that the Soviets had signed a pact with the Germans before they had been double-crossed and invaded, Curtiz's adaptation of Ambassador Joseph Davies's book has Walter Huston playing Davies with all the starry-eyed sincerity and belief in Soviet resilience that the actor brought to a host of political roles during the 1930s.

The reward for Curtiz, as for screenwriter Howard Koch (the pair that brought us *Casablanca* only a year before), was to be investigated and blacklisted by HUAC after the war. By then, anti-communism, as well as the Cold War, was moving into full swing but the movies of the war years, different as they were from spy thrillers, assassination movies and, most crucially, the paranoid conspiracy narratives to come, did lay the groundwork for the sort of developments that would come to fruition by the 1960s.

POST-1945: COLD WAR CONSPIRACY

In the immediate post-war era, it appeared that social-consciousness cinema had a future in Hollywood. On the back of propaganda documentaries and wartime intrigue, a series of films emerged that linked realism and melodrama in an effort to consider the effects of war (*The Best Years of Our Lives*, 1946), military racism (*Crossfire*, 1947) and a combination of the two (*Home of the Brave*, 1949). For film historians like David Cook, these movies and others, such as *Boomerang!* (1947, directed by Elia Kazan) and Henry Hathaway's *Call Northside 777* (1948), created a heady period in Hollywood after the war that saw filmmakers imbibe the style and influence of European neo-realism and expressionism.[10] With the creation of *film noir*, Hollywood also slowly began to give an American spin to revenge stories challenging modern conventions and tipping their hat to the cinema of Renoir, Zavattini and, of course, Lang.

Brian Neve presents a whole number of writers and directors who were responsible for this post-war race towards radical realism and persuasive politics. Carl Foreman and Dore Schary, Jules Dassin and Albert Maltz, Joseph Losey and Abraham Polonsky: all of them were affected by war, by European cinema, and by their ideological commitment to more left-wing, indeed in some cases communist, themes and beliefs.[11]

From *They Drive by Night* (1940), *The Maltese Falcon* (1941) and *Double Indemnity* (1944) to *The Killers* (1946), *The Big Clock* (1948), *D.O.A.* (1949) and Lang's own *The Big Heat* (1953), Hollywood created a series of angular pictures that promoted the aspirations and interest of other prominent directors too, like Billy Wilder, Nicholas Ray and John Farrow. Together with Otto Preminger, these men were important protégés who signalled the emergence of the post-war political thriller. What they and their films all had in common was a psycho-analytical framework from which they to began to examine individual conscious-ness and reactions to power and control, scenarios that would be later incorporated into the paranoia movies of the 1960s and 1970s. Once these themes had been joined by the emerging threat of the Cold War, Hollywood looked further afield towards the possibility of domestic infiltration and began to incorporate ideologically darker, un-Ameri-can characters into its pictures, though it would take a decade for this to be fully realised. In addition to Wellman's *The Iron Curtain*, then, already mentioned, movies such as Hathaway's *Diplomatic Courier* (1952) became locked in Cold War European settings with master spies (here played by Tyrone Power) seeking to expose treacherous Soviet plans for invasion of, in this case, Yugoslavia. With beautiful double-agents in tow and a jaunt across the European landscape on hand, Hathaway's film was, if anything, a precursor to the wit and gadgetry of James Bond that would follow in the wake of these sorts of pictures.[12]

No film, however, defined the combination of American and European sensibilities, visual construction and ideological contempla-tion in quite the manner of Carol Reed's *The Third Man* (1949), the nas-cent and truly original Cold War thriller. Of course, Reed's film was not strictly a Hollywood production. The partnership of David O. Selznick and Alexander Korda commissioned the movie for the British-based London Films (just as they had done for Reed's previous effort a year beforehand, the brilliant *The Fallen Idol*) and the only real Hollywood input was Selznick's contracted players, Joseph Cotten and Alida Valli, as well as the monumental presence of Orson Welles.

With a script by Graham Greene from his own story and strong sup-porting British character actors like Trevor Howard and Bernard Lee, the film could barely be equated with Hollywood fare at all, although that did not stop Selznick attempting to have a hand in virtually every stage of the production. But what does give the picture its link into Hollywood generally, and the emerging paranoia and conspiracy genre in particular, is its recall of a post-war Vienna toiling under the weight of wartime destruction, black market racketeering and, cru-cially, American optimism. The narrative, characters, stylistic touches and Selznick's constant hankering after a more upbeat ending all preyed upon an American philosophy of forward-thinking, Marshall Plan-inspired progress for the city and for Europe more widely. But

what Greene and Reed concentrate on instead is the beginning of subterfuge, concealment, spying and bipolar diplomacy in the post-war
era.

Vienna is subdivided into sectors, just as Berlin was at this time,
trust runs very low on the streets of the city, and the new world order
appears opportunistic, manipulative and exploitative. In the midst of
this, bright-eyed American novelist Holly Martins (Cotton) arrives on
a speaking engagement but also on the lookout for his friend Harry
Lime (Welles), who has, it seems, disappeared. Almost immediately,
Martins is presented with the news that Lime is dead and makes contact with his friend's girlfriend, the desperately mournful Anna (Valli).
She is certainly not optimistic about the future, nor about Holly's
rather idealistic view of Lime. When Martins then belatedly discovers
that Harry is not dead, his world, the new 'American Century' world,
is forced to confront harsh realities. The British army personnel, led
by Major Calloway (Howard), believe at first that Martins is tied up
in Lime's murky business dealings; Martins then learns that those
dealings involve the illegal trading around the capital of penicillin that
is impure and causing the deaths of sick children; and to top it all,
Martins's literary seminar, which is his reason for being in Vienna in
the first place, is a disaster. His western dime-store style of literature is
laughed at and dismissed out of hand in favour of contemporary tastes
for European philosophy and existentialism.

Using the gothic intensity of an old European city brought to its
knees by war, and filming in sparse light and at acute angles (a process
that rightly won an Oscar for cinematographer Robert Krasker), Reed
and his crew gave *The Third Man* its *noir*-ish contours and ideological patina. By the time we reach the climax, which sees Lime hunted
down through the sewer system below the city streets, the metaphors
of labyrinthine politics and complex personal relationships are already
well established. Even Harry's inevitable death, after his fake one has
been exposed, does not provide nearly enough comfort in conclusion,
and certainly was not enough for Selznick.

The final scene after Lime's funeral has Calloway driving Martins
away out of the cemetery and past Anna. Martins urges him to stop,
and then asks Calloway to look after her when he has gone. Both know
that in Vienna now, where she has been acquainted with a black mar-
keteer and child-killer, Anna is marked as undesirable and it is a hollow
promise that cannot be guaranteed. *The Third Man* ends with the Cold
War truly beginning and Holly Martins's American-induced optimism

Noir *photography in Carol Reed's classic,* The Third Man

in a world in which fascism and totalitarianism have been vanquished has been completely punctured by his experiences in Austria.

If Hollywood found it hard, then, to come up with anything quite as tense and immediate as *The Third Man* during the 1950s, it was not because there was a shortage of talent, as the list above demonstrates. Directors like Carl Foreman, as well as George Stevens, Fred Zinnemann and, of course, Hitchcock and Lang, produced important films that had a flavour of the currents of the time. But the arrival of HUAC in Hollywood, the rise of Joseph McCarthy and the blacklist that followed, corrupted and then cauterized the film community of its political inclinations for the best part of a decade. When it was all done, a new mood of filmmaking did emerge in Hollywood, but it was one now prompted by apocalyptic features such as Stanley Kramer's *On the Beach* (1959). As G. Tom Poe points out, the significance of Kramer's nuclear war film was that it arguably asserted its importance as an 'event' far more than it did as a 'text' in its own right. The initial reviews of the film were only moderately good, but caught as it was in the middle of heightened Cold War tension, *On the Beach* put down a cultural marker for attitudes towards American–Soviet relations that began to question the righteousness of the cause on both sides. Parent company United Artists came up with the smart idea of holding a premiere for their picture in Moscow just to exemplify the hold both superpowers had on the world's future. Government bids to undermine the significance and impact of the film's realisation of the aftermath of atomic conflict, as Poe attests to, then backfired and only contributed to more positive notices after the picture had arrived in cinemas, and respectable box-office returns started to follow. For the morbid subject it was and the premise it provided, the response was extraordinary and a secondary discourse that involved people, some of whom had not even seen the movie, sprang up and provoked debate and commentary in newspapers, magazines and in society more generally.[13]

On the Beach set the agenda for a more questioning and reactionary Hollywood discourse to emerge in the 1960s, as well as a new generation of activist filmmakers that were headed by the 32–year-old John Frankenheimer. Already a director of such acclaimed pieces as *The Birdman of Alcatraz*, Frankenheimer turned his attention in 1962 to Richard Condon's recent best-selling novel and engaged George Axelrod to adapt a screenplay for this contemporary thriller. In doing so, Axelrod and his director laid the groundwork for much of what was to follow in political movies over the next forty years. The film, released in October 1962 and starring Frank Sinatra, Lawrence Harvey and Janet Leigh, was *The Manchurian Candidate*.

Leonard Quart and Albert Auster identify the film as a neat balancing act for the liberal elite emerging in Hollywood after nearly a decade of inquiry and inquisition. The left wing that had looked to be in the vanguard of the new Hollywood after the war had largely dissipated in the face of HUAC and McCarthy, and Frankenheimer's film had more than a thing or two to say about the rumour and scaremongering that had done such damage. The film is at pains to expose the powerbrokers in Washington masquerading as patriots or rational figures, but it is also, Quart and Auster feel, too timid to contest the orthodoxy that had grown up around untouchable control freaks like J. Edgar Hoover.[14]

Both writers challenge some of the film's ideological combativeness precisely because the nature of its conspiracy seems to allow only one character, Major Ben Marco (Frank Sinatra), to understand the threat at hand from his army colleague and Korean War hero Raymond

Shaw (Lawrence Harvey), as well as Shaw's stepfather – the buffoon-ish Senator John Iselin – and his mother – the cold and calculating Eleanor Shaw Iselin (Angela Lansbury). It is, in Quart and Auster's opinion, a film that on the surface appears radical and reactionary, and yet lurking underneath are common conservative instincts. Like *On the Beach*, *The Manchurian Candidate* was also set to become as much an 'event' as a film standing on its own reputation, but even if this and the charge that it only rehearses the conditions for Cold War paranoia and infiltration are true, it is still a picture whose profound effect on political filmmaking in Hollywood is continuously being felt.

Raymond is a war hero returned from Korea and back in the bosom of his politically ambitious family. While he is anxious to distance himself from the aspirations of the Iselins, however, his platoon com-mander, Marco, is hired as a press liaison officer in Washington. Here he gets to witness the ineptitude of Iselin first-hand at a news confer-ence where the Senator mimics McCarthy's accusations of communists within the walls of government itself. Marco is also having nightmares, though: dreams of atrocities and indoctrination at some secret location in Manchuria. Frankenheimer's brilliantly conceived scene of hallu-cinogenic proportions has Raymond strangle one of his company at the orders of an opposing psychologist, Dr Yen Lo (Khigh Dhiegh), watched in docile fashion by his brainwashed comrades, including Marco. But the scene/dream keeps spinning and the Manchurian lec-ture hall, populated by military generals of Eastern or Asiatic persua-sion amid pictures of Stalin and Mao, slowly morphs into a meeting of the New Jersey Garden Club, where pruning roses is the order of the day. At once confusing and disorientating, Frankenheimer's rough-and-ready comparison of the garden club with Senator McCarthy's first high-profile speech to the women of Wheeling, West Virginia, in 1950 is an apparent causal link that only progresses still further as the film continues in its bid to lambaste the extremism of both left and right in the heart of the Cold War moment.

But Quart and Auster's point about the enclosed conspiratorial plot is well taken as the narrative proceeds. The list of people winding up dead rises, including the astute Senator Thomas Jordan (John McGiver), whose daughter Raymond has subsequently married and then mur-dered as his brainwashed mission nears its completion, and only Marco seems capable of stopping any of it. When the Major learns that it is playing cards, and the Queen of Diamonds especially, that are the trigger for Raymond's actions, he tries to intervene, to 're-programme' his friend not to carry out the task and save the political convention about to take place in Madison Square Garden from disaster. Iselin is to be a supporter and running mate to the presidential candidate, Benjamin K. Arthur (Robert Riordan), but when an assassin strikes during the acceptance speech, he is to rise up in Arthur's place, receive the nomination, and be carried into the White House on a wave of sympathy and grief from the public. The plotter, handler of Raymond and mastermind behind this devious 'communist' conspiracy, is none other than Raymond's mother, working for Moscow.

As the appointed hour nears, the convention starts, and Marco desperately hunts down Raymond in the rafters of the Garden. Shots ring out, yet Raymond has not trained the rifle on Arthur after all, but on Iselin and then his mother before turning the gun on himself. Has Ben's 'reverse brainwashing' worked or did Raymond know and reject the 'conditioning' all along? Is his war record legitimate or simply concocted as part of the plan? The questions hint at that which cannot be trusted any longer in public life: military service, government authority, or ideologies of any kind.

While Quart and Auster's theory of narrative enclosure is a fair summary of the events, conversely, the playing out of Raymond's pre-ordained plan amid lethargy and incomprehensibility arguably adds to the spirit of confusion and displacement. Are the general public aware of such developments as brainwashing in the Cold War and do they feel powerless to prevent state-sanctioned plots in any case? Is history a reliable guide to anything? The clever use of the Benjamin Arthur moniker provides chinks of historical recognition and memory by linking an American leader of the past with a fictional one of the present. But in history it was President Chester A. Arthur who ended up the beneficiary of assassination, and not the potential victim of it, as the successor to the murdered James Garfield in 1881. In a sense the Arthur here becomes a beneficiary too and Frankenheimer suggests that all these things – history, memory, ideology – can be usurped, swapped around, misremembered; and that the public are not as aware of the Soviet threat from within as they might be, not that this rescues the US from criticism either. As Jonathan Kirshner so succinctly puts it, 'Any film that can end, logically, with its central character murdering his mother while dressed as a priest wearing the Congressional Medal of Honor, can be fairly labelled "un-American".'[15]

Susan Carruthers's fascinating exposure of the 'brainwashing' aspect of *The Manchurian Candidate* also presents us with two further important contentions. First of all Carruthers details the more obvious aspect of this ploy in the 'conditioning' of Raymond and his platoon by Yen Lo; it is a plot device taken wholesale from events in Korea, where thousands of captured prisoners of war were allegedly being exposed to similar experiments and 'oriental techniques'.[16] An even more interesting aspect however, is the way the film itself subjects the American people to brainwashing through the series of staged events that kicks off with Raymond's return to the US and the hero's welcome that is organised by his mother and stepfather. This carries on through the press conference in Washington that Ben is ostensibly in charge of but which Iselin hijacks to demand just how many communists there are lurking in the corridors of government. Quoting Thomas Doherty, Carruthers sees the scenes as part of a media construction that echoes the staged or 'pseudo event' talked of in Daniel Boorstin's book, *The Image*, released in the same year as the movie.[17]

Where Carruthers crosses the path of the conservative outline discussed by Quart and Auster is in the political content of the movie. Having already stated that Frankenheimer's film really set the agenda for political thrillers to come, Carruthers is keen to question where the politics actually exists in the story.[18] The conspiracy to take over the White House is not explained, Mrs Iselin's treacherous motivations even less so, and the Senator's bumbling tendencies only suggest that politics is increasingly filled by inept and incompetent ciphers for someone else's aims and intent. Where Quart and Auster see the narrative bottled up in Marco's lone sleuthing, Carruthers suggests further motivations and explanations are hard to come by at times.

Whatever the confusions might have been, Frankenheimer himself delighted in the furore the movie created and the claims and counter-claims that came from all wings of the political spectrum. He often said that he knew he had done his job well when, at the opening of the movie at a theatre in California, members of both the right-wing John Birch Society *and* the Communist Party found themselves shoulder to shoulder on the pavement, protesting against the film for entirely opposite reasons.[19]

But if the film, and indeed Frankenheimer, found it hard at times to explain all the goings-on in the plot, that was nothing compared to the array of coincidences and rumour that swept the movie after its release. Sinatra's backing and unofficial capacity as an executive producer reportedly got the film made in the first place when United

Raymond Shaw, brainwashed in The Manchurian Candidate

Artists were lukewarm about it as a proposition. But it was also Sinatra, almost exactly a year after its cinematic release (by which time the film had grossed a little over $4 million), who was supposedly behind the film's 'withdrawal' from public exhibition in the wake of the Kennedy assassination. There is no doubt that the star had been shattered by his friend's death, but more unnerving than that was Sinatra's reported worry about *The Manchurian Candidate*'s link to a previous film the star had made a decade before.

In Lewis Allen's low-budget thriller, *Suddenly* (1954), Sinatra played John Barron, a hired hit man who turns up in the small town of Suddenly with a couple of buddies intent on assassinating the President when his train stops at the community's tiny railway station and he travels on by car to his vacation destination. Barron and the hoods acquire a hilltop house overlooking the station, where Ellen Benson (Nancy Gates), her son 'Pidge' (Kim Charney) and father 'Pop' (James Gleason) are living. Together with Sheriff Tod Shaw (Sterling Hayden), who has stumbled on the scene and is taken hostage too, Barron and his captives wait out the time until the appointed 5 o'clock arrival of the train.

The script is occasionally ponderous and the assassins' perfect plan quickly unravels. But the film's tension keeps the action taut and intriguing all the way to its climactic moment. Barron is a professional killer, a loose cannon who was discharged from the army in World War Two for his love of combat. He does not know why he is killing the President, we know nothing of the target and Barron is so apolitical as to be virtually psychotic. Shaw reminds him that presidential assassins have never got away and, as the fateful hour nears, Barron's masterplan is revealed as fatally flawed: not because he has not thought everything out, but because history and his degenerative mental state begin to conspire against him. It is one of Sinatra's best acting performances and even though, or possibly because, he never gets his chance to shoot the target – the train rolls straight on through the station at the last minute – Barron's demise is gripping and something of a taster for the conspiracy plots to come.

Two assassination films, nearly ten years apart, that Sinatra had been involved in: the alleged coincidence that spooked him was the perception that art had come to imitate life rather too intimately. In interviews after the shooting in Dallas in 1963, Marina Oswald stepped forward and reportedly explained that a motivation for her husband to shoot President Kennedy had been his viewing of *Suddenly* on television in the weeks prior to the presidential visit. Whether true or otherwise, as Art Simon recounts, the story entered into mythological folklore in the years that followed, being related in, amongst other publications, Don DeLillo's take on the life and actions of Lee Harvey Oswald in *Libra*. Only deepening the mystery still further, later investigation of Marina Oswald's story found that *Suddenly* had indeed been screened on 19 October 1963, but not on every affiliate network and not, interestingly enough, in the Dallas suburb where the Oswalds were residing at the time.[20]

The events in Texas and Sinatra's fears about the circumstances he seemed embroiled in were certainly a motivation of sorts for *The Manchurian Candidate* to be shelved. But the curiosity of the historical link does not end there. When the film finally re-appeared on video a quarter of a century later, it was touted as the movie that had not been seen since 1963. That was not quite true. As Michael Scheinfeld uncovered, Frankenheimer's picture had been aired on the CBS network in 1965, less than two years after the Kennedy assassination, was screened again in 1966, and was then sold on to NBC, which broadcast the film at least once in the early 1970s.[21] But the mythology and uncanny coincidences fell in with the film's representative nature: as a movie that signalled decline and fall, changing political aspirations, the very doubts that were thought to be indicative of America's fall from grace in the later 1960s. The journal *Positif* concluded that Sinatra's turn to the right at the end of the 1960s and into the coterie of supporters that followed Ronald Reagan into the White House a decade later, was the symbolic gesture emanating out of the film: a previous high-profile Democrat now defected to the Republicans, which signalled the collapsing liberal consensus that Ryan and Kellner pursued in their theoretical assessment of the movies of this time.[22]

Frankenheimer was not put off by the experience of *The Manchurian Candidate*, however. If anything, it galvanised him to pursue conspiracy and intrigue still further in his follow-up, *Seven Days in May* (1964), starring Burt Lancaster and Kirk Douglas. A gung-ho air force general, James Scott (Lancaster), seeks to overthrow an appeasing president and create confrontation with the Soviet Union, which, he believes, will be on the verge of world domination if a nuclear disarmament treaty is signed between the two superpowers and the Soviets choose to renege on the deal. Fredric March plays President Jordan Lyman with a resoluteness and upstanding dignity that manage to save the day, aided by one of Scott's friends and comrades, Colonel Martin Casey (Douglas), who punctures the attempted military coup.

Edmond O'Brien was awarded an Oscar nomination for his portrayal of southern Senator Clark, acting as loyal confidant to the President while remaining humorous and rancorous all at the same time in the face of military takeover. 'The entire plot, a fantasy of disaster, is totally believable in the manner in which it is portrayed, due to Frankenheimer's calm, assured direction,' observed one reviewer, revealing just how widely acclaimed the film was at the time, and what a box-office smash it proved to be, in a manner largely forgotten thanks to its proximity to the director's earlier, now more acclaimed and controversial work.[23]

Nuclear war still remained the defining motif in a number of movies of the time, not least Sidney Lumet's *Fail Safe* (1964), where Henry Fonda is the unnamed President dealing with technological mal-functions and aircraft heading for the Soviet Union. The planes fly beyond their 'fail safe' position of the title – that is, after the point at which they can be recalled – and on towards their target where the deadly payload will be dropped. The President makes a bargain to save the world even while his aides – and in particular nuclear sci-entist Groeteschele (Walter Matthau) – urge the President to use this moment as the chance to 'win' the Cold War and go for all-out attack. Instead, the President agrees to the bombing of New York as retalia-tion, even though he knows his family are there and that millions will die. Lumet's taut, hair-raising scenario made the earlier *On the Beach* look positively tranquil by comparison, and Fonda and Matthau give two of the best performances of their careers.

Charles Maland has argued that this collection of mid-1960s nuclear narratives began to refocus attention on the perceived ideological con-sensus at the heart of Cold War doctrines. An alternative conscious-ness, he suggests, was starting to pervade people's minds; it challenged the conformity of the immediate post-war years and was throwing out the old rules about political engagement in Hollywood, and political realities of bipolar conflict further afield.[24] Frankenheimer himself had talked of the 'absurdity' of the claims and counter-claims between left and right wings, capitalist and communist ideologies, but no film brought this absurdity home in more startling and hilarious terms, as Maland points out, than Stanley Kubrick's *Dr. Strangelove* (1964).

These films did not exactly rebuke the establishment for its endan-germent of mankind. As Susan Sontag wrote of Kubrick's movie at the time, no one was standing outside the theatres raging about the immi-nent collapse of democracy and life as we knew it, as if Hollywood had broken some sacred taboo and dared criticise establishment doctrine. Indeed, Sontag felt that the kids who queued up for *Dr. Strangelove* understood the mentality of the film, its dark humour, pseudo-psy-chological references to sex and permissiveness, its devil-may-care attitude to the end of the world, far better than the commentators and intellectuals who were caught up in a frenzy over the picture's release.[25]

Originally intending to make a straightforward thriller adaptation of Peter George's best-selling novel, *Red Alert*, Kubrick with screenwriter Terry Southern opts for black humour and farce instead, verging on the absurd. Peter Sellers plays multiple roles as President Merkin Muffley, an Adlai Stevenson type-figure; Lionel Mandrake, a British RAF Group Captain straight out of World War Two; and the eponymous anti-hero of the title, a play on Groeteschele from Lumet's film, who himself bore more than a passing resemblance to Nazi turned NASA rocket scientist, Wernher von Braun. As with *Fail Safe*, the round-the-clock airborne nuclear arsenal receives the wrong instructions and heads for Moscow at the behest of Sterling Hayden's Jack D. Ripper, who attempts single-handedly to take over a military installation, with Mandrake for company. In 'The War Room', Muffley finds Russian premier Kissov drunk on the phone and, while trying to explain the problem, is advised to call directory inquiries in Omsk, who might be able to help him. Arch-conservative General Turgidson (George C. Scott) manhandles the Russian ambassador, only to be reminded by Muffley that 'Gentlemen! You can't fight in here . . . this is the War Room.'

The best compliment Kubrick thought paid to him was from critics who took the tongue-in-cheek liberties at face value and accused the director of celebrating nuclear holocaust, rather than exposing its appalling ideological determinism.[26] The conclusion to such comments might be that paranoia had not quite invaded the American conscience by the mid-1960s, but it would not take long to arrive.

One of the defining characteristics of *noir* movies, and indeed of the arrival of the thriller as a dedicated genre in its own right from the 1940s through to the 1960s, was the pervasive presence and authority of the cop/detective/private eye character. Distinguishing features included reckless abandonment of procedure, complicated private lives and an almost incessant trust in instinct and hunches. As Ray Pratt puts it, 'as the myth of the private detective diminished, the expanding genre of paranoia thrillers developed.'[27] The certainties that came from these personality tics faded in the 1960s and 1970s as a concentration on institutional authority was brought to bear on screen characters like those mentioned above – generals, scientists, politicians – who had once been part of the institutional fabric, were still part of it or thought they were part of it, but who now seemed to be embroiled in conspiracy from the outside. As with Raymond Shaw in *The Manchurian Candidate*, what once had seemed certain and assured was now questionable and usurped.

ALAN J. PAKULA AND THE CLASSIC PARANOIA STYLE

Rarely can there have been a group of films that caught the imagination and the atmosphere of the times in quite the manner of the paranoia collection that surfaced in the 1970s. From a decade that still located its conspiracies in the wider Cold War arena, a set of films released roughly between 1971 and 1976 transformed the outlook, ideologically and visually, of the paranoia thriller in dramatic fashion. David Miller's *Executive Action* (1972), which took its inspiration from Mark Lane's *Rush to Judgement*, a book-cum-documentary that tested and rejected the conclusions of the Warren Commission investigating Kennedy's death, was pure assassination narrative. In its attempts to re-open the investigation into Kennedy's death in Dallas, it parades doubts and conspiracies that Lane's documentary and book had called to attention, but the tone, atmosphere and intent of the picture was to have nothing like as profound an influence as that which was to come from other filmmakers in the decade. Likewise, Robert Aldrich's *Twilight's Last Gleaming* (1977), intriguing and quite gripping though it is, seems, like Miller's film, to belong more to the 1960s catalogue of nuclear thrillers. Burt Lancaster is a disillusioned ex-Vietnam veteran Lawrence Dell, on the run from prison; he holes up in a nuclear silo and demands money and concessions from the President, as well as the public airing of a secret conversation held between Dell (Lancaster) and the White House right at the outbreak of the war in South-East Asia.

Both films share the desire to leave their audience in bleak, somewhat fatalistic territory as they exit the cinema, but the paranoia unleashed in other films of the period made the political thriller even darker and more morbid in its societal outlook. Francis Ford Coppola's subtler *The Conversation* (1974) and Sidney Pollack's tense *Three Days of the Condor* (1975) brought social dislocation, political anxieties and cultural terror to the fore in films that sat uneasily with traditional Hollywood notions of linear narratives, satisfactory resolutions and traditional heroic protagonists. But the man who really developed all these traits was Alan J. Pakula, in a triumvirate of pictures. From the cool allure of *Klute* in 1971, to the mind-bending and sinister *The Parallax View* (1974) and masterful *All the President's Men* (1976), Pakula headlined a style and vision for the political thriller that forsook many trademark Hollywood elements and yet at the same time demonstrated the historical precedents and key influences that directed his work and this sub-genre of political movies during the decade. Pakula's films provided the thread for an examination of American politics and society from beyond authority and accountability in the 1970s and in the process created cinematic form and content that would define the agency of paranoia cinema in its entirety.

So, while an early example of the form, such as Miller's film, calls on established stars in the form of Burt Lancaster and Robert Ryan to assemble a rogues' gallery of capitalists and unhinged assassins who plot the Kennedy assassination in the absence of compelling evidence from the Warren Commission in a tidy but obvious selection of scenarios leading to the killing, movies skirting the boundaries of Pakula's fascination with alternative social and political reality, such as *The Conversation*, were far more scathing of the secret societies, surveillance culture and dubious corporations that dictated American life as the 1970s begin to unwind. Coppola's modestly budgeted take on an outsider culture of disparate loners on the margins of American society sees Harry Caul (Gene Hackman) as an electronics expert who takes on a seemingly innocuous job of following a couple presumed to be having an affair, only to stumble upon what he is convinced is a murder plot. Coppola's cinematography makes even San Francisco seem somewhat drab and demure while Caul's almost limitless capacity to reveal very little about himself, his past or his family unnerves and disorients the viewer even more. There are times when the film seems to meander, when the investigation and bugging he is pursuing amount to nothing; and the cinematic tension is entirely vacant at times, left hanging by long absences of incidental music or, indeed, sounds of any kind occasionally.

When the denouement kicks into gear, however, the shock to the senses becomes even more acute as a result of the absence beforehand. Not only do Caul's worst fears come true, but also the acoustic assault from the soundtrack is sometimes deafening and on more than one occasion terrifying. Coppola's shot of Caul anxiously looking at a perfectly ordinary hotel bathroom toilet that suddenly fills and overflows with blood is surely one of the most affecting paranoia scenes in 1970s cinema. In the end Caul is told that his services are no longer needed by the corporation that has engaged him, but they know he knows that something terrible has happened to Robert Duvall's unnamed 'Director'. In the final moments, as Caul immerses himself in his beloved jazz music, he is phoned at home only to have his saxophone played back to him by a recording machine that has been hidden in the apartment. Trapped in his own surveillance world and by his peers, Caul pulls the apartment to pieces in an attempt to find the bugging devices but is left defeated and forlorn as the credits roll.

In Sidney Pollack's *Three Days of the Condor* (1975), Joe Turner (Robert Redford) is a man similarly out of his depth in the unfolding conspiracy in which he is caught up. It has a screenplay by Lorenzo Semple, who had also written *The Parallax View* and in between worked on the Paul Newman thriller, *The Drowning Pool* (1975). Turner is a desk-bound CIA operative who reads books and documents for the agency. He works as part of a small team analysing data somewhere in the heart of New York, rides to work on a motor scooter and has a casual disregard for the ethics of his job. When his boss asks him why he is so reluctant to accept the fact that he cannot tell people what he does, he replies, 'Because I trust in people.' Early in the story, he shoots out of the back entrance to fetch lunch for his colleagues, only for a hit squad to arrive, led by the independently contracted assassin, Joubert (Max von Sydow); they decimate the staff, including Turner's girlfriend, Janice (Tina Chon).

What is so compulsive about the first fifteen minutes of Pollack's movie is that everything is so demonstrably normal and ordinary, to the extent that when Turner returns from the deli with lunch to find his colleagues slain, the paranoia that engulfs him and the film so immediately is absolute, rather like that which closes in on Caul in Coppola's finale. Turner walks out of the nondescript brownstone building his CIA unit has been operating in, under the guise of the American Literary Historical Society, and transforms into a man who cannot trust anything or anyone. Immediately on the street, a woman approaching him with a pram who happens to be wearing sunglasses triggers every suspicious instinct his association with the agency has now engendered. He contacts 'control' in the blind belief that he will be 'brought in', but successive phone calls reveal to him how little he can rely on people he realises he does not know. When an alleyway meeting with two agents – including an old friend – goes wrong because one of the agents is rogue, Turner's friend is shot and later dies in hospital, and the rogue agent then tries to eliminate Turner himself, he loses all faith in anything associated with the agency and authority. Hijacking a woman, Kathy Hale (Faye Dunaway), on the street, Turner holes up in her flat and begins to piece together the plot in which he is engulfed.

Once again, power and responsibility are merged symbolically in

Three Days as Pollack offers some cinematic pointers for Pakula's night-time settings in the following year's *All the President's Men*, which Redford was helping to bring to fruition as he made this movie. Conversations amongst the conspirators are set against the backdrop of a brightly lit Lincoln Memorial as well as downtown Washington streets and offer a template for the imagery Pakula was to employ so successfully.

And, just as with Coppola's cinematography and style, the scarcity of incidental sounds and the often bare, occasionally dingy cityscape speak to a decade drawn and hag-ridden by the military and political traumas engulfing the country. In contrast to the capital, the New York locations are often on streets that look untidy and dishevelled until, that is, a scene at the World Trade Center, which the film offers as a setting for a CIA field office. One was indeed located in 7 WTC, a building damaged and destroyed by the September 11th attacks twenty-six years later. In addition, Turner remarks that professional photographer Kathy's pictures in her flat show sparse, desolate scenes of burnt-out cars, empty streets and general decay: an allegory of the times surely, he implies. Michael Coyne quotes possibly the film's best line in this regard, arguing for its social and political summation in the scene when the unaccountable director Wasbash (John Houseman) informs Turner's contact Higgins (Cliff Robertson) that his intelligence career dates back to just after the Great War. What do you miss about that time? asks Higgins. 'The clarity,' Wasbash replies.[28]

Turner, meanwhile, finally confronts Joubert at the house of a CIA director, Atwood (Addison Powell), who is compromising the Company by pressing for conflict in the Middle East over oil, and who turns out to be the instigator of the whole conspiracy, as well as Joubert's last target. His assignment to kill Turner has been superseded at the close but, as he explains, that does not mean Turner has 'much of a future' in New York in any case. He will still be followed, and probably hunted down at some point. His only recourse, thinks Joubert, is a long trip to Europe. Turner leaves him, remarking that, unlike Wasbash, he does seem to have some clarity about it all. His own job is easy, Joubert replies: 'I don't have to believe in any side.'

Like *The Parallax View* and *The Conversation* before it, *Three Days of the Condor* is unwilling to throw up any convenient closure. Turner meets Higgins on a corner just off Times Square, by the site of the *New York Times* building. He informs Higgins that he has given the story to the paper, to which his handler despondently asks why. Part of the game, rationalises Turner, but as he walks away Higgins plants doubt in his mind. 'How do you know they'll publish it?' he asks. 'How do you know?' The picture freezes with Turner melting into the crowd and the credits commence.

The brilliant mix of ideological complexity in these films with the simplicity of their cinematic presentation was every bit as important as what was actually going on in the narratives and with the characters. It was this that Pakula really perfected across the first half of the 1970s. First off with *Klute*, which was in effect a psychological thriller whose political aspects only surfaced at the margins of characters aware of their surroundings and of the turmoil going on around them in early 1970s New York, but little else, Pakula made incredible use of sound, settings and atmosphere to get the feel of the movies right. In *The Parallax View* he uses the modernist landscape of 1970s Seattle to create a sense of distance and perspective from the centres of power, but still manages to implicate all parts of the institutional environment in a story of assassination, brainwashing and political unaccountability. Bookended by two scenes featuring shadowy assassination commissions who are located in totalitarian settings and who refuse dialogue or questioning of any sort, Pakula concocts a chilling tension from the off in his 1974 movie that sees a popular Senator murdered at the top of the city's recently constructed Space Needle. This was 'Kafka's America', he later said. 'Tossed up and turned into some kind of surreal nightmare.'[29]

Newspaper reporter Joe Frady, who is refused entry up to the top of the Needle prior to the assassination, becomes more and more convinced of the plausibility of an unknown organisation working to undermine the emergence of crusading politicians. Many of the witnesses to the murder wind up dead, and we next meet Frady in the scene directly after the opening sequences when he is looking to avoid the authorities who are raiding homes and trying to track him down three years on from the event. Eventually, he himself is supposedly brainwashed by the shady Parallax Corporation and induced to commit yet another assassination. Pakula's often subliminal cinematography almost hypnotises the audience, and the great persuasive nature of these films, and the style employed by him as director, were such that they almost seemed to offer the answers to real-world problems off screen.

As Art Simon positively articulates, paranoia-style Hollywood could easily be made to seem like paranoia-style real life with suspicious gunmen, seedy politicians and dark, dangerous urban landscapes set up as a collection of images (later mimicked and much clichéd) that might explain the real predicament of the nation in the mid-1970s.[30] Ryan and Kellner further point out that while our crusading individuals are somewhat ostracised from the rest of society, the movies do provide some kind of catharsis whereby resolute individual action can be asserted, even if it is never as successful as it was in political movie eras gone by.[31]

As *The Parallax View* reaches its denouement at an empty aircraft hangar of a building where a political rally is due to take place, power, patriotism and presentiment all merge together. Frady ends up in the rafters of the building with a rifle, just as Raymond Shaw does in *The Manchurian Candidate*. National symbols adorn the whole area, with balloons and tables decked out in red, white and blue. But, as well as the picture of the aspiring new candidate, George Hammond (Jim Davis), behind the stage we see other images of America's great and good, including Lincoln and Teddy Roosevelt; these are almost giant grotesque caricatures, imagined faces, as though painted by the likes of Lucien Freud. While Pakula seems to associate Hammond with these historical heavyweights, they are nevertheless horribly oblique visions of an iconic past seemingly tainted by the politics of the present. Hammond is assassinated while travelling from the stage on a buggy in the near-empty arena and Frady, who we suppose did not fire the bullet, is trapped before he can escape and is shot himself.

The sparse and desolate space that is created by the arena, the reverberations of the bullet, and the marching band music in the background engender just the kind of fearful symmetry Pakula was looking to achieve. But as he himself admitted, it was not quite meant to be that way.

> There was going to be this huge fundraising banquet, mobbed with people [he explains]. I went into the hall and said 'God, just put red, white and blue tablecloths on the tables. Keep this endless empty space here because that's much more of a nightmare quality.'[32]

To reinforce his point the commission returns in epilogue, summarising Hammond's death as the result of Frady's unhinged state, and the camera slowly tracks away from them as the film ends. No glorious resolution, no redemption, little meaning or hope: the film offers no

Political imagery in Pakula's The Parallax View

sense at all that the state of affairs and controlling forces can in any way be held to account.

If Ryan and Kellner's point about the heroes finding some meaning in the events taking place around them is hard to accept in *The Parallax View*, it is somewhat more apparent in *All the President's Men* (1976). Pakula's account of journalists Bob Woodward and Carl Bernstein's investigation into the Watergate scandal that brought down Richard Nixon is grounded in actual events, of course, but even this does not make it immune from moments of danger and disunion as the protagonists track down their quarry. He even attempts a similar sort of on-the-record proclamation to that which concludes *The Parallax View*. Just as in that film the assassination committee unveils its findings in a dimly lit room of some menace, affirming their version of the 'official' record of Joe Frady's death, so in *President's Men* Pakula concludes not with shots of Nixon's resignation speech nor his exit by helicopter from the White House lawn, but with a tight close-up of a typewriter banging out the sentences that fill in the rest of the story between late 1973 and Nixon's resignation in August 1974, and the consequences for some of the perpetrators. The film, like the investigation by the

Washington Post reporters, is thus made official in that the typewritten words are, as the film is at pains to stress, journalistic and source-based confirmations of facts and details about the president's corruption and duplicity towards the American people. It is, as Pratt surmises, 'a civics lesson in why freedom of the press is so important'.[33]

But elsewhere, dimly lit streets glossily coated by rain, moody stairwells that give all the impression of an Edward Hopper painting, and empty underground car parks with the odd screech of tyres and occasional footsteps, all play to Pakula's recurring fascination with that which is unknown, concealed and buried deep by officialdom and bureaucracy. In the Library of Congress, Pakula's celebrated shot that starts at the table where the journalists are looking at papers and evidence before panning out to reveal the size and scope of the building itself, and therefore its secrets, is a brilliantly conceived piece of cinematic rendering that makes the story fresh and immediate, even though its conclusion and legacy were already known in 1976 and even more so over thirty years later. Yet it still sets the standards and continues to be the inspiration for a host of imitators.

In the midst of this conspiratorial scheming and Hollywood fascination with the sights and sounds of paranoia in the mid-1970s, there were sceptical voices. Indeed, pre-dating what was to appear twenty years hence, critics like Fred Kaplan were less than convinced by the 'conspiracy craze' of the mid-1970s and what paranoia movies were trying and able to achieve. He went even further in asserting that the ideological premise of these films, at least, simply did not work. The pictures were a travesty of conspiracy, he said, because if there was a global or at least a large 'corporation' pulling the strings behinds the scenes, why were they biding their time in the inevitable drift toward takeover? If the capability existed, this was paradoxical paranoia, opined Kaplan, that 'neither necessitates nor logically implies the notion, or even the efficacy, of conspiratorial assassination as a means of domination'.[34]

Writing about *Executive Action* and *The Parallax View*, with a nod to inspirations like *The Ipcress File* and *Our Man in Havana*, Kaplan found it hard to rationalise the motivations and insecurities on which the films' premises lay. In both movies, the implication is that liberal politicians are being murdered. Why? he asks. Because they offer some greater threat to the establishment than other politicians? 'Nothing truly political is made of this,' he protests. 'The candidates are variously liberal but their views are never expressed.'[35]

Picking up the threads of the wider political and historical themes developed by C. Wright Mills and Richard Hofstadter, Kaplan concludes that the wave of paranoia which hit Hollywood in the mid-1970s did have an impact, but only because it was tapping into already established 'neurotic patterns of behaviour' in a society less sure of its future, and more suspicious of its past. 'As long as political cinema remains on this level of wanton non-thinking, it can make no contribution to enhancing the conditions of this country's political reality,' he damningly signed off.[36] Kaplan's points about narrative and character are not entirely unfounded and it is a position that rests on that which is most often the critical base for attacking many different types of political movie. If they are not setting the agenda, only reflecting the zeitgeist, playing with it, then what use are they truly?

The question is surely legitimate and ideologically this sub-genre of political films especially could be accused of being on the shakiest of ground when trying to conceptualise and theorise what paranoia actually represents or is about. But as with any cultural form, the art itself always adds something to the mix and these movies were no exception. After all, the conclusion of Pakula's trilogy of films was not fiction in any respect; even some of the paranoiac intention with which Woodward and Bernstein occasionally look over their shoulders in the darkened crevices of the director's Washington had its grounding in the investigation as it actually unfolded. With Pakula, Coppola and Pollack, therefore, the films reflected the stable and impressive style of filmmaking each was interested in pursuing. If paranoia could be described as an aesthetic mix of both political intrigue and visual menace, then the conscious use of sound – as already intimated – was at least as important in determining the atmosphere and intent of these pictures in this era of political movies as were the plot and screenplay.

In 1971, Pakula commissioned a young, aspiring and very genial New York jazz pianist to score the music for *Klute*. Michael Small wanted to be a theatrical composer but instead struck up a rapport with Pakula's style of directing and his movies' themes, becoming in the process, as Kyle Renick's appreciation of his work suggests, 'the unrivalled master of movie-music paranoia'.[37]

When it came to *The Parallax View*, Small's mixture of eerie mood music juxtaposed against 'faux patriotic' marching bands, as Renick describes it, made the emotion genuine and the manipulations of the Parallax Corporation frighteningly real, especially in the final assassination scene already described.[38] Although an outstanding composer in his own right, David Shire and his score for the final part of the paranoia trilogy, *All the President's Men*, owe much to Small's intuition for the genre, and his technique has been copied persistently down the years. Pakula found a cultural affinity with his audience to the extent that *All the President's Men* joined *One Flew over the Cuckoo's Nest* as the two top-grossing films in Hollywood during 1976, and the 'New Hollywood' elite came up with a list of movies – *Taxi Driver*, *Chinatown*, *The Godfather*, *The Last Picture Show* and so on – which challenged the dynamics of the film industry in the early 1970s as much as they did the traditions of social and cultural inquiry. But the mood for paranoia and re-appraisal of America's political system would not last. A year later the two biggest movies were *Rocky*, Sylvester Stallone's all-conquering boxing film, and a science-fiction epic by a developing but little known filmmaker in Hollywood, whose only previous hit had been the minor success, *American Graffiti*, in 1973. The director was George Lucas and the film *Star Wars*. Escapism was returning to the screens and the political conspiracy film would wait nearly a decade to re-emerge.

POLITICAL THRILLERS IN THE CONTEMPORARY ERA

It was extremely hard, if not impossible, for the political thriller to avoid the watershed ending of the Cold War as the 1990s got under way. The classic Cold War narrative, as well as dictating the way Hollywood dealt with foreign policy, was equally as relevant to the kind of para-noia and conspiracy thrillers that had emerged after *The Manchurian Candidate* and continued through the 1970s. Beyond these eras, how-ever, movies like *Red Dawn* (1984) with a young Patrick Swayze, Taylor Hackford's previously mentioned *White Nights* (1985), *No Way Out* (1987) and *The Hunt for Red October* (1990) all perceived the enemy of the United States to be recurrent communist ideologues mixed up in sometimes less than believable scenarios. And domestically too, the dark corners of Washington and the shady dealings of insider forces and Machiavellian villains owed much to the threat from outside the borders of America, the same kind of spies and infiltrators that had first shown their hand in the espionage thrillers of World War Two.

   If a movie like *The Manchurian Candidate* had its cinematic follow-ers and impersonators, however, no film, and no director, has served to redefine a genre and an era for political filmmaking quite as much as Oliver Stone's *JFK* (1992). Prior to its release, conventions of ide-ology and cinematic style had largely been set. Subsequent to it, *JFK* kick-started a whole new generation of engaged and posturing thriller pieces, each one owing something to Stone's radical agenda, if not his astonishing cinematographic presentation. By the start of the 1990s, Stone was already no stranger to controversy or to penetrating and caustic inquires into American policy, especially abroad. He won an Oscar for his script for Alan Parker's *Midnight Express* (1978), and in succession his films *Salvador* (1985), *Platoon* (1986), *Wall Street* (1987) and *Born on the Fourth of July* (1989) pulled no punches in their devastating critiques of Central American foreign policy, Vietnam, corporate capitalism and post-war recuperation and social unrest. Two of these pictures won him Best Director Oscars and the rest earned accolades and nominations in equal measure.

So it is fair to say that, when Stone announced at the turn of the decade that he was developing a three-hour-long epic about the Kennedy assassination, based primarily around Jim Marrs's somewhat controversial treatise, *Crossfire: The Plot That Killed Kennedy*, and Jim Garrison's recently published memoir, *On the Trail of the Assassins*, the project created a fair amount of interest. Garrison actually ended up appearing in a couple of scenes of the movie as Chief Justice, interviewing Jack Ruby in one while he is held in jail. So the media speculation became intense before the film even hit the screens. After its release, with the further involvement of historians, cinema scholars, politicians et al, the frenzy made sure that the movie produced as much debate and copy as any film might reasonably expect to create in an era before the internet, movie sites and political/fan blogs. In many ways, Stone himself revelled in the attention during this time, having acquired the moniker of America's most significant and important political film-maker of his generation, but he probably was not prepared for the kind of critical backdraft that met *JFK* upon its release. Clocking in at just over three hours eventually (with a director's cut that later added a further seventeen minutes) and including a fully annotated and unprecedented 'book of the film' that incorporated ninety-seven separate pieces about the picture and the assassination from reporters and academics, *JFK* quite simply became the most talked about and controversial movie of this and possibly any other decade in Hollywood's history.

As well as using Garrison as a source and part-time actor, the movie took as its focal point the story of the former New Orleans District Attorney. The assassination is persistently seen through Garrison's eyes, as played in lugubrious and heroic mode by Kevin Costner. As the evidence building up in New Orleans starts to make less and less sense, Garrison chases lead after lead with the determination of someone uncovering the very essence of American fabrication and crisis. Eventually, despite the attention of government sources and individuals, a trial emerges, played out around the somewhat fey character of Clay Shaw (Tommy Lee Jones), a onetime CIA operative who is hard to pin down.

Stone's defence in the face of increasing accusations that the film played fast and loose with known facts, or simply inserted insinuation as if it were fact, was to retreat back to his style and nature of presentation. But, as Peter Knight pointedly remarks, that was not always a convenient sanctuary either. 'Stone's insistence on his postmodern approach to representation and about being endlessly open to interpretation and revision, betrays at times a residual naïve faith in the power of images to speak for themselves and tell the truth.'[39] Knight refers to the constant repetition of the Zapruder film – the famous twenty-six seconds of 8 mm silent colour film taken by amateur cameraman Abraham Zapruder in Dealey Plaza – as though it were the definitive last word on the 'truth' of the event, despite its own controversies and contentions.

But Knight also concedes that, when it comes to the pivotal scene in the whole picture, the confrontation between Garrison and Colonel 'X' (Donald Sutherland) in Washington in preparation for Shaw's trial, the film is a 'tour de force of synthesis', bringing together footage, facts, assertions, documentary inserts, reconstructed pieces, still photography and more to create a thirty-minute sequence that is breathtaking in its cinematic construction and even more so for those less than sold on its premise.[40] And for those who did remain unconvinced, there were other scholars such as Robert Brent Toplin, who stepped forward to defend Stone still further by claiming that the greater part of the 'evidence' unleashed in the film was already well known and/or available in the public domain, even if it took some time to uncover.[41]

On the back of *JFK*, the Kennedy myth and the enigma of the events in Dallas filled screens in movies such as *Ruby* (1992), which told the tale of the former nightclub owner and the events leading up to his slaying of Lee Harvey Oswald in the Dallas County Jail, just three days after the shooting, and *Love Field*, with Michelle Pfeiffer. Most especially in Wolfgang Petersen's 1993 thriller, *In the Line of Fire*, the ghost of Kennedy's past and the mythic indoctrination of the events of that day are actually reinforced and torn apart almost at the same time by a plot that recalls lead character Frank Horrigan's (Clint Eastwood) failure to get to Kennedy before the 'fatal shot is fired'.

Petersen's film was really the first in a series during the decade that reinvigorated the conspiracy/assassination thriller as both an ideological and a commercial proposition. Horrigan is still on presidential protection duty thirty years after Dallas (and the film's publicity and marketing made a lot of the date); he is joined by a new partner, Lilly Raines (Rene Russo), after his existing one, Al (Dylan McDermott), is shot by prospective assassin Mitch Leary (John Malkovich) in a bungled attempt to capture the man who is openly threatening to kill the President. Leary and Horrigan establish a connection which preys on the senior agent's version of the events in Dallas and allows Petersen to use the emerging technology of the time by morphing a young Eastwood into the stock footage taken at Love Field and in downtown Dallas that day. Horrigan nicknames Leary 'Booth', after Lincoln's assassin, and Leary in turn reminds Horrigan of his failing in the moments after the first shot rang out, all the while assuming that the events are as detailed in the Warren Commission's report: that is, that the shooter was Oswald alone and that Horrigan was 'the nearest to Kennedy but didn't react', as Booth reminds him. The cat-and-mouse game is thus played out over the remaining moments of the film until Horrigan can be redeemed for the tragedy thirty years beforehand by stopping Leary/Booth in his tracks.

In *Murder at 1600* and *Shadow Conspiracy* (both 1997), dubious and deadly bargaining is going on right in the White House itself. In the former, Dwight Little's film has Wesley Snipes playing a Washington cop, Harlan Regis, called in to investigate the murder of a young intern; he is shadowed by a Secret Service agent, Nina Chance (Diane Lane), who is in effect there to report, and if necessary undermine, his inquiries. Regis and Chance form an unlikely partnership, however, as she comes to distrust her superiors almost as much as Regis does. They stumble across a wider plot to unseat the President because he is felt to be too weak to deal with a diplomatic crisis involving North Korea. His political enemies try to incriminate the President's wayward son (Tate Donovan) in the assault and death of the girl, Carla Town (Mary More), and as Regis and Chance uncover the pieces of the jigsaw, they square up to the perpetrators operating right under the nose of the President in the Oval Office itself.

A similar scenario unfolds in *Shadow Conspiracy*. Charlie Sheen's special assistant to the President, Bobby Bishop, has a plot to kill the President revealed to him by an old professor from his college days whom he happens to bump into on the street and who is almost immediately killed. Bishop goes on the run and now has to find the people responsible for the assassination plot because his boss is about to be sacrificed for announcing dramatic spending cuts in the defence budget, to the consternation of some of his colleagues. Again the plotters are working from within, and Alan Alda's hawkish National Security Adviser Alvin Jordan in Little's movie and Donald Sutherland's scheming Chief of Staff Jacob Conrad in director George Cosmatos's film are powerbrokers intent on usurping the power of the Chief Executive, Congress and the Constitution, if necessary, to get their way.

In *Absolute Power* (1997), a further take on the late 1990s White House corruption angle, Clint Eastwood's career thief Luther Whitney is accidental witness when the President (Gene Hackman) assaults his mistress, who is then killed by Secret Service agents investigating the disturbance in the woman's home. A cover-up ensues, while Whitney grabs evidence as he is fleeing the house and the President's staff and agents attempt to track him down. Thus a renewed game of philosophical plotting and engagement is played out until Whitney can corner President Richmond and expose his utter unaccountability to anything and anyone.

While the 'heroic quest' model is as much in play as one might envisage with these sorts of texts, they do falsify the traditions of the paranoia genre in denouements that make the likes of *The Parallax View* look highly plausible. But they do at least attempt to ground a part of their institutional power structures within the iconic refuges of the capital, like many other films we have examined. Regis has a meeting with Jordan at one point in *Murder at 1600*, for example, set against the backdrop of the Jefferson Memorial, and sweeping aerial vistas of Washington and its monuments crop up in all the films.

Together with Edward Zwick's dramatically prophetic *The Siege* (1998), a film about the imposition of martial law in New York after a series of terror attacks, which then pits institutional forces against each other in a bid to stop the bombings, these movies were entertaining enough in their plotting, if entirely dissolute when it came to any philosophical or ideological commentary on political culture. And as the 1990s moved into the 2000s, this showy, often gimmicky kind of conspiratorial presentation got renewed traction in TV shows like *24* (2001–10), where the outlandishness of the plots over each set of twenty-four episodes (one for each hour of the day covered each week) was part of the attraction.

While foreign policy and overt military pictures did arise (see Chapter 6), the Bush era provided surprisingly few other openings for credible domestic conspiracy narratives to flourish and the immediate ramifications of 9/11 tell a good deal of the tale of why that might be so. David Mamet's somewhat underrated *Spartan* (2004) was an early decade exception. As with many of Mamet's scripts and directed features, dialogue, character and an almost meditative contemplation of the settings and scenario for his movies are incredibly important. With a script that is far more literate and sophisticated than many of its predecessors from the 1990s, Val Kilmer plays a secret government operative, Scott, secretly assigned to uncover the whereabouts of the daughter of a high-ranking US government official. (One might presume it is the President's offspring but the words are never spoken.)

Mamet immerses his character and audience into a nether world of spying, global networks of informants and underworld communities that never bother the surface life of much of the rest of the population. The story focuses a lot of its attention on strategy, negotiation and pursuance rather more than on bombs, guns and action. *Spartan* is therefore quite a fascinating take on an alternative world that lives beyond the reach and comprehension of normal existence. Its story does not always offer satisfaction to the audience but Mamet is forever seeking the human actions and reactions in his story rather more than the visceral intent of other narratives, even if the final ten-minute denouement requires some convenient coincidences to tie up its loose ends.

There is also quite a bit of human reaction in Andrew Niccol's script and direction for *Lord of War* (2005), a rip-roaring yet morally dubious take not on government conspiracy, but on the interlocking global arms trade. The Orlov brothers, Yuri and Vitaly (Nicolas Cage and Jared Leto), realise that they are very good at being arms dealers for all manner of underhand clients around the world. From the end of the Cold War through the 1990s to the turn of the new millennium, they escape the confines of Little Odessa in New York and become rich and influential in the world's deadliest shipping industry, only for Yuri's conscience to get the better of him and his luck to run out. Niccol's film is not only having its cake; it made the cake, is eating it and patenting the recipe too. Part-thriller, part-satire on conflict and collusion, part-action film, part-cautionary tale, it is hard to know whether we are to feel sympathy or sorrow, anger or angst for Yuri in the conclusion, as he is compromised, recruited and forced into 'official' government circles by joining and advising the good guys.

If *Lord of War* could at best be seen as a morally vacant take on Bush-era doctrines, then little else could match some of its other nihilistic pretensions. Movies like *The Sentinel, Shooter* and *Vantage Point* followed, as Chapter 7 outlines, revisiting innumerable cinematic œuvres and plotlines to condition their serviceable if uninspired routines of assassination and insider duplicity. It was left to the British, ironically enough, then to provide an alternative perspective on the Bush years at the end of the decade, as well as an introduction to the Obama era of rededication to the causes of truth, honesty and justice in politics and wider establishment circles. For both *State of Play* (2009) and *Edge of Darkness* (2010) were, in fact, Hollywood reinventions of British political thrillers made by Brits and/or, in the latter's case, the director of the original BBC series.

Phillip French's review of Kevin MacDonald's film provides a very satisfying conclusion to the way the whole genre had moved and changed in the years since World War Two. Citing Robert Warshow's maxim that the key to the enjoyment of genre filmmaking was not in wholesale reinvention but subtle, evolutionary change, French thinks that in the arena of the political thriller, *State of Play* was a rarefied form of that artistic expression.

> The political thriller has been developing in a fascinating manner over the last fifty years [he said]. *State of Play* gains from the way it draws, consciously and unconsciously, on an established repertoire of characters, situations and themes. The movie, an admirable and indeed exemplary instance of the genre, begins by presenting two apparently unrelated incidents occurring within a few hours of each other in a paranoid Washington DC.[42]

Kevin MacDonald himself described his Hollywood remake of Paul Abbott's 2003 BBC mini-series as being more about journalism than anything. In fact, the revamped *State of Play* is about journalism in the same way as *All the President's Men*, the movie closest to its visual and ideological aesthetic. That MacDonald's film stands comparison with Pakula's is a testament to how well it translates the wider Hollywood canon and aspires to the compliment paid to it by French, as well as standing comparison with what has gone down in the annals as a definitive piece of British television. At play here, as French quoting

Warshow observes and MacDonald himself admitted to, is, of course, a homage to the 1976 picture that the contemporary film knowingly incorporates by having scenes at the Watergate building as well as in anonymous underground car parks. Indeed, MacDonald and his cinematographer Rodrigo Prieto went so far as to recreate a lot of the photographic experience that had so informed Gordon Willis's shooting of both *President's Men* and *The Parallax View*, including filming in widescreen.[43] The offices of the *Washington Globe* newspaper in the story are meticulously constructed and the lighting of the building, as well as the night-time settings in DC – including shots of the Lincoln Memorial, the congressional offices and associated ephemera – are all given their own colour palettes and discrete tone and imagery. 'To represent Cal's world,' for instance, said Prieto, 'we decided to enhance the film grain and shoot hand-held.'[44]

The film also keeps being updated by press reports and newspaper headlines focused on the screen, as though the traditions of crusading journalism could almost be reconstructed by the sheer will of the movie. MacDonald describes it as a 'little last hurrah' for the press as it was once known and understood, and, although modern, slick and at times cynical – especially as embodied by Helen Mirren's excellent editor, Cameron Lynne – one can appreciate why Peter Bradshaw called it an 'old fashioned political thriller'.[45]

The two incidents that the film kicks off with are the murder of a young man in a decrepit side-street, witnessed by a cyclist who is himself shot, and the death of Sonia Baker (Maria Thayer) on the Washington subway. Baker is congressional aide to rising Representative Stephen Collins (Ben Affleck), and her apparently accidental death initially comes as a major shock to him, not least because we learn that Baker and Collins were having an affair, behind the back of the Congressman's wife, Anne (Robin Wright Penn). *Washington Globe* reporter Cal McAffrey (Russell Crowe) is soon on the story but is personally involved because he knows Stephen and Anne, and had a relationship with the latter in the past. As McAffrey uncovers more about both deaths, aided by ambitious cub-reporter Della Frye (Rachel McAdams) on her first big assignment, the obvious scenarios become less credible and Collins's story to Cal about his relationship with Sonia, what his committee is investigating on Capitol Hill, and who the mysterious PointCorp corporation is begin to weave the unlikely plotlines together.

Although the exposure of a conspiracy from within business

conglomerates looking to exploit defence contacts in Iraq and Collins's involvement in a duplicitous relationship with Sonia slightly undermine the weight of the argument, Billy Ray, Matthew Michael Carnahan and Tony Gilroy's script is sharp and caustic enough to pull off the depressing confirmation that short-term economic gains were being generated in exchange for long-term military and personal suffering in war and business. Members of Congress, aides and TV reporters speak with an inside-the-beltway mentality to each other, as though politics barely registers beyond the end of Pennsylvania Avenue. The *Washington Globe* is, in places, a hotbed of ambition, suspicion and weary cynicism about where news is going, full-stop – let alone about the prospects for old-style investigative journalism. And even its own characters knowingly want to undermine the premise of the paranoia effect being created by the movie. 'You give him 24 hours, dead body in an alleyway and this geezer will give you a full-blown corporate conspiracy,' mocks Lynne to Cal in one early scene in the picture.

As an examination of the previous eight years of Bush in Washington, therefore, *State of Play* lays out many of the indictments that were familiar from Pakula's exposure of the Nixon Administration in *All the President's Men* all those years before. And in even starker fashion, New Zealand-born Martin Campbell's updating of his own BBC series from the 1980s, *Edge of Darkness*, directed by himself, plots out an ever more vicious and unrelenting campaign of multinational conglomerate power, aided, abetted and protected by sources closest to government. If the Hollywood version lacks the subtlety of the original, as well as some of the style and panache of MacDonald's *State of Play*, it does not let up, at least on its critique of corruption and suppression at the heart of government. The slightly renamed Tom Craven (Mel Gibson) in the film – originally Ron when played by Bob Peck – witnesses the murder of his mysteriously ill daughter when she returns home to Boston to visit him. Craven is traumatised by the experience and by the lack of any real motive for the killing.

But with persistence, strong-arm tactics and not a little help from a somewhat out-of-kilter version of government hit man/informant/ protector, Darius Jedburgh (played as a London gangland heavy by Ray Winstone), Craven discovers that his daughter was involved in radical environmental politics and had already contracted radiation poisoning from a facility her campaign group were trying to expose, even before the shooting. Craven's own downfall, though not before he kills various protagonists, and exposes and generally causes ruptures within his own police force and the wider establishment, reinforces the critical and downbeat slide towards conclusion and ambiguity.

As Philip French has said, *State of Play*, and to some lesser extent *Edge of Darkness*, reveal how the 'cinematic seeds of this kind of expressionist thriller were sown by Fritz Lang in the 1920s' and why the viability of the genre has remained pertinent in Hollywood.[46] Each succeeding generation beyond Lang – Pakula, Stone, MacDonald – has taken the template and reinvented the model for modern times: allegorical of, critical of, and a mirror for each subsequent political era. But is history enough to explain the ideological passage of paranoia and conspiracy beyond the realm of cinematic fantasy and out into the real political world? Peter Knight concludes his work on conspiracy culture by stating that if society is willing to believe in a 'frightening cluster of infiltrating forces', then it is only making real that which it fears, which may be paranoiac but is not necessarily reliable if there is no evidence of 'actual conspiring'.[47]

As Kaplan explored many years ago therefore, and the likes of Romney, Barker and Pratt have subsequently reiterated, the political thriller in its most conspiratorial, paranoiac mode occasionally flirts with the creation of that which is, by its very design, illogical, unsubstantiated and just hubristic in its all-encompassing plotting. But it also occasionally taps into a momentum that reflects, articulates and prophesies that which is to come in American political culture, and for that alone its excitement, reach and potential are acknowledged and important.

NOTES

1. *Enemy of the State* topped the $100 million mark in the US in early 1999 and was fractionally short of $112 million at the end of its box-office run, with over £6 million being taken in Britain. The film did, however, have a $90 million production tag. Figures quoted from iMDB.
2. Jonathan Romney, 'They're Out to Get You', *The Guardian*, Media Section, 19 October 1998, pp. 6–7.
3. Adam Barker, 'Cries and Whispers', *Sight and Sound*, vol. 1, no. 10, February 1998, pp. 10–11.
4. Michael Ryan and Douglas Kellner, *Camera Politica: The Politics and Ideology of Contemporary Hollywood Film* (Bloomington: Indiana University Press, 1988), p. 97.
5. Ray Pratt, *Projecting Paranoia: Conspiratorial Visions in American Film* (Lawrence: University of Kansas, 2001), pp. 8–9.

6. Tony Shaw, *Hollywood's Cold War* (Edinburgh: Edinburgh University Press, 2007), p. 2.
7. Tony Shaw, p. 11.
8. Tony Shaw, p. 9.
9. Michael Foley, *American Political Ideas* (Manchester: Manchester University Press, 1991), pp. 180–1.
10. Cook describes neo-realism as a 'cinema of poverty and pessimism' that socially could never outlast the growing prosperity of the 1950s, but its influence and legacy cinematically have survived and prospered. See David A. Cook, *A History of Narrative Film*, 3rd edn (London: Norton, 1996), pp. 424–38.
11. Brian Neve, *Film and Politics in America: A Social Tradition* (London: Routledge, 1992), pp. 112–36.
12. Tony Shaw, p. 249.
13. G. Tom Poe, 'Historical Spectatorship Around and About Stanley Kramer's *On the Beach*', in *Hollywood Spectatorship: Changing Perceptions of Cinema Audiences*, ed. Melvyn Stokes and Richard Maltby (London: BFI, 2001), p. 99.
14. Leonard Quart and Albert Auster, *American Film and Society Since 1945* (New York: Praeger, 1991), pp. 79–80.
15. Jonathan Kirshner, 'Subverting the Cold War in the 1960s: *Dr. Strangelove, The Manchurian Candidate* and *The Planet of the Apes*', *Film and History*, vol. 3, no. 2, 2001, p. 40.
16. Susan L. Carruthers, '*The Manchurian Candidate* (1962) and the Cold War Brainwashing Scare', *Historical Journal of Film, Radio and Television*, vol. 18, no. 1, 1998, p. 78.
17. Susan Carruthers, p. 78.
18. Susan Carruthers, p. 84.
19. Paul Monaco, *History of the American Cinema: The Sixties* (London: University of California Press, 2003), p. 171.
20. Art Simon, *Dangerous Knowledge: The J. F. K. Assassination in Art and Film* (Philadelphia: Temple University Press, 1996), p. 161.
21. Michael Scheinfeld, 'The Manchurian Candidate', *Films in Review*, vol. 39, no. 11, November 1988, p. 545.
22. Review of 'The Manchurian Candidate', *Positif*, no. 335, January 1989, pp. 68–70.
23. Beverly Merrill Kelley, *Reelpolitik II: Political Ideologies in '50s and '60s Films* (Oxford: Rowman & Littlefield, 2004), p. 137.
24. Charles Maland, '*Dr. Strangelove* (1964): Nightmare Comedy and the Ideology of Liberal Consensus', in *Hollywood as Historian*, ed. Peter C. Rollins (Lexington: University Press of Kentucky, 1983), pp. 190–210.
25. Sontag is quoted in J. Hoberman, 'When Dr. No met Dr. Strangelove', *Sight and Sound*, vol. 3, no. 12, December 1993, p. 20.

26. Kubrick, somewhat archly, suggested that just because he recognised the insanity of the physically afflicted doctor, it did not mean that he was celebrating his madness, merely exposing the sham. Louis Giannetti, *Masters of American Cinema* (Englewood, NJ: Prentice Hall, 1981), p. 401.
27. Ray Pratt, p. 124.
28. Michael Coyne, *Hollywood Goes to Washington: American Politics on Screen* (London: Reaktion, 2008).
29. Darrell L. Hope, 'Alan J. Pakula and the Parallax Reviewed', *Directors Guild of America Magazine*, vol. 23, no. 3, September 1998, p. 24.
30. Art Simon, pp. 167–9.
31. Michael Ryan and Douglas Kellner, p. 101.
32. Darrell L. Hope, p. 24.
33. Ray Pratt, p. 130.
34. Fred Kaplan, 'Parallax View, Political Paranoia', *Jump Cut*, no. 3, September–October 1974, p. 5.
35. Fred Kaplan, p. 4.
36. Fred Kaplan, p. 5.
37. Kyle Renick, '"The Poet of Paranoia": An Appreciation of the Late, Great Michael Small', *Film Score Magazine*, September–October 2005, p. 30.
38. Kyle Renick, p. 32.
39. Peter Knight, *The Kennedy Assassination* (Edinburgh: Edinburgh University Press, 2007), p. 157.
40. Peter Knight, p. 158.
41. Robert Brent Toplin, *History by Hollywood: The Use and Abuse of the American Past* (Chicago: University of Illinois Press, 1996), pp. 58–9.
42. Philip French, Review of 'State of Play', *The Observer*, 26 April 2009 at: http://www.guardian.co.uk/film/2009/apr/26/state-of-play-review.
43. Jon D. Witmer, 'On the Record', *American Cinematographer*, vol. 90, no. 9, May 2009, pp. 38–40.
44. Jon D. Witmer, p. 38.
45. Peter Bradshaw, Review of 'State of Play', *The Guardian*, 24 April 2009 at: http://www.guardian.co.uk/film/2009/apr/24/state-of-play-review.
46. Philip French, Review of 'State of Play'.
47. Peter Knight, *Conspiracy Culture: From Kennedy to The X-Files* (London: Routledge, 2000), p. 244.

Chapter 5

POLITICAL BIOGRAPHY IN FILM

The life of a man and his significance in history cannot be described with clear and judicious definition in broadly pictorial terms – especially when the subject is one of great depth and scope.

Bosley Crowther, review of *Wilson*, *New York Times*, 2 August 1944[1]

One might be forgiven for thinking that the revered film critic Bosley Crowther was setting up Henry King's portrait of America's twenty-eighth president for a fall when he sat down to write his review of the director's film following a lavish New York premiere at the Roxy Theatre in the Summer of 1944.[2] Signposting the difficulty of cramming all the 'significant' events of a public life into a picture of even two and a half hours' length, Crowther highlighted, and in one phrase summarised, the dilemma for the aspiring cinematic biographer. How could you bring clarity and justice to the subject when so much needs to be left out in order to construct a tale that is fluent but concise? And there were certainly some objectionable omissions from the President's career in this movie, he thought, not least the quickly dismissed ploy of not asking the Senate for help in drafting and selling the Fourteen Points to the American people, as well as the disagreements with French premier Clemenceau at Versailles, both of which are glossed over as the narrative progresses. All in all, however, Crowther's review of 20th Century Fox's *Wilson*, starring the relatively unknown Canadian actor Alexander Knox, was nothing like as harsh as the *Times*'s doyen was sometimes noted for when reviewing films he especially disliked. The sumptuous settings were acknowledged, for example, as was the attention to visual and historical detail, and the spirited ideological and rhetorical endorsement of Wilson's vision for a new world order in the form of the League of Nations that climaxes the movie was given full weight and import.

In fact, Crowther thought that the intentionality of the picture as a whole was extremely creditable. 'For a stirring, eye-filling panorama of the hot political world in which he [Wilson] lived and for a warm appreciation of his humanity, it would be hard to beat this glowing film,' he boldly declared.[3] Other reviews were equally, if not more, complimentary. 'It comes forth upon the screen in sequences of great pageantry and interludes of poignant intimacy stranded together with skill and over spread with the patina of glamour that only Hollywood can achieve,' noted Terry Ramsaye in the *Motion Picture Herald*.[4] Kate Cameron in the *New York Daily News* described the film as a 'beautiful production in Technicolor, superbly acted by a large cast that does its level best to project real people on the screen'.[5] There was just one problem: even with all these facets and an approximation of Woodrow Wilson by Knox that was at times uncanny in its resemblance and mannerisms, the film was rather dull in places! Some of this appreciation might be obscured by time and retrospect, of course. The film does not move along with anything like the pace of modern cinema – 'lofty but ponderous' is how Terry Christensen and Peter Hass describe it – and certainly it bears only a passing resemblance to the kind of visual and aesthetic pyrotechnics that biographical presentation has subsequently seen applied by a contemporary director such as Oliver Stone.[6] And while Michael Coyne, like Christensen and Hass, might be stretching the point a little when he says that the movie was a 'sumptuous but soporific paean' to Wilson, especially when some reviews of the time concluded that it moved at a 'spirited pace' with few 'draggy moments', it is nevertheless true that certain episodes in Wilson's career appear to stretch beyond a screen time that does not appear absolutely necessary.[7]

What Crowther in effect recognised and criticised at the time, and even Ramsaye gave a nod to in the headline of his review, 'Romanticising Political History', was the quality that director King, star Knox, producer Darryl Zanuck and screenwriter Lamar Trotti were actually striving for in their recreation of the President's career. They had the idea of *Wilson* being the definitive political biography to end all political biographies: a kind of *Birth of a Nation*, *Ben Hur* and *Gone with the Wind* all rolled into one. It was to be filmed in Technicolor and would cost $3 million to make; it was going to recreate the Hall of Mirrors at the Palace of Versailles for the 1919 peace conference; and it would portray Wilson's dramatic nomination victory at the 1912 convention.[8] In short, it was going to be epic, lavish and ultimately tragic.

Darryl F. Zanuck's **"WILSON"** with ALEXANDER KNOX, CHARLES COBURN, GERALDINE FITZGERALD, THOMAS MITCHELL, RUTH NELSON, SIR CEDRIC HARDWICKE, VINCENT PRICE, WILLIAM EYTHE, MARY ANDERSON   In Technicolor

Professor Woodrow Wilson gets ready to embark on a political career

In all this visual drama, at least, *Wilson* represented something else as well, and this was as important to the time it was made as it was to the history and the man it was purporting to represent. In the spirit of C. Wright Mills, its aim – the aim of any biography in reality – was to merge and mirror history, social movements and personal recall into the life of one individual. In other words, biography is there to tell us something about the current age and the forces and predilections at work in the here and now; it is not just an opening into the past that gives us a clue as to why some subjects and characters emerge over others. In *The Sociological Imagination*, in the aftermath of the Second World War, Mills wrote that the 'very shaping of history now outpaces the ability of men to orient themselves in accordance with cherished values'.[9] Publishing his work more than a decade on from King's picture, Mills identified what the literary, if not cinematic, form felt compelled to do: 'We have come to know that every individual lives out a biography,' he suggested.[10] Biographical portraits, by this interpretation, therefore display an understanding of the values and ideals at play in the contemporary era. At the same time they galvanise opinion as to the intentions and movements of the past moulded into a recognisable form: in this case, the life and times of a chief exponent who lived, breathed and shaped those movements, literally or metaphorically. Bosley Crowther's problem with all that, from a film critic's point of view, was that if you followed all those intentions with a strict adherence to the public record on screen, you were not likely to have a very attractive or exciting film, even if it could lay claim to being an accurate one.

And so it proved with *Wilson*. The President's tortuous brooding over America's entry into World War One and the losses that then ensued, and his zealous campaigning for the Fourteen Points and the League, are vital historical moments in the twentieth-century world. But in the hands of King and Zanuck, they do become slightly laborious, not to say preachy final acts in a saga that in the end just goes on for too long. The film did give a nod to recent epic Hollywood sagas that were cinematically bolder than they were historically accurate: notably, Orson Welles's breathtakingly ambitious *Citizen Kane* (1941). Donald Staples, for one, suggests that the New Jersey gubernatorial speech early in *Wilson*, as the future President sets out on his political career, is framed in a manner not dissimilar to Welles's construction of the larger-than-life personality of Charles Foster Kane delivering his campaign speech in Madison Square Garden: all low-angle shots, giant pictures of the candidate as a backdrop to the drama of the rhetoric, and sumptuous attention to the crowds and the political paraphernalia of the time.[11]

But complementing these stylistic flourishes, the vital ingredient for adding authenticity to this tale, as seen by Zanuck and screenwriter Trotti, was a factor that somewhat put the nail in the entertainment coffin: the historical record. Fox hired Wilson's biographer, Ray Stannard Baker, who had compiled eight volumes on the President's life and times and won the Pulitzer Prize for his efforts in 1940, to act as a consultant in Hollywood. He read and reread Trotti's treatments, which, from the screenwriter's position, were striving for the human dimension in the man that Zanuck had been so keen to bring to the surface since he first had the idea of doing the film. In fact, so committed was Zanuck to making sure his creative team gelled that Henry King remembers being stunned by his producer turning up on set when filming started, to observe how things were going – the sort of visit Zanuck never usually undertook.[12] The result was that Alexander Knox does bring a frightening resemblance to the role, as well as personal characteristics and some warmth that lighten the former academic's alleged style. Staples talks of Knox's 'commanding stature, imperious look, and mellifluous voice', all of which were features that brought him a deserved Academy nomination for Best Actor.[13] Wilson gets to cheer on his beloved Princeton at football, plays golf badly, and even does his bit for morale by serving hot drinks to doughboys on their way to France at an embarkation point outside Washington. But he also appears in a total of 294 scenes, delivering 1,124 lines and 'recreating' 338 verbatim speeches that existed in the public record.[14] Wilson was certainly going to put biography on screen with this treatment, but was it going to bring its subject to life? Would it create drama, pathos and excitement for audiences? Archer Winsten, in his New York Post review of the time, was sceptical. He suggested this approach tended towards a 'montage of historical tableaux' rather than a complexity of performance and possibility.[15]

If the suspicions of Winsten and Crowther did not amount to much for other critics, the inclusion of Baker as a consultant, and the focus on actions taking place a quarter of a century before, did accede to Wright Mills's maxim in other ways. Whatever the protestations about the movie as wartime propaganda, it did say something about America in its current age, about the choices one needed to make when the war was over and about the legacy that a contemporary figure like Franklin Roosevelt – as a successor to Wilson's political conscience – would leave for generations to come: all of the similar contentions that the nation faced as Wilson's era had drawn to a close in 1920.

But many other critics really did not seem to mind whether Wilson set standards for political representation or not, even whether the film was as achingly accurate as the statistics suggested. The acclaim the movie generated for its 'absorbing' and 'intellectually stimulating' portrayal of the President was quite extensive enough and could lead the reviewer to no other conclusion than, as Thomas Knock suggests, 'the critical response to the film was unprecedented.'[16] Some saw it as fourth-term propaganda for Roosevelt with an election coming later that year, as much as it was a battle cry to America to steel herself for the final tests of the latest world war; yet many more tapped into the mood of nostalgia, peace and reflection that clearly resonated with the times and the audience's craving for an end to the drudgery of the current conflict.

But the extent of Wilson's commercial and indeed wider cultural success is somewhat harder to determine. Knock positively asserts that the film contributed substantially to a spirit of internationalism in America. It brought public opinion much closer in line with Europe as the Second World War drew to a close and the need for rebuilding began. It was almost a confirmation of America's need not just to preach new world order and then leave the European powers to it, as had happened in 1919 against Wilson's wishes, but to engage actively in that rebuilding process, literally and politically, amidst the post-war rubble. Citing the movie's record-breaking run at the mammoth Roxy in New York, which held 6,000 patrons, Knock suggests that emotions ran so high for many who came out of the theatre having been inspired by the film that they recognised immediately that the errors of the past should never be repeated.[17]

Leonard Leff and Jerold Simmons, on the other hand, put the film's total box-office takings into a slightly different context. They point out that, initially, Zanuck spent some $250,000 just advertising *Wilson*'s presence at the Roxy, 13 per cent of its overall publicity budget. That kind of saturation was bound to call attention to the movie and generate ticket sales, but often at no more than an immediate regional level. Furthermore, the film's gross receipts at a little over $4 million might have looked very healthy on the face of it, but they told only a portion of the tale. As Leff and Simmons further argue, *Wilson*'s ticket prices were slightly inflated to represent the pedigree of the film, the production costs and advertising were 600 per cent higher than the average Fox movie of the time, and, more crucially still, the good box-office returns in New York, Los Angeles, San Francisco and Philadelphia did prove regionally located because they were somewhat offset by poor returns in the Mid-West especially, where smaller chains and independent cinemas could mean the difference between overall profit and loss.[18] For all its good reviews initially, then, and encouraging returns at selected movie theatres on the East and West Coasts, *Wilson* ended up making Fox a record they did not want: a $2.2 million loss.[19]

Zanuck spoke up for his grand experiment through much of his life and it was true that the effort to bring the President's life to the screen was as much a noble, idealistic undertaking as it was a commercial one. 'Of all the pictures I have made in my career, *Wilson* is nearest to my heart,' he explained.[20] It should not be forgotten, either, and Zanuck never did, that the film received ten Academy Award nominations, winning five, though all these were in minor categories. This was an achievement of sorts but also one that highlighted the film's great problem. Few pictures with that level of critical acclaim have been largely forgotten to the extent that *Wilson* has over the years, and it was the very grandiosity of Zanuck's endeavour that was also its Achilles heel, damaging the movie's lasting reputation, however unfairly.

Coyne concludes that at '154 minutes, like many other self-styled messiahs, [Wilson] outstays his welcome'.[21] It is a dilemma that has befallen a number of political biographies in Hollywood's history and is one reason why, from the visual medium's point of view, biographical mini-series proliferated far more as television came to dominate in the post-war era, and cinematic presentations were treated increasingly cautiously. Episodic engagement with a subject buys space and time to flesh out character and events while seemingly carrying the audience along in a spate of specific engagements, each of which can have its own climax and denouement. It is a successful formula that has worked remarkably well for ground-breaking series such as *Kennedy* in the 1980s and *John Adams* in the 2000s.

But the biographical mini-series has often felt obliged to present linear, 'cradle-to-grave' narratives too, which can be well intentioned and detailed, but not necessarily audacious or sparkling. The two mini-series mentioned above do not pursue a whole life story, as a matter of fact, though they do take up their subject's narrative at a particular moment in their careers and proceed from there in more or less chronological order. Thanks both to their subject matter and to the leading performances, however, they still manage to stand as absorbing accounts of the political life and times that they are documenting: rarely preachy or dull, often focused and intricate. So if television would appear to be the natural home for the biography to work, why have some Hollywood filmmakers persisted with the motion picture formula?

One secret behind the preference for and sustainability of feature-length political biographies is concealed within the initial inspiration for *Wilson*, which Zanuck was so taken with when he first saw the production that it drew him immediately to America's World War One leader. Howard Koch and John Huston's play, *In Time to Come*, opened in New York during December 1941, the very month America entered the Second World War, and was directed by future Hollywood luminary, Otto Preminger. In many ways, it had all the idealism and contemporary signification of events of the day that the *Wilson* team were later keen to instil in their film. The difference was that Koch and Huston's drama about the President revolved around just one event:

the battle for the League. Reviews were generally very positive but the timing of the play was not. In the aftermath of Pearl Harbor, a stage play that prompted thoughts of the Great War, of humanity's failings when it came to peace and stability, and of a president that recommended neutrality for so long, even if his inclinations were naturally anglophile, sounded hollow and self-reverential in a new era of global threat. The production lasted for a short period only.

Nevertheless, one of the keys to the praise generated from reviewers was the fact that Wilson was often portrayed in the play as, in Leff and Simmons's phrase, 'an exclusively political animal'.[22] In retrospect, it was some of this depth of character and duality of conscience tempered by ambition that made the drama so specific to a particular moment and interesting for the audience, but it was ultimately what Zanuck seemed keen to wash away. His aim to lighten Wilson's historical reputation for being somewhat cold, aloof and often academic (which is exactly what he was) was a project that the film achieves on one level. In short, Zanuck's intention was to make entertainment, to offer Wilson as an engaging and charming character, not someone increasingly distant, pensive and driven, and he ends up trying to do this by opening up the man's whole political career to scrutiny as a means to explain his position at the close of that career.

The picture is arguably a psychological profile, then, as much as anything. How do great leaders become driven by causes and how far will they go in pursuit of their principles? The trouble with such a philosophy was that, in a time of further global conflict, with the invasion and liberation of Europe under way, the idea of a movie escaping the significance of itself as a political and propaganda film event was hard to avoid. Upon release, the film was banned for a time by the War Department because it infringed the Soldier Voting Act, which forbade distribution of work classified as propaganda within the armed services.[23] And while it was true that the picture did not go so far as to attempt to relate the events of Wilson's whole life, the decade it did focus on was large, multifarious and full of portent and influence. While the stage play confined itself to the League and Wilson's take on the old powers' ideological renewal, the film took in the whole decade of Wilson's political career in monumental and minute form. As a later mini-series, it could no doubt have been hugely successful; but as a condensed motion picture, it was almost too much to take, and that dilemma has been the bane of the political biography in Hollywood ever since.

Zanuck's screenwriter Trotti, who was charged with brightening Wilson's persona, had his own experience to call upon in writing within this field. His Oscar-nominated script for John Ford's *Young Mr. Lincoln* (1939) also measured the biographical imprint, like *In Time to Come*, by recall of only one part of a famous life, and then transposed that allegorical lesson into a feature of personal destiny, impact and future greatness. Trotti might have been trying to follow the same agenda for *Wilson* but whether he was baulked, won over by the epic sweep, or just saw the two presidents in different ways, the portent and drama were far more obvious and less contemplative than in *Young Mr. Lincoln*. The film, in short, was on an altogether grander scale than Ford's vision, and ultimately, while the reach of its ambition and the scope of its visual splendour could be admired, *Wilson*'s success as a ground-breaking piece of cinema that brought the crises and drama of one moment in American political history to life remained debateable.

ORIGINS AND EVOLUTION

While the subject of Woodrow Wilson set a cinematic marker for Hollywood's lavish take on presidential lives up until the 1940s, the President himself had already contributed to the debates and controversy that emerged as film biography first appeared during his own time in office. As Hollywood was finding a home for itself on the West Coast in the early part of the century, and makers of films about great figures in American or world history were slowly waking up to the fact that the movies could be about more than simple historical recreation, more than the narrative re-enactment of a public life and times, Wilson contributed to the debate with his assessment of one of American cinema's early landmark productions. For while D. W. Griffith's epic and notorious *The Birth of a Nation* (1915) could hardly be described as outright political biography, its rendition of Abraham Lincoln and the President's place in the defining moment of the nation's history during the Civil War of the 1860s prompted Wilson, upon viewing the picture at the White House during a private screening, to remark famously that, 'it was like writing history with lightning.'[24]

While Wilson marvelled at the cinematic scope of Griffith's presentation, biography was starting to find inspiration in a variety of cultural sources. Early Hollywood 'silents' had utilised presidential lives and events as grandiloquent statements about the grandeur of America's political experiment and the nobility of its leaders. William McKinley had been filmed in the year or so before his death, and Teddy Roosevelt had featured on screen too, treated almost as if they were immediate documentary sources, and the moving images were cultural artefacts already preserved in nitrate (ironically not to prove terribly durable) in their own time. But it was in the mythic and idealistic presentation of Lincoln, represented as an almost unimpeachable paragon of virtue and goodness, that the defining features of biographical representation and influence were to be carved. From the silent era onwards all the way through to the outbreak of World War Two, as several monumental recollections devoted to the man in a number of different forms appeared, Lincoln's myth grew heavy and overwhelming. As Coyne suggests, perhaps the most persuasive and certainly the largest of these literary canonisations was Carl Sandburg's four-volume account of the president, *The War Years*, published around the same time as two of Hollywood's foremost realisations: John Ford's aforementioned *Young Mr. Lincoln* (1939) and, just a year later, John Cromwell's *Abe Lincoln in Illinois*.[25]

But the endeavour to put Lincoln on screen started with silent film-makers, and with Griffith in particular. *The Birth of a Nation* envisioned the President as a semi-tragic figure, who would never have allowed the South to drown in the sea of corruption, economic blight and racist intent over which his successor, Andrew Johnson, held sway. But Griffith was stung by critics who saw him as somehow lining Lincoln up with the director's idea of the redeemers in the story of Southern reconstruction: the Ku Klux Klan. So affected was Griffith by this state of affairs and by the scandal that rocked his picture that he resolved that one of his first sound movies fifteen years later was to be a wholesale biography of Lincoln. With the up-and-coming Walter Huston in the lead role, *Abraham Lincoln* (1930) gave the man the sort of legendary presence that had, by the start of that decade, already come to be expected. Huston's Lincoln is honourable, self-deprecating and saintly, even. His death is regal, tragic and prophetic, all the way down to the cold that seems to whistle through his bones, as if the cool chill of destiny on the night of the Ford's Theatre drama has come to wrest him away from his people. It is at times a stilted picture by 1930s standards, with Griffith's cinematic technique, as well as characterisation of his players, being held up to scrutiny in the coming sound era in which his filmmaking style would quickly lose its gloss. Indeed, a year later, *The Struggle* (1931), a rather modest tale of a couple dealing with the effects of alcoholism, scripted by Anita Loos, was, in effect, the last

Hollywood film Griffith ever made, as his resources dwindled and the industry excommunicated him.

Nine years later, John Ford shied away from the historical largesse and defining political moments of a career that Griffith's vision had attempted to portray. Ford was forever interested in myth and legend, rather more than historical truth and accuracy. Use of the symbolic countenance of Lincoln, for his most enduring silent film, *The Iron Horse* (1924), was typical of a director who immersed himself in the stories and folklore that had, in particular, forged a persistent myth about the West, which Ford built up still further in so many of his most enduring movies. Starring Henry Fonda, *Young Mr. Lincoln* portrays Abe as a gangling, slightly awkward young man, who comes across some old law books given to him by the poor Clay family when they first arrive in town (and whom he will repay as the narrative proceeds). Reading Blackstone's commentaries inspires Abe to make something of himself, even while he contemplates running for the Illinois legislature. It is his self-deprecating campaign speech that kicks off the narrative and lays the groundwork for Lincoln's common-sense, no-nonsense approach to the law later in the film.

Thus recounting only a mythological imprint of Lincoln's early law career in Springfield, the film takes his defence of the two young Clay brothers, whom he meets at the beginning of the film and who are later accused of murder, as a springboard to examine honesty, endeavour and the Mid-Western frontier temperament amid the metaphoric insertion of greatness and predestination. Matt and Adam Clay (Richard Cromwell and Eddie Quillan respectively) are charged with the slaying of Scrub White (Fred Kohler Jr) at the county fair. Abe prevents a mob from hammering down the door of the jail to lynch the two boys, who appear guilty as charged even before their trial. Asserting his home-spun philosophy and biblical scripture to prevent the boys from being attacked, Lincoln takes on the seemingly impossible defence of the Clays, who are reluctant to tell their side of the incident.

As Joseph McBride asserts in his biography of Ford, '*Young Mr. Lincoln* seamlessly and paradoxically melds the romantic "great man" theory of history with a Tolstoyan sense of historical determinism.'[26] Assuming Ford's implacable belief in free will, McBride contends that the predetermination of the actions and narrative is driven by Lincoln's unique persona. At each and every juncture of the film, for example, Lincoln's future political adversary, Stephen A. Douglas (Milburn Stone), makes an appearance to offer a succinct appraisal of the man's gifts and foibles, all the way preparing the ground for the later majestic confrontation of the two in their future political careers. Despite Douglas's reservations, Lincoln continues with the defence, takes on the trial, and finally puts John Palmer Cass (Ward Bond) on the stand: the only man to witness the incident and to see White lying on the ground, fatally stabbed. Thanks to the *Farmers' Almanac*, Abe proves that the moonlight was not shining down on the event that night as Cass asserts, so he could not have seen what had happened in the fight between the Clays and White. At the last minute, Lincoln, while letting Cass walk away from the stand, accuses him of the crime. Cass, in his confusion and shock at being discovered as the perpetrator, confesses to stabbing White for greed and money; and before anyone knows it, the homespun Abe has won the day.

As McBride might have it, the sense of good triumphing over evil and Lincoln's innate logic and fierce will overcoming the odds are none the less driven by an implacable determination to succeed and prove the truth of the matter. The closing line of the court scene, Abe's nonchalant rejoinder to the prosecuting counsel, 'your witness', somewhat camouflages a ruthlessly persistent streak in him as he sets out to destroy the blasé Palmer Cass as the key witness and badgers him into a confession that never seemed apparent only a few moments before.

In the aftermath of the trial, Douglas apologises for his earlier accusations about Lincoln's standing, to which Abe replies, 'I don't think we'd better underestimate either of us from here on in, Steve.' The predestination is completed by Lincoln's spiritual and metaphoric walk up a hill with thunder and lightning spilling all around him, as he bids farewell to the Clays and suggests that he might 'walk on apiece'. The Battle Hymn of the Republic strikes up on the soundtrack and the scene dissolves into a contemporary image of the Lincoln Memorial as the credits roll. The fact that the rain really did start falling on the Fox backlot as Ford concluded the scene proved, as McBride notes, to be one of those 'happy accidents' that recurred throughout the director's career. 'The tears of the multitudes', commented Ford, knowing exactly the impression he was conveying.[27]

Cromwell's take on Lincoln was an adaptation of Robert Sherwood's Pulitzer Prize-winning stage play, which had premiered only two years before the 1940 film. Raymond Massey takes Abe on a longer journey than Fonda through adolescence, preaching the law, and his confrontations with Douglas (Gene Lockhart) that lead us to the 1860 election. But the rite-of-passage, predestined arrangement of Lincoln is still very much in place, and while Massey's performance seems at times to be almost too sage in its pose and recall of common sense and ideals, the film nevertheless follows a breathless trawl through history that confirms the 'Spirit' of the man and the people, as the film was titled in territories outside the United States.

Almost fifteen years later, the same pretensions, as well as a similar structure, adorn Henry Levin's film, *The President's Lady* (1953). Here Charlton Heston plays a young, ambitious and go-ahead Andrew Jackson, as a robust lawyer and pioneer of the American West in the early years of the republic. His military accomplishments are enhanced and his rugged individualism foregrounded, while the racist outlook on Native Americans and the penchant for violence – which included permitting military executions – are virtually abandoned in favour of an enduring love affair with divorcee Rachel Donaldson Robards (Susan Hayward). Jackson's political scheming, which would land him later in the White House, is largely confined to a final section following his triumphant victory at New Orleans in the War of 1812. In Levin's hands, Jackson's political philosophy is less an education in heroics and dealing with frontier settlement than it is a restless and persistent protection of Rachel, the scandal emanating from his alleged illegal marriage to her, and the fight to have the wider echelons of society recognise them both. It drives him on toward the presidency and, inevitably, personal tragedy.

Reviews of the film at the time acknowledged its rite-of-passage intent, the sense of great and important American history passing before the protagonists' eyes, with Jackson's predestination, rather like Lincoln's, never too far away in the background. But the likes of the *Monthly Film Bulletin* also perceived the movie to be nothing more than a historical romance, following in the footsteps of earlier pieces such as Frank Lloyd's *The Howards of Virginia* (1940), set a generation or so earlier with Cary Grant. Heston was certainly a worthy incarnation of Jackson, all loud suppositions and wild gestures, but the passage of time left a lot to be desired, thought the reviewer. 'Due to some grotesque make-up, both players age rapidly, particularly Susan Hayward, who takes to knitting long, shapeless articles [as a result],' was how they rather dismissively put it.[28]

Political ideas do emerge, then, in this final section of the film as Jackson's political career begins to take shape and John Patrick's screenplay offsets the emerging 'Western tradition' with Eastern reaction to and suspicion of the frontiersman's vaulting ambition. The brief campaign scenes that are featured see Jackson accused on the stump of stealing another man's wife and having committed murder in the past, their importance a reflection of the new sensibilities of the age. Levin and Patrick conceive of a political confrontation between East and West that perceives Jackson as bringing the lawlessness of the frontier to the genteel respectability of Washington: a not dissimilar tactic to the one employed by British director Lloyd in the aforementioned *Howards of Virginia*, where Cary Grant's Matt Howard is equally impetuous and dismissive of Washington society in the post-revolutionary era.

But *The President's Lady*'s social and political aptitude seems a long way from Ford's intent in *Young Mr. Lincoln*, as Tag Gallagher has noted. While Ford also manages to acknowledge the ideas of the Jacksonian age in which his film is set, the Lincolnian traits of spiritualism and truth garnered from nature are very much apparent here, giving a hint of the transcendentalist philosophy and Second Great Awakening movement from which Lincoln took comfort and ideas, thinks Gallagher. In Ford's film the ghosts of Thoreau, Emerson and Whitman seem very much alive and well, while in Levin's the bawdy nature of costume melodrama does not seem to expand beyond the confrontational and personal.[29]

In fact, Levin's film did have an agenda that was vital and constitutive of its make-up and structure, and one akin once again to the theories at the heart of C. Wright Mills's observations. *The President's Lady* was nothing if not a commentary on 1950s America, and more specifically on the anti-communist witch-hunts that plagued the Hollywood community of the time, the spectre of McCarthy looming large in people's imagination, if not their real lives. The picture may not have consented to examine the nature of political change and participation as it was unfolding in the 1820s and 1830s, but it did touch on notions of exclusion, perceptions of personality and the construction of image; and it was ultimately a film about sacrifice and endeavour. These were endemic themes that were terribly important to American society in the 1950s, and they were issues and conceptions that took this type of movie about as far as any political biography might reasonably go in the atmosphere of the times.

In fact, the era was so corrosive that political films in general had a hard time being made in 1950s America. In a period when the powers-that-be began to question the legacy of the New Deal and the role of state intervention in an American political heritage that, up until the

1930s, had been wary of such participation, it might come as some surprise to see the dawn of the 1960s kick off with a biography of Franklin Roosevelt. But Vincent Donehue's adaptation of Dore Schary's stage play, *Sunrise at Campobello* (1960), did not focus on Roosevelt's crowning political career. Instead, taking its cue from the Ford and Cromwell pieces, it looks at the future President's earlier life and especially his contraction of polio in the early 1920s. Using his battle back from illness and incapacity, Donehue's film displays the Roosevelt grit and focus as he resolves to re-enter political life and deal with his disability. Indeed, the film's denouement, the 1924 Democratic political convention where Roosevelt gave a rousing speech in support of Al Smith's doomed bid for the presidency, is arguably somewhat anticlimatic, given the outcome; but the message of courage, persistence and character is there for all to see and once again prophesies that which is later to come.

Schary adapted his own work and Ralph Bellamy reprised his role as Roosevelt, which had won him so much acclaim on Broadway. Greer Garson is Eleanor Roosevelt in the film, giving an extraordinary performance that sees her attempt a sometimes unintentionally funny mid-Atlantic English drawl. Sounding like Miss Marple in some scenes, the voice was no doubt a reminder of Eleanor's English finishing school education when she was young. To her credit, she responds to Roosevelt's assistant, Louis Howe (Hume Cronyn), who is pressing for her to share some of the burden of Franklin's public engagements, by saying that her voice flies all over the place at times and she never sounds confident or secure in front of audiences, thus conveying the sense that maybe the voice is deliberately strained and discordant for the character.

Myron Levine describes *Sunrise at Campobello* as an 'uncritical hagiography' and it certainly moves in a constantly flattering light, as befits the subject.[30] Warners, as parent company, might have expected this tactic to help the film do better than it did at both the box-office and in the awards season that followed, especially given its subject and reputation on stage. But if anything, the movie did give some impetus to John Kennedy's 1960 presidential campaign, which was going on at the same time. Released in late September, just as the main presidential election season was getting into gear, the film re-affirmed why the young Massachusetts senator had such an admiration for his predecessor and for the Roosevelt philosophy more generally, and it seems reasonable to prescribe some of the Kennedy momentum that year to a film that, as the future President might say, profiled the courage and resolution of one of his and America's great heroes and leaders.

Three years later, Leslie Martinson's film of Robert Donovan's book, *PT 109* (1963), similarly tackles early-life experiences, in this instance of J. F. K. himself. The military service that made his name and laid the groundwork for his political career is conveyed in a series of engagements with the enemy on board the attack cruiser of the title in the Pacific during World War Two. Cliff Robertson plays the young Kennedy, and while the portents for political destiny are slight, the action and adventure of wartime heroics are heightened at every turn in a passable, if somewhat melodramatic, picture.

One could hardly describe the movies highlighted above as a glut in the aftermath of the war, and the paucity of films through these decades really signals the direction of political biography in the era to come. During the 1970s and 1980s an ever-growing number of mini-series projecting the great and the good back on to the nation started appearing on television rather than in movie theatres. That many lacked some of the reverential sympathy of past years now that civil rights, Vietnam and Watergate had broken the spell of White House trust and faith was itself evidence of a wariness of the formula, as much as it was a need to revise some of the history. Leading the way was a docu-drama in which only the names and faces were changed: the hugely successful *Washington Behind Closed Doors* (1977) with Jason Robards. The actor, straight off the back of playing Ben Bradlee of the *Washington Post* in *All the President's Men*, stars as President Richard Monckton, a barely concealed interpretation of Richard Nixon. Ironically, the film is an adaptation of John Ehrlichman's 'fictional' thriller, *The Company*, and Robards, Robert Vaughn (winning an Emmy), Andy Griffiths, John Houseman and Nicholas Pryor give bravura performances as White House insiders indulging in any amount of corrupt and unguarded practice. An adaptation of White House counsel John Dean's book, *Blind Ambition*, followed in 1979, with Martin Sheen playing Dean and the whole Watergate tale being played out over eight hours of prime-time television and anchored by a veteran director of these types of series, George Schaefer.

Likewise turning performance into a manifesto for character assessment, though here for something more than political infighting, Randy Quaid won an Emmy for his portrayal of Lyndon Johnson in *LBJ: The Early Years* in 1987, by which time the Reagan era had attempted to return some of the gloss to the tarnished reputation of the Chief

Executive. Following in its wake, Nigel Hamilton's controversial biography, *JFK: Reckless Youth*, was adapted in 1993 by Harry Winer, another long-standing filmmaker in American television. Patrick Dempsey takes up the role of the adolescent J. F. K. and notable stars such as Loren Dean and Claire Forlani lend support to a story which, at the very least, probes the inner psychosis of Kennedy's political ambition and romantic, nay, sexual attachments during his early life.

Perhaps the height of the mini-series boom was reached in 1995, when David McCullough's exhaustive biography of Harry Truman was brought to the small screen. Not only a ratings success but a phenomenal awards contender too, which racked up several Emmy and Golden Globe nominations and wins, notably for lead actor Gary Sinise, who offered a refined portrayal of the man from Missouri, *Truman* was less a series than an extended, one-off, made-for-TV film. Chasing McCullough's extensive research, it was also a movie more akin to *Wilson* than it might have liked to let on. The movie covered a slightly longer trajectory of Truman's life than King's movie did in 1944, but it followed a similarly prophetic path to destiny, from humble small-town beginnings to the man who authorised the use of the atomic bomb and emerged from F. D. R.'s shadow.

Time and space to build character were not as critical in *Truman* as in other bio-pics, but this only served to emphasise the authoritative presence of Sinise in the lead role, which he carries brilliantly through episodic engagements from beginning to end when lesser actors might not have been up to the task. One issue that benefited this film especially was that most problematic but often crucial element for the aspiring political biographer to take on board: the subject's reputation. No small thanks to McCullough's epic work, Truman was going through something of a renaissance by the time he reached TV and the movie takes full advantage by engendering a sympathetic feel for the man and the events portrayed.

Back in Hollywood, by 2001, Roger Donaldson's under-rated *Thirteen Days* (2001) could not be described as overt biography in the manner of *Truman*. Nevertheless the making and unmaking of reputation and the Kennedy legacy suffuse much of the action. In detailing the inside story of the Cuban Missile Crisis of 1962 in near-documentary mode at times, Donaldson and executive producer Kevin Costner actually fashion a pretty convincing 'clock-is-ticking' political thriller out of real historical events. Those real events are culled from Robert Kennedy's own account in the book of the same name, from Costner's character Kenny O'Donnell's private papers, and most particularly from Ernest May and Philip Zelikow's book, *The Kennedy Tapes: Inside the White House During the Cuban Missile Crisis*. As Art Simon's review of the movie tellingly asserts, all this produced any amount of attention to detail. But Donaldson and Costner also revert to issues focused upon in *Wilson* nearly sixty years beforehand. 'With six hundred pages of transcripts drawn from tape-recorded discussions held by the Executive Committee of the National Security Council, the filmmakers certainly had no shortage of material,' confirms Simon. 'But such sources are only history in a limited sense.'[31] He believed that the film was pretty faithful but then forsook some of the graphic cinematic style that so troubled critics of *JFK*, yet thrilled viewers with the visual assault on their senses. Once again, the biographer is in a no-win situation; drama, accuracy and visual panache are never easy tricks to pull off all in one go.

And whatever the history was doing, none of this further prevented reviewers from focusing in on Bruce Greenwood's intriguing personi-fication of John Kennedy; nor did it stop the film being accused of play-ing up to the myths of the 'Camelot' legacy so closely attended to by the family and friends of those involved in the events portrayed. John Patterson, for one, cared not at all for the construction of character and the manner of historical evaluation in the movie.

> Donaldson and his screenwriter David Self dig Kennedy out from under a mountain of dead dogs and retroactive slander [he claimed]. Settling not for the real Kennedy, a deeply flawed but adept politician, but the one sold to us as a part of that sudsy package deal stamped 'Camelot'.[32]

It might not be entirely clear what Patterson means when he says that Greenwood's Kennedy is 'one of those eerie performances that erase and replace the real man before your eyes', but one thing is certain: the myth, legend, construction and obscurity that make up the person J. F. K. are very difficult to escape from when one is attempting to document history as definitive as this episode of edge-of-your-seat diplomacy.[33] The filmmaker is trying to fashion heroic and personable grace under pressure and the reviewer/historian is arguing for the cover-up of now clearly known flaws and failings. It becomes a biographical impasse that cannot easily be bridged. Nevertheless, Todd Purdum's review of the time asserted that the film 'did its bit to return some of the lustre to the legend of Camelot', in no small way due to the integrity of its leading players and the desire of Donaldson to foreground the story as much as the people involved.[34]

Simon was complimentary too about the claustrophobic feel of the movie and the suggestion of 'the invisibility of the people on whose behalf policy is supposedly being enacted'. But he also feels that it is too long, exactly the same complaint that befell *Wilson*. Costner's O'Donnell uses the actor's previous experience on *JFK* to mould a character that builds family drama and an insider's personal eye on the action as it unfolds in the Oval Office and beyond. Just like Knox before him, though, it is still Bruce Greenwood who manages to pull the film through to its nail-biting finale. 'To his credit, Greenwood acts rather than impersonates Kennedy and whatever credible drama emerges throughout the film is, in large measure, due to his perform-ance,' concludes Simon.[35]

Acting, too, in HBO's acclaimed 2002 mini-drama is Michael Gambon as Lyndon Johnson in John Frankenheimer's *Path to War*. As the title implies, the film concentrates its efforts upon the escalation in Vietnam after Johnson's 1964 landslide election result over Barry Goldwater. But domestic issues get an airing too, not least with the appearance of Gary Sinise again, this time as Governor George Wallace of Alabama, determined to stand up to the civil rights movement sweeping his state. Johnson and Wallace's confrontation in the Oval Office is played out in all its dramatic insouciance with the president's famous remark, 'You're a very persuasive man, Governor. I was watching you on television and hell you almost made me change my mind.'

In fact, Frankenheimer, directing this final work before his untimely death only weeks after the film had been aired, was not only no stranger to TV movies, but also no stranger to the related subject matter. Including Sinise was a smart way to conjoin this drama with the direc-tor's earlier TV biography, *George Wallace* (1997), which earned both him and his lead actor Emmy Awards. Wallace is only a marginal sub-plot here, used as a stepping-stone to Johnson's successful attempt to pass civil rights legislation through Congress. The war takes over the story for the remainder of the picture, and while sticking faith-fully to the historical record, Gambon's performance, ably supported by Alec Baldwin (as Defence Secretary, Robert McNamara), Donald Sutherland (Clark Clifford) and Bruce McGill (George Ball), is perfectly pitched as a man increasingly haunted by a historical legacy he seems to have no control over writing.

First Ball and then Clifford spend their time arguing increasingly desperately for restraint on Vietnam against the persuasive powers of McNamara. Johnson falls into the routine of escalation, though, and by the beginning of 1968, as Clifford had prophesied, it is tearing him and his administration apart, as demonstrations take to the streets and casualties mount on the ground.

Frankenheimer occasionally uses stock footage from the time but for the most part the drama is played out in (some) smoke-filled rooms, departmental offices and the White House itself. Through its two-and-a-half-hour length, he never loses a sense of pace as doubt, apprehension and fear fall upon many in the administration. The film is therefore conventional in one sense: it never presents any bravado imagery or sweeping timeline that flits back and forth between events. Instead, Frankenheimer captures the iconic moments and photographs of the time and translates them into a persuasive historical drama – including the President's famous bowed-head moment when we see him with his glasses out in front of him, drawn, beaten and exasperated. Unlike *Truman, Wilson* and others before it, *Path to War* does not assess Johnson so much as it does White House politics and Pax Americana, ground into the dust of defeat in Vietnam. Michael Coyne describes the film as 'Shakespearean tragedy' in a manner, he argues, that Oliver Stone's *JFK* was not.[36] Certainly, Frankenheimer casts Johnson as an increasingly lonely individual prowling the halls of the White House and hearing nothing but mounting doubt and indecision from his advisors. But it is still a drama that privileges the desperate questions of policy above any psychological probing, and the collapse of the politician is conclusively about the loss of judgement as much as it is the unravelling of a destabilised leader.

The latter half of the film, as the war develops and American society grows increasingly fractious, focuses more, in fact, on Robert McNamara up to the point of his departure from the administration. He gives testimony to Congress that reveals the division within the cabinet as even he himself comes to doubt the wisdom of the Operation Rolling Thunder bombing programme he had originally endorsed, and the way is paved for his exit from the Pentagon. It bears some comparison, then, with a portrait of the man more than thirty years after the events, in Errol Morris's Oscar-winning documentary, *The Fog of War* (2003).

Partly biographical recollection, partly psychological profile by way of Morris's famous Interrotron method/machine, the film is indeed a *mea culpa* for McNamara's decision-making, in Vietnam at least; but, like Frankenheimer's film, the eleven lessons of life implied by the film's sub-title are also an investigation of how policy decisions are made in the context of late twentieth-century global *realpolitik*. McNamara recalls how close Kennedy came to making the wrong move over Cuba in 1962 while wiser heads – notably Tommy Thompson, the former Ambassador to Moscow – were urging the President to temper his opinion of what Premier Khrushchev was trying to achieve. McNamara is honest enough to concede that the administration 'got lucky' in its decision-making at that point and twice more when conflict with the Soviets seemed likely. That dicey dance with death is, for McNamara and the film, the dilemma of the modern world.

Morris's film is about as far as you might travel from the conventions of Henry King's *Wilson* sixty years beforehand. Yet, in its way, the questions and resolutions remain the same. How does one cope with grace under pressure? What are the demands made of leaders who bear such huge responsibility for the policies of states and their effect on the world? And who accounts for the aftermath? Morris answers these questions by employing a style that combines a single but compulsive talking head with impressively coordinated footage and graphics that instil in the audience both fascination and horror at how war, decision-making and politics combine. Proportionality is everything, argues McNamara, but he leaves you with a nagging doubt as to whether the rules of war are ever truly followed, let alone defined.

DRAMA AND POLITICS: THE BIOGRAPHIES OF OLIVER STONE

Commenting in 2008 on the dilemma that has plagued much of his directorial career, Oliver Stone said, as part of the publicity that heralded the arrival of his new political biography of George Bush, *W.*, that he showed the movie to a senior journalist ahead of its preview screenings. The journalist told him to expect controversy as usual because there were quotes from Bush out of context. 'They'll say Bush didn't make that comment in his pyjamas,' said the unnamed journalist, who nevertheless remarked that the spirit and projection of those comments were not ill founded or designed to manipulate the historical record in any fundamental way. Stone used this exercise as an example of his own philosophy in interviews for the film. 'Good historians understand that dramatists who deal with history have a licence they don't have,' he explained, wondering aloud why Hollywood and history still found it so hard to get along.[37]

In fact, rather than political controversy as usual, Stone's *W.* brought the presidential biography full circle in the 2000s. Neither as contentious as *JFK*, nor as cinematically dazzling as either that film or *Nixon*, the latest document of presidential life from Hollywood's pre-eminent political filmmaker of the last twenty-five years operated on a more conventional level structurally, and bore resemblances in its form and features to the work of D. W. Griffith, John Ford and Henry King in the earlier twentieth century. *W.*'s flashbacks and early life experiences are altogether more prosaic in this film than in Stone's previous efforts. They provide a perfectly aligned binary link between youthful lessons learnt and later presidential decision-making implemented. Early scenes contrast the debates with staff about the merits of a new war in Iraq with, for example, Bush's initiation into his college fraternity in the 1960s. Rather than disorientate viewers or make them work harder for a clear rationale of the man and the events surrounding him, *W.* is perhaps conventional to the point at which Stone himself felt disinclined to document Bush with similar widescreen historical virtuosity to that employed with Kennedy or Nixon, for fear that the effect would look incongruous set beside these earlier presidents.

Douglas Kellner is one commentator who describes Stone's presentation as 'uncharacteristically restrained' in this picture. But he also acknowledges that there are subtleties at work in the movie that are designed to leave the audience with the bitter taste of 'How did this all happen?'[38] The scene when Dick Cheney (Richard Dreyfus) hands Bush (Josh Brolin) the draft document that will allow the torture of prisoners and violation of their human rights, for example, as the 'war on terror' kicks into full gear, is where the President insists on trying to read the evidence and make sense of the complicity into which he is entering. Cheney talks of the control of Iran in an extended scene in the Situation Room that posits an administration serious about the renewed concept of 'Empire' and Bush slowly but incrementally being sold on the whole idea.

But his apparent helplessness at resisting this right-wing *coup de grâce*, in Stone's eyes at least, is as hopeless and baffling as the audience's own acceptance of the actions and policy carried out in their name during the eight years of the Bush Administration. The final moment of bemused misunderstanding in the film, situated in the fabled baseball field (a metaphoric scene which keeps recurring throughout the picture), is also one that delivers and confirms that undercurrent of susceptibility and manipulation by the 'handlers' of the President in pursuit of their own objectives rather than his. Both scenes suggest Stone is trying to contrive a movie that, at his own behest, is nothing like as ambitious and complicated as his previous efforts because Bush is nothing like as ambitious or interesting as the men who preceded him.

Long-time collaborator Julie Monroe, who has been a film editor for the director on a number of his most prominent pictures, confirmed that the piecing together of scenes and imagery for this movie was much more straightforward, compared to others. 'It was a lot simpler, in that he [Stone] shot a lot less and the story was more specific. It was still a lot of footage, but it was definitely dialog telling the story more than imagery.'[39]

Ultimately, Kellner perceives *W.* as fitting into a historical and cinematic moment at the end of the Bush era where biography, contemporaneously framed or set in the past, is marked by turmoil and tumult, rather than nostalgic reverence and remembrance. Citing Steven Soderbergh's two-part *Che* with Benicio del Toro (2008); Gus Van Sant's *Milk* starring Sean Penn (also 2008), which, closer to home, engages with the restless bigotry of domestic politics; and Ron Howard's *Frost/Nixon* (2009), an adaptation of British playwright Peter Morgan's stage success about the televised confrontation between the former President and celebrated talk show host David Frost, Kellner argues for a collection of bio-pics that 'open up discussion and debate rather than comforting ideological closure'.[40] Monroe again confirms that Stone wanted to employ a more 'fly-on-the-wall approach' to Bush and did not want to be 'caricaturey' for fear of simply disengaging with the character from the off.[41] Instead, the sometimes objective, distanced approach that Stone employs speaks to Kellner's theory about bio-pics trying to leave their ideology and opinion of the subject as a matter of discretion for the audience to take stock of in a bewildering first decade of the twenty-first century.

Frost/Nixon, as well as presenting another facet of the President that Stone himself wanted to transfigure in the 1990s with Anthony Hopkins, is also something of a complementary piece to another film from the 2000s: Niels Mueller's *The Assassination of Richard Nixon* (2004), starring Sean Penn. Both are ardent recreations of 1970s America; one is all economic dislocation, the Watergate hearings on TV and social decay, while the other is California hedonism, large shirt collars and discos, with the faint whiff of *Saturday Night Fever* about it. Just as *JFK* is more about paranoia than politics, so both these films are exercises in 1970s nostalgia as much as they are inquiries into Nixon as leader. That is not to denigrate the intensity and insight both bring to a nation confused about its purpose at the time or an ex-President unsure of what his legacy could ever be, having been the first Chief Executive to resign. Their tone, therefore, the almost relentless aesthetic intensity of their spectacle, does say something about Nixon the man, and almost as much as that implied in earlier bio-pics. The restless, fractured state of society in 1970s America, the birth and rise of a new media celebrity-dom that would make interviewers almost as famous as their guests in the coming decades: all of this works towards a re-imagination of the US in the Reagan and later Clinton years that conjoined politics and Hollywood in a fashion few during the mid-1970s would have lent much credibility.

Mueller's film title is necessarily metaphoric. Sam Bicke (Penn) is a fidgety, restless individual who is being swallowed up by the American Dream in the recession-led 1970s. As Nixon preaches on TV about trusting in the White House and not being a crook, Bicke loses his livelihood in the family tyre company and proceeds to disintegrate as the bank refuses him a loan to start his own business. The office furniture store he works at is only about hard selling and little ethical management, and his marriage to the less than empathetic Marie (Naomi Watts) collapses entirely as she falls for another man and attempts to escape the life with Sam she openly admits was a catastrophic mistake. Bicke's brother, Julius (Michael Wincott), serves notice of Sam's less than reliable state of mind when he uncovers the truth about fraudulent sales receipts, and any residual sympathy the audience has for Sam starts to wither away as he concentrates his mind on Nixon and concocts a plan to hijack a plane at Baltimore airport which will take him to Washington and his date with infamy. Of course, the attempt itself is botched, violent and ultimately sadly baleful: not a bad analogy for Nixon himself.

By contrast, Howard's film offers the supposedly glamorous side of the 1970s and the media stardom that beckoned for people as able and beguiling as David Frost. If anything, *Frost/Nixon* is about that transcendent moment between the instigation of celebrity entertainment in the 1960s when the interviewees still remained the stars, and the later 1980s incarnation when talk show interviewers/presenters not only began to dictate the pattern of show-business but also made news in their own right. It is no coincidence, for example, that on Nixon's side, almost as important to the negotiations as his political aides, is the larger-than-life presence of talent-maker and deal-breaker, Irving 'Swifty' Lazar (Toby Jones). That David Frost's series of interviews with the disgraced Nixon, back on the former President's home turf of California in 1977, managed to include elements of both entertainment and political spectacle only made the original discussion and Howard's brilliant translation to the screen of Morgan's play that more pertinent.

Mueller's film perceives Nixon at the head of a monster chewing up American morals and morale in an era of decline and decay that he captures intently on screen. Howard has his players discover a moment when fallibility can be unveiled on television and trust is washed away forever from politics. Even hard-boiled journalist James Reston (Sam Rockwell) is unconvinced that Nixon will reveal anything dramatic in the interviews, let alone that Frost is the man for the job. So when the moment arrives, and Nixon inadvertently admits illegal activities but tries to justify them by saying that when the President does it, it is not illegal, the whole of Frost's crew look at each other, knowing full well the implications not just for television, but for politics as a whole.

Strong and insightful as both of these films are in their particular revelations about America and Nixon at a specific moment in time, Oliver Stone's canvas has always been wider, the events even more deeply rooted in American history and psychosis. And this rendering of historical verisimilitude has always been an intimate part of his political agenda. Indeed, actor Toby Jones, who worked on both *Frost/ Nixon* and *W.*, commented that the styles of the two directors reflected the way material ended up on screen and the ideologies of the protagonists were pursued. *Frost/Nixon* was already a 'complete narrative' with fully formed characters who had real-life personalities to fall back on, as well as having Morgan's characterisation of them in the stage play to work from, which Howard then carefully and precisely plotted out on screen. On *W.*, real though the characters were, they were also subject to a certain manipulation and experimentation as Stone groped for the right feel and tone for the scenes. It was, Jones said, much more like 'guerrilla filmmaking', working on the edge with the script and scenes, and testing the waters of how characters might grow, develop and adapt to the story.[42]

The insinuation that the actors themselves have always been encouraged to put themselves out on a limb to accentuate the intensity of their characters, as well as Monroe's earlier contention that Stone shot far more footage in his previous movies, add to the evidence of the ambition at the heart of his 1990s bio-pics. Both *JFK* and *Nixon* were films in the first half of that decade that, by Andrew Pepper and Trevor McCrisken's reckoning, were attempting nothing less than to bring the whole 'meta-narrative of American history crashing down'.[43] If *The Assassination of Richard Nixon* and *Frost/Nixon* were smaller cameos of the American experience documenting the disintegrating consensus at the heart of American society in their narratives, then Stone's movies, by contrast, have always been about a much larger, breath-taking sweep of history attempting to answer bigger and more imponderable questions. Both *JFK* and *Nixon* arguably accelerated that acceptance of an America in thrall to its leaders and institutions, yet all the while being led down a path to destruction and despair from the mid-1960s onwards.

With *Nixon* (1995), the resultant structure saw the director borrow from the classic heritage of the political bio-pic while staying true to much of the conspiracy make-up that had registered so successfully with *JFK*. As Gavin Smith observed, Nixon's manic depressive secret history is composed from a century of cinematic technique, encompassing Griffithian associative superimposition and *Forrest Gump* digital compositing, Soviet montage and Wellesian *mise-en-scène*, the Sixties American avant-garde and *March of Time* newsreels.[44]

The mood of destruction at the heart of the administration is additionally offset by scenes in the film of increasing darkness and night-time sequences that allow Stone's cinematographer, Bob Richardson, to roam the hallways of the White House, establishing the mood for the demons that Hopkins's Nixon conjures up in his mind. With no pretence at a chronological order following the subject, the film offers up flashbacks – sometimes in colour, mostly in black and white – and composite scenes where White House discussions are occasionally mixed in time and order. The array of technique and composition allows for the distortion of logic that is suffusing Nixon's mind as well as the administration's policies, and it is this breakdown and pressure of concealment, the 'dirty tricks', illogical decision-making, infighting and subterfuge that Stone sees acting as a physical presence – the mythical beast – destroying the Nixon presidency in its last two years.

While directors like Griffith and Ford professed greatness and the spirit of American renewal cut short by tragedy in their films, Stone signals descent and personal affliction repetitively playing on Nixon's mind and leading to an inevitable political fall from grace. The

flashback dreams of Nixon's childhood confer much of the responsibility for this tragedy on him, just as spectacle and early foresight suf-
fused the Presidents of Ford and Levin's earlier pieces. Nixon's 1930s
California is paraded by Stone as the last frontier of America, while
the obsessions of his mother, the anger of an omnipotent father and
the deaths of his two brothers, Arthur and Harold (Joshua Preston
and Tony Goldwyn), constitute symbolic staging posts on the young
Richard's ladder of ascent.

The difference is that these early life experiences offer some hope
mixed with ambition but they are contrasted against the later Nixon,
listening to the White House tapes that will spell his doom, alone and
unnerved. He is visited by the apparition of his mother, Hannah (Mary
Steenbergen), while sitting in the Lincoln Room, his health deteriorat-
ing and his aides slowly falling around him.

At the heart of the film, then, remains an auteur vision that is hard
to displace in Stone's canon. He has long felt susceptible to charges
of fabrication, and the experience of *JFK*, by his own admission, profoundly shocked him to the extent that he felt compelled to begin to
expound on his theory of the cinematic historian as a way to justify the
approach to his subject in *Nixon*. 'Whenever you start to dictate to an
artist his "social responsibility", you get into an area of censorship,' he
explained, when asked about the filmmakers' obligation to the historical record.[45] Terry Golway is a little more pragmatic in his explanation.
With *JFK*, he reasons, 'the historians, conventional sorts, demanded
proof. That's when Stone decided he was an artist after all, not a docu-
mentarian.'[46] Whether Stone took that convenient position or not is
less important than some of the consistent patterns that have emerged
in his films over a longer period than the 1990s focus on presidential
figures. 'Kennedy, Nixon, Jim Morrison, they're all part of his uncon-
scious,' explains Richard Rutowski, a long-time friend who identifies
the disintegration of American life in the 1960s and early 1970s as a
psychological trauma that has long informed Stone's filmmaking, all
the way back to *Midnight Express*.[47] For Stone's part, it is clear that
interpretation, myth and perception have always been fundamental
and that position does not separate him too far from luminaries like
John Ford and his vision of the nation's great leaders, and the country's
mythic contestation.

As if to anticipate such criticisms, actor James Woods, who returned
to work with Stone on *Nixon* after a decade away from the director,
confirmed the later impressions of Jones, who played Karl Rove in *W.*

Woods noted that the style in the intervening time between *Salvador* and *Nixon* had become a lot looser, scenes and dialogue were constantly subject to change and alteration, and the desire and capacity to research more material were never-ending.[48] Just as he had done with Zachary Sklar for *JFK*, Stone, together with Christopher Wilkinson and Stephen Rivele, produced an annotated screenplay, articles and commentaries tied together as a general historical companion to *Nixon*.

Despite this historical fame of reference, the film itself still laid the groundwork in its initial scene for a somewhat fabricated and disassembled strategy towards the history it was documenting. *Nixon* begins with the Watergate break-in, constructed as a fake business lunch where the 'plumbers' mask themselves as business associates who are watching a training film about becoming a salesman before they embark on the burglary of the Democratic National Committee headquarters. The trope of Nixon as 'used car salesman' is thus invoked in the very early moments of the picture and this 'pop art' technique of Stone's, to mix the historical record with pastiche and analogies to events and personnel, sparks the imagination and signposts the drama as much as it provokes contention and derision in some.

One might have expected Stone to follow the same Manichaean line as *Wilson* where the President's opponents are berated for their bipartisan spite and for refusing to work with him on the Versailles Treaty and the League of Nations especially. But in *Nixon* the President's opponents are all around him, as even his aides and friends are presented as more of a threat to Nixon than any political opponent, and we see few Democratic contenders, except for the Kennedys, of course. Instead, Nixon's staff become something more than co-conspirators to the unfolding events. H. R. Haldeman (James Woods) and John Ehrlichman (J. T. Walsh) assume the role of grand schemers, while Mitchell, Ziegler and Dean (E. G. Marshall, David Paymer and David Hyde Pierce respectively) remain sceptical, concealed, unreliable and ultimately treacherous comrades in Nixon's war, as Theodore White termed it.[49] Yet, as Stryker McGuire and David Ansen commented at the time of the release, despite the unravelling of his political judgement, *Nixon* does discover ambiguity in the man and a twisted humanity and tortured history that liken themselves to non-political biographies at the very least. The result was that Stone delivered a more ambiguous political agenda than many critics suspected but one that still could not escape criticism from those who railed against its fabrications and composite scenes.

*Plotting and collusion within the White House are the hallmarks of
Oliver Stone's* Nixon

Despite the scenes of triumph that accompany the trips to China
and the Soviet Union and register achievement and empathy, Stone
ultimately brings it all crashing down in waves of psychological and
philosophical allegory. The part-Shakespearean, part-Greek tragedy
denouement to *Nixon*, with the President looking at the famous portrait of Kennedy hanging on one of the White House walls and asking
why he became so revered when Nixon will not, speaks to the illusory
quality at the heart of all political biography. How can the public be
made to understand what drives leaders and great figures? What leads
rational and intelligent politicians sometimes to make dangerous or
misguided choices?

The same kinds of questions, claims and ethical issues feature as an
integral part of Stone's *W.* But the film came at the end of a year when
the biographical mini-series had gone through yet another transformation and this one did not even involve Stone. With the release of
HBO's *John Adams*, a sweeping account of the second President's life
and times, inspired again by one of David McCullough's best-selling
books, political biography took on acute historical re-enactment visited upon a burgeoning republic aspiring to the mantle of power while

its perpetrators figured out what the reins of power might entail, even before they could cling to them. British director Tom Hooper brings even-handed empathy to Paul Giamatti's delivery of Adams and the President's concern that too much is lost of old colonial heritage in the rush to assent.

Hooper's impressively coordinated vision of eighteenth- and early nineteenth-century America does what political biography has long hoped for: to show how leaders become the people they are and remain in public consciences, and occasionally, as with Stone, how that mercurial facade is destroyed. As the director himself said of Richard Nixon, 'In the end . . . it's tough not to feel some compassion for a guy who just never thought he was good enough to join the establishment, even when he emblemised that very entity.'[50] The history of biography on screen is, then, one of reinforcement for the pantheon of great American leaders, but it has also increasingly become an investigation into other neglected figures in the nation's history as well as a reading of that established canon that asks how and why certain figures continue to hold the imagination and interest. As a film like *W.* and a TV series like *John Adams* exemplify, historical and social reconstruction, the personal and political reinforcing each other, have always been and continue to be vital components of a sub-genre that exalts and acclaims the political greats with equal force.

NOTES

1. Bosley Crowther, '"Wilson", an Impressive Screen Biography, in which Alex Knox is the Star, has its World Premiere at the Roxy', *New York Times*, 2 August 1944, cited in the collection, *New York Motion Picture Critics Reviews*, 7 August 1944, p. 284.
2. Producer Darryl Zanuck reputedly spent $250,000 on the premiere alone, as much as 13 per cent of the film's whole publicity budget. See Leonard J. Leff and Jerold Simmons, '*Wilson*: Hollywood Propaganda for World Peace', *Historical Journal of Film, Radio and Television*, vol. 3, no. 1, 1983. p. 9.
3. Bosley Crowther, p. 284.
4. Terry Ramsaye, '*Wilson*: 20th Century Fox – Romanticized Political History', *Motion Picture Herald*, 5 August 1944, p. 63.
5. Kate Cameron, '"Wilson" at the Roxy Fine Historical Film', 2 August 1944, cited in the collection, *New York Motion Picture Critics Reviews*, 7 August 1944, p. 285.
6. Terry Christensen and Peter J. Hass, *Projecting Politics: Political Messages in American Films* (London: M. E. Sharpe, 2005), p. 102.

7. Michael Coyne, *Hollywood Goes to Washington: American Politics on Screen* (London: Reaktion, 2008), p. 60. The review is from Alton Cook, 'Wilson Offers Colourful Panorama of War Era', *New York World-Telegram*, 2 August 1944, cited in the collection, *New York Motion Picture Critics Reviews*, 7 August 1944, p. 285.
8. Leonard J. Leff and Jerold Simmons, p. 3.
9. C. Wright Mills, *The Sociological Imagination* (New York: Oxford University Press, 2000), p. 4.
10. C. Wright Mills, p. 6.
11. Donald E. Staples, 'Wilson in Technicolor', in *Hollywood's White House: The American Presidency in Film and History*, ed. Peter C. Rollins and John E. O'Connor (Lexington: University Press of Kentucky, 2003), p. 120.
12. George F. Custen, *Twentieth Century's Fox: Darryl F. Zanuck and the Culture of Hollywood* (New York: Basic, 1997), p. 276.
13. Donald E. Staples, p. 117.
14. Thomas J. Knock, '"History with Lightning": The Forgotten Film *Wilson*', *American Quarterly*, vol. 28, no. 5, Winter 1976, pp. 526–7.
15. Archer Winsten, 'Zanuck's Monumental "Wilson" Opens at the Roxy Theatre', 2 August 1944, cited in the collection, *New York Motion Picture Critics Reviews*, 7 August 1944, p. 286.
16. Thomas J. Knock, p. 533.
17. Thomas J. Knock, p. 538.
18. Leonard J. Leff and Jerold Simmons, p. 11.
19. Leonard J. Leff and Jerold Simmons, p. 14.
20. George F. Custen, p. 280.
21. Michael Coyne, p. 62.
22. Leonard J. Leff and Jerold Simmons, p. 5.
23. Leonard J. Leff and Jerold Simmons, p. 12.
24. Everett Carter, 'Cultural History Written with Lightning: The Significance of *The Birth of a Nation*', *American Quarterly*, vol. 12, no. 3, Autumn 1960, pp. 347–57.
25. Michael Coyne, p. 45.
26. Joseph McBride, *Searching for John Ford: A Life* (London: Faber & Faber, 2004), p. 304.
27. Joseph McBride, p. 306.
28. Review of 'The President's Lady', in *Monthly Film Bulletin*, vol. 20, no. 232, May 1953, p. 70.
29. Gallagher is particularly keen to observe that the scenes of Abe's courting of Ann Rutledge, and her subsequent passing away, play to these transcendentalist themes and philosophy very strongly. See Tag Gallagher, *John Ford: The Man and his Films* (Berkeley: University of California Press, 1986), pp. 167–9.
30. Myron Levine, 'The Transformed Presidency', in *Hollywood's White*

House: The American Presidency in Film and History, ed. Peter C. Rollins and John E. O'Connor (Lexington: University Press of Kentucky, 2004), p. 371

31. Art Simon, 'Thirteen Days', *Cineaste*, vol. 26, no. 2, 2001, p. 43.
32. John Patterson, 'In the Bay of Fibs', *The Guardian Review*, 12 January 2001, p. 5.
33. John Patterson, p. 5.
34. Todd S. Purdum, 'A True Story of What Now Seems Incredible', *New York Times*, 5 November 2000, p. 19.
35. Art Simon, p. 44.
36. Michael Coyne, p. 75.
37. Oliver Burkeman, 'W and I', *The Guardian Weekend* magazine, 4 October 2008, p. 23.
38. Douglas Kellner, *Cinema Wars: Hollywood Film and Politics in the Bush–Cheney Era* (Oxford: Wiley-Blackwell, 2010), p. 253.
39. Gabriella Oldham, 'Cutting Remarks on *W*', *Cineaste*, vol. 34, no. 2, Spring 2009, p. 34.
40. Douglas Kellner, p. 250.
41. Gabriella Oldham, p. 33.
42. Author's interview with Toby Jones, 16 December 2009.
43. Andrew Pepper and Trevor McCrisken, *American History and Contemporary Hollywood Film* (Edinburgh: Edinburgh University Press, 2005), p. 141.
44. Gavin Smith, 'The Dark Side', *Sight and Sound*, March 1996, pp. 6–9.
45. Susan Mackey-Kallis, *Oliver Stone's America, 'Dreaming the Myth Outward'* (Boulder, CO: Westview, 1996), p. 41.
46. Terry Golway, 'Enslaved by the Beast', *The Guardian*, 14 December 1995, p. 2.
47. Holly Milea, 'All the President's Men', *Premiere*, March 1996, p. 80.
48. Chris Salewicz, *Oliver Stone: The Making of his Movies* (London: Orion, 1997), pp. 111–13.
49. White's analysis concludes, somewhat with Stone, that the aides were at least as culpable, if not more so in some respects, of the events that took place. 'The villains were clear-cut – Haldeman and Mitchell and Magruder and Dean, and the lesser hustlers of the underground.' See Theodore White, *Breach of Faith* (London: Jonathan Cape, 1975), p. 34.
50. Michael Singer, 'Interview with Oliver Stone', *Nixon: An Oliver Stone Film*, ed. Eric Hamburg (London: Bloomsbury, 1996), p. xvii.

Chapter 6

HOLLYWOOD AND AMERICA IN THE NEW FOREIGN POLICY ERA

If the presidency managed to be something of an obsession for Hollywood as the 1990s progressed, and assessments of the comedic/action/thriller genres as well as biography threw up particular lines of inquiry about what Americans were looking for in their President, how much they wanted narratives that were fulfilling and wistful rather more than contemplative and questioning, then how do we assess the crop of foreign policy/thriller narratives for the end of the last century and now the new post-9/11, Iraq War generation? Back in the early 1990s the Tom Clancy-inspired crop of Jack Ryan novels-turned-movie-franchise, particularly *Patriot Games* (1992) and *Clear and Present Danger* (1994), both defined and surveyed an America looking for a new direction in the post-Cold War world. With the certainties of bipolar conflict at an end, and hence the tone of messages inherent in the likes of *The Manchurian Candidate*, *Dr. Strangelove* and *No Way Out* increasingly redundant, Cold War thriller-writers and Hollywood producers sought new ways to determine America's on-going mission to rescue the world from itself.

Whether it was rogue terrorists in the former Clancy story or Colombian drug barons in the latter, Ryan was sent on missions where the US military and intelligence were attempting to act as some kind of arbiter in the world's trouble spots. With a screenplay by W. Peter Lliff, who at that point had gained notoriety for his slacker-surfer-heist movie script, *Point Break* (1991), and directed by Australian action-helmer, Philip Noyce (*Dead Calm*, 1989), *Patriot Games* had all the foreign policy reinvention one might hope for in Jack Ryan's thwarting of an IRA assassination attempt on a member of the British royal family. Ryan's successful intervention to prevent the bombing makes him a target for revenge and threatens the activation of terrorist activity on American soil itself. In *Clear and Present Danger*, Ryan is immersed in an illegal war against Colombian drug cartels that smacks of the Reagan and Bush Administrations' attempts to hunt down and close off the business of the Medellín cartel of Pablo Escobar in the 1980s. The later film hints at Washington double-dealing, even from within the White House, but Ryan's hefty principles always save the day. Both pictures nevertheless set the tone for a roguish collection of forces and groups who became the target of American retribution around the world, carried on in the likes of James Cameron's *True Lies* (1994), John Woo's *Broken Arrow* (1996), and even the *Lethal Weapon* franchise with Mel Gibson and Danny Glover.

As complements to the Ryan franchise, *Independence Day* and *Air Force One* (the latter, of course, also starring Harrison Ford) were not so realistic but they did at least encourage a new generation of blockbuster fans to think about the presidency and politics to some extent. All of these movies paid due reverence to traditional generic devices used in Cold War thrillers and many fell in with the mood of the decade for ever larger and more lavish Summer blockbuster productions that attracted large demographics and put the emphasis on thrills and spills rather more than on ideological or diplomatic engagement.

If the spirit of these initial 1990s re-assessments of America's place in the world created a template that was as much about explosions and entertainment as politics and power, later movies towards the close of the decade, the likes of *Proof of Life* and *Behind Enemy Lines*, attempted to extract a little more ambiguity, if not subtlety from their stories of corporate kidnapping in South America and American/UN peacekeeping operations during the decade's divisive Balkan War. Arguably, even if a little simplistically, here were scenarios 'inspired by' real stories that were closer to the mark in their search for a policy agenda on 1990s US foreign policy, set against the backdrop of Soviet collapse.

Indeed, assessments of Hollywood's realisation of foreign policy adventures like these have often been couched in terms of their historical acuity to events and personalities of present or previous eras. As Andrew Pepper and Trevor McCrisken argue, 'The question for these films is how they work to produce or unsettle established or consensual views about US military actions and how they undermine or reinforce traditional understandings of the benign meta-narrative of American history.'[1] On one level, McCrisken and Pepper are interested in the way film can be used as pedagogic text in a bid to understand the world and the events taking place in it. But on another level, they are also discussing the means by which certain 'texts' interpret and re-assign particular codes and discourse towards key moments in history. Their examples, as we will consider below, do more than historicise events on film; they contemplate political choices, diplomatic engagement and military intervention as part of the cultural firmament surrounding those events, no more so than in David Russell's *Three Kings* (1999) and Ridley Scott's *Black Hawk Down* (2001). Russell's and Scott's films dealt handily enough with the major global issues that immersed the US in the 1990s: namely, the first Iraq War in 1991 as well as peacekeeping missions which went disastrously wrong, such as in Somalia in 1993. What they did not and could not anticipate was an event on the scale of 9/11 and how it would alter the perception of everything in the following decade.

J. Hoberman observes that the first film of the post-9/11 era was the event itself, a confirmation of the myriad of commentaries that likened the collapse of the Twin Towers to a movie in the catastrophic tradition. If the horrendous events of that day seem trivialised by the Hollywood connection it did not seem to bother either the film industry or Washington unduly. As Hoberman confirms, in the days that followed, the *Los Angeles Times* reported that Hollywood was fearful of the public accepting any more action, terrorist and disaster movies such as Schwarzenegger's *Collateral Damage*, which itself was postponed for fear of offending with its terrorist network scenario and its narrative featuring Arab assailants being pursued by Arnie's all-too-familiar man-on-a-revenge-mission agenda. But the fear never really materialised in quite the manner filmmakers might have thought. 'Hollywood expected to be punished; instead, it was drafted,' as Hoberman succinctly puts it.[2] And although the type of scenario that appeared in *Collateral Damage* also subsequently saw even comic superhero adaptation *Spiderman* recut so as to exclude the Twin Towers from the publicity and climactic sequence of the movie, the Pentagon proceeded to fund the Institute for Creative Technologies at the University of Southern California significantly in the aftermath of 9/11, convening meetings with screenwriters and directors in order to test the efficacy of terrorist scenarios appearing on the big screen.[3]

Although already slated for release before the events of 2001, Phil Alden Robinson's *The Sum of All Fears* (2002), updating the Clancy/Ryan novels and giving the franchise a sense of the real events surrounding the production, was the first to test the new waters of public acceptability and response to these sorts of films. By recasting the main lead with the younger and slightly more impressionable Ben Affleck while sticking with the book's premise of a nuclear attack on America, the movie went a step further in prophesying what Americans themselves now feared was a real possibility in the light of 9/11. Published way back in 1992, the novel originally had Islamic terrorists setting off a small nuclear device in Denver; this was then changed in the pre-9/11 months before the release of the film to feature neo-Nazis detonating an explosive in Baltimore, partly because the former were not seen as having the capability to carry out such an attack. The final film version appeared in the US in August 2002, eleven months after the attacks made the terrorist conspiracy eerily prescient despite the rather counter-intuitive side-stepping of Clancy's original set-up. Written by Paul Attanasio, the film took nearly $120 million in the United States alone and quickly answered Hollywood's question about the value and appeal of such productions.

Ridley Scott's *Black Hawk Down* (2001), a movie that in pre-publicity the director did his utmost to distance from any kind of political commentary, sits in an even more awkward ideological position than Robinson's picture. Certainly the film, handled by anyone else other than an Oscar-winning British director, might have been accused of being even more jingoistically right-wing than it actually was. Nevertheless, in trying to tell the tale of a group of US Special Forces, sent into Mogadishu, Somalia, in 1993 as part of a mission to hunt down rebel warlord Mohamed Farrah Aidid, the movie does become conditioned into the formula components for 'war movies' of a small force holed up and heroically trying to secure a small neighbourhood in the capital until other forces arrive. The soldiers were ordered to capture several of Aidid's aides. The mission was to take thirty minutes, but when it took a terrible unexpected turn with the helicopter crash, it turned out to be a lot longer. The greater part of the movie tells the tale of the soldiers' long and violent fight to stay alive.

Hoberman remarks that the film as it stood, headlining the first array of military movies after 9/11, was an 'exercise in virtual combat, inviting anti-war protest and inspiring European ridicule'.[4] Ridicule or not, Scott's film took almost $110 million at the American box-office and over £5 million in Britain. Taking up Hoberman's notion of virtual combat, Andrew Pepper has attempted to understand and define *Black Hawk Down*'s combination of ideological intent and aesthetic visual pretension that made it so popular with audiences. Pepper's argument centres on the visceral presentation of modern war movies: the now accepted norm for Hollywood of 'battle-conditioned realism' masquerading as political detachment, as he puts it. What he

suggests is that, in adopting the kind of kinetic visual kaleidoscope
that was becoming familiar at this time in movies like *Saving Private
Ryan*, *Windtalkers* and *The Thin Red Line* – MTV editing, virtually inau-
dible dialogue, confusion, mixed point-of-view shots, the violent realism of death and maiming – the film offers a gritty sub-text to the
horror of warfare, but this is its disclaimer from any attempt to analyse
the overall point of missions, actions and wider American policy in
such arenas. In other words, Jon Lewis's contention that technological and spectacle-induced texts omit the motivation, cause and effect
of modern foreign policy adventures, is arguably the cinematic legacy
of American hegemonic power in these sorts of movies. The sophisticated visual discourse is such that it asks the audience to care only
about the fate of these characters, not about the overall consequences
of American foreign policy power.[5]

One further observation to make, leading us into an analysis of other
movies, is that from an ideological point of view, even if we accept
the political implications of a narrative as best interpreted, it remains
almost impossible not to draw parallels from both wings of the political spectrum over a movie like *Black Hawk Down*. The US as world's
guardian policeman or ill-judged and poorly defined arbiter of the
peace in territories and among cultures it does not know well enough
and cannot comprehend? You decide, it almost seems to be saying,
and it is a point worth returning to in a number of other pictures from
the time just beyond 9/11. *Black Hawk Down* certainly worked as 'con-
sumable spectacle' but the array of computer games, DVDs and other
merchandising it spawned only further complicated the way such films
could be seriously analysed for their political and cultural significance
in modern Hollywood.[6]

Bruce Willis's action-adventure, *Tears of the Sun* (2003), directed by
Antoine Fuqua, is a case in hand. Although nothing like as commercially successful as Scott's effort, it certainly laid the most claims to a
flag-waving patriotic foreign policy agenda in the wake of 9/11. Philip
French's review in *The Observer* summed up the pros and cons.

> The one good line in *Tears of the Sun* is the epigraph by Edmund
> Burke: 'The only thing necessary for the triumph of evil is for good
> men to do nothing.' This line explains the change of heart under-
> gone by US Navy Seal Lieutenant Waters (Bruce Willis) when he
> is parachuted into war-torn Nigeria to rescue Dr Lena Kendricks
> (Monica Bellucci), an American national working for Médecins

Sans Frontières. Instead of sticking to this limited mission, he undertakes to escort a party of Nigerians to the safety of Cameroon to save them from the bloodthirsty Islamic rebel forces who are raping and slaughtering everyone they come across. The fire fights are well handled, the dialogue is terrible, the callow political tone mildly offensive. Bruce Willis, who would not even take a plane in America after 9/11, let alone venture abroad, seems to have recovered his nerve, though the movie was shot on location in Hawaii where life has been relatively safe since Pearl Harbor.[7]

Peter Bradshaw in *The Guardian* was even more caustic in his assessment, noting the comparison to other films of the time. 'It's a kind of Black Hawk Up fantasy of short-term, pain-free military intervention,' he remarked. 'This kind of thing was brought off with more panache in Taylor Hackford's *Proof of Life,* with Russell Crowe or, indeed, John Moore's *Behind Enemy Lines* with Owen Wilson.'[8] While we should remember that these are British reviews observing American actions and cultural discourse from a distance, there are enough lessons to be learnt from the assessments to extend a synopsis of the foreign policy action thriller. The first point is perhaps obvious but worthy of reiteration. September 11th remained an over-arching reference point for any Hollywood vehicle with pretensions to show 'America's place in the world'. Virtually any film, whatever its intentions might be, was going to suffer comparison in the 2001–6 period for believing that it could somehow rationalise American actions subsequent to that date. Of course, none could, and the only recourse was to believe that the movies were jumping on the patriotic bandwagon, whipping the audience up into a frenzy over how righteous, laudable and just the US cause was, should or could be.

The second aspect is that both *Black Hawk Down* and *Tears of the Sun* would have certain American audiences believe that, by simply setting foot in Africa, one was transporting oneself back not to the twentieth but more likely to the nineteenth century. That Conradian sense of the pervading 'Heart of Darkness' very much suffuses the atmosphere and visual aesthetic in each of the films. Lawlessness mixed with and fighting against a tangible sense of justice and tolerance for human life is brought to the narratives by our upstanding central protagonists, very much in contrast to an indigenous society that is perceived to be both deadly and unfeeling.

The third element brings together all the themes we have discussed so far. By instigating narratives about individuals – the Special Forces unit in Scott's film, the aid worker in Fuqua's – the films offer an opt-out clause from any responsibility even to talk of America's place in the world, let alone take a position on it. Neither definitive in saying that America could make the world a better place, nor critical in questioning why the US persists in taking on such incursions, the films sit in that no-man's land between guns-and-bombs action entertainment and informed critique of unilateral American power without ever being able to articulate or negotiate a stance between the two. Not quite *Rambo* but not really anything close to *Dr. Strangelove*, either. Such was the state of the twenty-first-century Hollywood foreign policy action movie in 2002–3. And if one were looking for confirmation of the confused and indeed frustrated response to these texts, then you could do a whole lot worse than consider a number of the reviews of *Jarhead* (2005), British director Sam Mendes's adaptation of Anthony Swofford's best-selling book on military stasis. Offering a similar conclusion about this movie as French and Bradshaw had done about the earlier pieces, Glenn Whipp suggests that the film went so far down the road of disengaging itself from any kind of political stance as to delay gratification and meaning to the point of boredom. 'The film's lack of meaning seems all the more egregious, particularly since even wartime inaction contains large doses of political consequence,' he concluded.[9]

To be fair, others praised *Jarhead*'s meditation on the tedium and fruitlessness of modern combat, but just as many were frustrated by a lack of position and message, even if its attention to the detail of Swofford's memoir made the movie a faithful rendition of the boredom. Mendes's film follows a tradition, therefore, that is not entirely unrelated to the periods of quiet contemplation and inactivity that are both a characteristic of war unknown to those who have not been at the front end, and a feature of movies as diverse as *Apocalypse Now* (which is featured itself in the film), Terrence Malick's version of *The Thin Red Line* and even *Catch 22*.

TRUST NO ONE

In 2004 two key events for the film industry changed the way American cinema approached diplomatic/foreign policy/political agendas, neither mutually exclusive of the other. The first was that Michael Moore's *Fahrenheit 9/11* was released around the world during that Summer and provoked such a furore even before it hit the screens that it quickly became the most talked-about feature of the post-9/11 era. As of January 2005, the film had grossed over $222 million worldwide, making it easily the most successful documentary release of all time. Like no other political film since *JFK*, it polarised opinion and courted controversy, from film festival to festival, multiplex to art house cinema, East to West Coast, Europe to America, and Hollywood boardrooms to the White House. Moore was hailed as the saviour of the left while at the same time being denounced as Satan in a baseball cap by the right.

Love him or hate him, admire the film or otherwise, there was no arguing that *Fahrenheit 9/11* caught the zeitgeist of the political times like no release since Stone's movie and before that possibly *All the President's Men*. The imagined dream sequence of the 2000 election and its endgame, the darkened screen during the moments recalling the attacks in New York, the unseen demonstrations on Inauguration Day against Bush's victory, and the caricaturing of the man himself as he vacationed in Texas during that now fateful Summer of 2001: Moore's images captured some sense of the disbelief and shock vibrating around America and the world in the years immediately after 9/11.

The picture provoked a wave of documentaries in its wake, some following similar routes to Moore's own conspiracy agenda, linking the attacks on New York, the war, business and financial corporations, Bush and the Saudi royal family together; others trod their own path towards political, military and corporate investigations into the state of America. This selection of documentaries springing up around the extraordinary success of Moore's offering also owed much to his 'cinematic' style of filmmaking. Inspired by an earlier tradition that wound its way back to World War Two and beyond, and which had perceived American documentary as every bit as narrative and visually drawn as mainstream features, filmmakers like Errol Morris and Eugene Jarecki directed films in the 2000s that were designed as much for the multiplexes – and younger audiences – as they were for older, contemplative TV-watchers. Featuring fast-paced imagery, mixing archive footage with contemporary film, offering data and statistics on screen, and presenting talking heads in swift and dramatic vein, they also used cross-cutting between speakers to tease out sound bites that really struck a chord with audiences.

Jarecki's title for his 2005 documentary about the history and influence of America's 'military industrial complex', *Why We Fight*, was itself an entreaty to remember and associate his work with the classic series of the same name, directed by Frank Capra during the Second World War. And slowly but surely, in the second half of the 2000s, this spate of politically charged documentary features inspired the mainstream within Hollywood also to contemplate change within itself and to start to question all manner of political and social assumptions, the like of which had been held in check since that fateful day in September 2001, after which the industry's 'relationship' with the government had been re-affirmed.

The second thing that happened was that George W. Bush was re-elected for a second term in office in November 2004, with all the implications that brought over the following four years. Five months earlier in May, Bush and prospective Democrat candidate John Kerry had been running neck and neck in the polls, while Bush's approval ratings in the White House were the worst he had experienced at 46 per cent, thanks to the turn of events in Iraq which had become bloody and violent. Public approval of the war itself started to collapse. Only 44 per cent of the public thought it 'worthwhile', a similar new low reflecting some of the highest casualty figures of the conflict that Spring.[10] By November, however, Bush was capturing just short of 51 per cent of the popular vote and managed a decisive-enough victory over Kerry, whose campaign was perceived to have faltered badly at key moments during the election battle. A year on, and a CNN/USA Today/Gallup poll in November 2005 had Bush's approval rating sinking to 37 per cent, widely reported as a figure lower than Richard Nixon's performance at the height of the Watergate inquiry in late 1973, though the same, in fact, as Bill Clinton's when he was six months into his term of office in 1993.[11] But set against the backdrop of the on-going war, ratings that pointedly questioned Bush's domestic as well as foreign policy agenda, and scandal in the White House itself – notably the resignation of Chief of Staff I. Lewis 'Scooter' Libby over charges that he had lied to a Grand Jury about the circumstances of revealing the name of a CIA operative, whose husband had criticised the administration's conduct of the war – it was easy to see why trust and faith in Bush ran very low indeed.

To equate the administration's fall from grace with the rise of a newly energised political cinema in Hollywood after 2005 is a little too simplistic. Some of the movies already mentioned, as well as other hard-hitting dramas such as Michael Mann's *The Insider* (1999) and Steven Soderbergh's *Traffic* (2000), hint at more than a little guile and complexity in business and government policy at home and abroad during an era before Bush had ever reached office and 9/11 had taken place. Nevertheless, in a series of features from 2005 onwards, the merging of the thriller aesthetic with hand-held *cinéma vérité*-style photography, multiple narratives, ambiguous closures, and central protagonists who neither seem nor are as heroic as yesteryear, gave credence to the belief that a perceptible shift was taking place. The Hollywood mainstream, we might suggest, was adapting to the momentum of the independent documentary movement by framing politics at home and abroad with a much more urgent and critical eye.

Some of these first alternative endeavours looked to present recent diplomatic and political discourse within the confines of histori- cal or pseudo-documentary historical constructions. Both of George Clooney's feature films of 2005, *Syriana* and *Good Night, and Good Luck*, for instance, concerned themselves somewhat more with the infrastructure and ideological context of Cold War and post-Cold War American history as affecting the nation at home, rather than over- seas hegemony. In the former film, an international context is set up in which Clooney plays Bob Barnes, a bureaucrat increasingly out of his depth in the murky world of Middle East politics and US oil interests where no one can be relied upon or trusted. Building upon this central plot strand, writer/director Steven Gaghan brings a similar kind of nar- rative melange to the piece, with several threads and numerous 'lead' characters, a technique that was very apparent in his script for *Traffic*, all pointing to the way domestic interests impinge on global activity.

Good Night, and Good Luck, by contrast, is a tour de force of style and cinematography, co-written by Grant Heslov and with Clooney directing himself. Using the story of CBS reporter Edward R. Murrow's investigation of Senator Joseph McCarthy in the 1950s, the film has been described as an allegory for the modern age.[12] If that is so, the comparison perhaps resides in Clooney's uncanny ability to capture the aura and mood of the period as a decade of faux calm, style and respect on the surface, only matched by ruthless politics, compromised business ethics and persecution underneath.

David Strathairn's portrayal of Murrow is semi-tragic: a media figure with a suave personality and an agenda of his own that is quickly being usurped in a broadcasting world that demands safe and predictable product, not crusading, socially conscious zeal. Murrow's other 'enter- tainment' show that he hosts as part of his obligations to CBS involves 'soft' interviews with showbiz favourites of the moment like Liberace. Clooney and Heslov emphasise the mood and ambience not only by having jazz singer Dianne Reeves provide musical interludes to the action, as though singing with her band in a nearby studio, but also by having Murrow muse on this period of McCarthyite censure and torment through a prologue and epilogue that feature him winning a lifetime achievement award a few years later as his TV career was waning and he announced he was wandering away into retirement.

In a similar vein, both *The Good Shepherd* (2006) and *Breach* (2007) investigate the United States Secret Service infrastructure in contemplative retrospect. One dates back to the early 1960s and the establishment of the CIA's heavy political influence over successive White House administrations; the second is a more recent true story and legacy of the Cold War, telling the tale of Robert Hanssen, a rogue FBI operative who was revealed to have been handing over secrets to the Soviets for more than twenty years. Again in allegorical fashion, both Matt Damon's young recruit, Edward Wilson, in the former film, thrown into the emerging world-view and dominance of the CIA from after the war until the early 1960s, and Ryan Phillippe's Eric O'Neill in the latter, as the rookie whose eyes are opened to the insider dealings of the FBI, and its treatment and exposure of one of their own, lead the audience down the path of stories that resonate with some of the themes of coercion, secretive forces and unaccountable actions conditioning the times in which the films were made. The performances in both pictures are subtle and underplayed, especially Chris Cooper as Hanssen in Billy Ray's movie, and the ensemble of Robert De Niro (who directed), William Hurt and Angelina Jolie in *The Good Shepherd*.

The retrospective fashion in which these films deal with America's foreign intelligence superstructure does not mean that contemporary international relations, counter-terrorist narratives and current affairs were absent at this time; in fact, their presence in a series of movies tailored Hollywood responses increasingly towards the shortcomings of the 'War on Terror' as the second term of the Bush Administration became ever more mired in conflict and instability. Focusing on global interlocking mechanisms and relationships between institutions and corporations, the adaptation of John Le Carré's *The Constant Gardener* (2005), by Brazilian director Fernando Meirelles, is a companion in some ways to Reed's *The Third Man* as much as it is to Gaghan's *Syriana*. Not really a Hollywood production, as it was funded by the UK Film Council although distributed by Universal, concentrating on a host of British characters played by leading actors such as Ralph Fiennes, Rachel Weisz and Bill Nighy, and with settings in London and Africa, the story is a conglomeration of international intrigue, African political manœuvrings and British/American relations abroad.

Principled and dependable High Commissioner Justin Quayle

(Fiennes) begins a relationship in London with a passionate activist, Tessa (Weisz). They marry, he is posted to Kenya, and she becomes involved with activists and doctors looking into the role of a multi-national pharmaceutical company (a British/American operation is implied) that is testing drugs on the local community. Tessa is killed in what at first seems a random act but Justin uncovers evidence of a wider conspiracy that runs into the heart of the British establishment, embodied by Nighy's Sir Bernard Pellegrin. In the same year and in a comparable manner, an American setting and cast for Sidney Pollack's *The Interpreter* (2005) implicates the United Nations in similar covert African diplomacy and corruption in a thriller that portrays the lead-up to an attempted assassination plot on a despised leader who is coming to the Assembly in New York to make a speech. Each of these movies stretches the diplomatic, political and cultural boundaries of the traditional Hollywood thriller out beyond its domestic confines into settings that mix politics with the personal, and business with bloodshed. But what of more specific American engagements with the 'War on Terror' and the aftermath of 9/11, and how did these shape a Hollywood assessment of the Bush years on film?

The war itself was handled in a number of narratives that took their cue from some of the *cinéma vérité* aesthetic that emerged in other areas of political film. Embedded camera work following soldiers on the ground and loose narratives that become a succession of episodic engagements are both to the fore in Brian De Palma's *Redacted* (2007), a highly realistic portrait of the Iraq conflict and insurgency. British director and documentary-maker Nick Broomfield brings a great deal of the immediacy that characterised his earlier films to the UK-funded *Battle for Hiditha* (2007), a recounting of the atrocity in 2005 that resulted in twenty-four dead Iraqis, murdered in reprisal for an earlier ambush of US marines. Broomfield does not just give the audience a similar battle-conditioned realism, but actually used Iraqi War veterans as actors whom he then put back into similar scenarios, often giving them only a modicum of script to play with. Fabled television writer/director Stephen Bochco gave us *Over There* (2005–6), also an on-the-ground account of soldiers dealing with the war on a day-to-day basis, played out over thirteen episodes on Fox Television; while most conspicuously Kathryn Bigelow's Oscar-winning *The Hurt Locker* (2009) pursues a group of bomb-disposal experts on a tour of duty as they deal with the lethal ordnance dotted about the conflict zone.

These films survey the conflict up close and personal without too much recall of the politics, diplomacy and machinations that carried on behind the scenes, be it in Baghdad or Washington. *The Kingdom* (2007), though, was the first in a series of pictures that directly engaged with American policy in the Middle East, the intricate politics of the region, and the implications of Bush-era ideology. Directed by Peter Berg and written by one of Hollywood's new breed of socially and politically conscious scenarists, Matthew Michael Carnahan (a former Washington lobbyist and later co-writer of *State of Play* for Brit Kevin MacDonald in 2009; see Chapter 4), the picture seems like a slightly inauspicious entry by the Hollywood mainstream into Middle Eastern terrorism and organised American institutional response. Starring Jamie Foxx, Chris Cooper and Jennifer Garner, it often looks like a Jerry Bruckheimer high-octane thriller, and – to use the parlance of the western – felt like the posse going back into town to hunt down the bad guys in a manner not dissimilar from that of the 1990s cohort of movies. But as Ron Fleury, Foxx leads a unit of trained government operatives into Saudi Arabia in the aftermath of a bomb in an American compound in Riyadh, only to find a much more ornate picture of culture and response than earlier narratives, and where mistrust, suspicion and tradition hamper the forensic-style 'Western' investigative methods of his team. Just as the movie appears to be winding up its narrative against a background of frustratingly poor leads, little cooperation and half-baked logistics, coupled with misguided and misinformed political assessments of the region, and seems set to end the operation to find the perpetrators, a roadside bomb and then attack on the Americans' convoy along the main highway back to the airport sets up a heart-pounding finale of kidnapping, car chases, explosions and all manner of shooting.

Berg attempts a humble-enough denouement in the aftermath of these action sequences, which strikes one as apolitical to a degree and somewhat open-ended. We follow Fleury as he returns to the child he left in America at the opening of the picture while some of the terrorist network remain at large in Saudi Arabia. But the film lacks subtlety in merging these familial plots of Fleury and Egyptian Colonel Al Ghazi (Ashraf Barhom) at the end, as if resorting to that tried and tested Hollywood formula of placing the future in the hands of the young and innocent is all that is required for an understanding of social and cultural divides to be bridged.

If *The Kingdom* seems not to assert its potentially strident views all the way through to the conclusion, though, the backdrop to the film and its making is a sobering reminder of how different a world Hollywood was operating in during the 2000s, even as it rediscovered some of its critical integrity after 2005. Screenwriter Carnahan gave a great deal of credit to Berg for just getting the film made in the first place. 'Consider a guy making a movie for Universal, a company owned by GE [General Electric] that does billions of dollars of business with Saudi Arabia, and he can get that movie out with that ending, with some of those questions and situations.'[13] Carnahan explained further that the studio told him in no uncertain terms that taking an hour of screen time for the investigation team to get into Saudi Arabia was not going to work; the pace of the film, never mind the politics, had to operate on a faster level. To top it all, the original ending was considerably bleaker and darker. It initially involved one of the Saudi military personnel assigned to the group going over to the side of the terrorists and becoming a suicide bomber; he potentially blows everyone up in a final scene where the blast can only be heard over Fleury's conference call to Washington before the picture fades to black and the credits roll. Carnahan's reaction to its jettisoning was sanguine, to say the least. 'You've got a major studio that's faced with the proposition of putting upwards of $100 million into an otherwise nihilistic film. It's not going to fly,' he reasoned.[14] The film's $50 million box-office take in the United States was respectable business for a movie that at least posits questions about America's relations with the region, but its compromises as a piece of cinema ultimately threaten some of its impact and longevity.

Rendition (2007), on the other hand, released at almost exactly the same time as Berg's film and written by relative newcomer Kelley Sane, was director Gavin Hood's attempt to expose the practice of extraordinary rendition that had been a feature of the Bush and previous Clinton Administrations for at least a decade. Jake Gyllenhaal's CIA operative, Douglas Freeman, is assigned to one such case of an Egyptian-born American national returning to the US from a business trip to South Africa; Anwar El-Ibrahimi (Omar Metwally) is detained following a bombing and flown off to a secret location. He is finally held in what we might presume to be a North African country, where, after several bouts of torturing from local, pro-American officials, he offers up little reason as to why his phone records can be matched to a Middle Eastern suspect in the bombing and why he might be a terrorist sympathiser operating incognito as an academic.

El-Ibrahimi's American wife, Isabella (played by Reese Witherspoon), comes to discover the truth about her husband's abduction and attempts to confront the instigator – or least protector – of this covert national security policy in Washington, CIA chief Corrine Whitman, played by Meryl Streep. Isabella has the door opened for her by an old friend, Alan Smith (Peter Sarsgaard), who is aide to Senator Hawkins (Alan Arkin), an ally of Whitman. Witherspoon gives one of her best ever performances as a wife and mother distracted to the point of exhaustion by the not-knowing and the intransigence of Washington bureaucracy. Arkin, meanwhile, offers up one of his typically under-stated performances as Hawkins, perfectly well-meaning but with a savvy Washington brain that gives nothing away and is always wary of being compromised by his position. When Alan confronts his boss with the problem of El-Ibrahimi, Hawkins says, 'Would you like me to talk with her [Isabella]? I mean I'd rather not, but . . .' The words are all that Alan needs to know; his boss does not want this to touch his office. Later, when Alan, out of loyalty to 'Isi', as he calls her, pushes the investigation a little further, Hawkins warns him off with the prom-ise of a file and evidence that makes Isabella's husband complicit in the actions of the terrorist network under surveillance.

The subtle Washington posturing is thus teased out and complicated by the nuances of language and diversion in a consistently smart way. Meanwhile, on the ground, Gyllenhaal's Freeman is out of his depth as a man condoning torture and being at best naïve in his understanding of the relationship the CIA and the American government has with its foreign hosts. As his conscience begins to prey on his mind ever more, it is this which provides the plot's dramatic turn as the film opts for a somewhat contrived ending; Freeman 'rescues' the captive El-Ibrahimi and puts him on a boat, presumably across the Mediterranean, and on to Europe and the freedom to return to America.

But nevertheless, even allowing for this unlikely resolution, the taut, often confusing displacement of people, time and place that has become detached from any sort of real-world politics (as the plot reveals itself to be a revised narrative epilogue that leads us back to the bombing that opens the film, which originally appears to be the reason for El-Ibrahimi's arrest, only to be ultimately revealed as a pre-emp-tive attempt to try to prevent it) is handled by Hood in a manner not dissimilar to the confusing and distorting conspiracies at the heart of 1970s Hollywood political cinema. Arkin's Senator and Streep's coldly calculating Whitman are brilliantly complex politicos used to wheeler-dealing and pulling the strings in Washington power games, and it is their scenes which stand out and give the film its authenticity and some of its questioning audacity.

Jim Threapleton's British production, *Extraordinary Rendition*, also from 2007, covers similar ground and was somewhat usurped by the Hollywood clout of Hood's movie. Nevertheless, on a smaller scale, and with a nod to the real-life case of Canadian Maher Arar, who was deported from Canada to Syria after similar allegations when an educational institution finds out about one of its staff touting radical terrorist rhetoric, the film is effective and claustrophobically plausible. Its plot involves a young Arab Lecturer, Zaafir (Omar Berdouni), who is whisked off the streets of London and then interrogated for much of the film's seventy-seven minutes by an unnamed questioner, played with a detached insouciance by Andy Serkis.

The last of this mini-slew of films in 2007 was *Lions for Lambs*, perhaps the most eagerly anticipated of all these pictures, casting a spotlight on post-9/11 American foreign policy in the second half of the 2000s. It was eagerly anticipated because of its powerful cast, the threat of it being the most caustic and critical of the movies that had appeared up to that point, and finally because it was slated as the first film to appear under the newly acquired banner of United Artists, a whole film studio in essence purchased by Tom Cruise and to be used as a vehicle for his own projects. *Lions for Lambs* was certainly the most literate, if not the most commercially successful, of the pictures appearing at this time. Again written by Matthew Michael Carnahan, it is about as far removed from *The Kingdom* as it could be in its style and execution, if not its politics. In fact, Carnahan's comment about having to up the action quotient in the former film was the key point of divergence for him when it came to writing this movie. He wanted to know how he could express more of the ideological contemplation going on behind the scenes that would lead up to the actions that dominated much of the screen time in *The Kingdom*. 'Lions for Lambs grew out of that frustration,' he suggests. 'My desire to stay in those offices longer was certainly part of the structure.'[15]

Including the former film's director Peter Berg in its cast, and with Robert Redford as star and director, *Lions for Lambs* is a triptych that alternates between West coast academia, the political world of a United States Senator's office, and the preparation and beginning of a military operation in Afghanistan, all occurring at one and the same time. The slow, reflective and academic ruminations of Redford's Professor Stephen Malley, who arranges to meet up with delinquent

Senator Irving and reporter Janine Roth confront each other in *Lions for Lambs*

student Todd (Andrew Garfield) early one morning before class at
a Californian university – ostensibly USC, which Carnahan himself
attended, although not named as such – fill the philosophical void as
Malley proceeds to question the young man's ethics, commitment and
overall awareness of where America, and the world, are heading.

The high-powered interview of a gung-ho senator (Tom Cruise) by
a once-crusading journalist (Meryl Streep) is the media-dominated
section: the opening up of the relationship between the press and
politicians as regards their selling of the 'War on Terror' and how
public bodies and investigative reporters are duped and manipulated
for their support. Senator Jasper Irving is flattered enough by Streep's
reporter, Janine Roth, who has written about him as the 'future of his
party', to take her into his confidence and exclusively reveal a new
surge in the war before anyone else in the media is privy to it. Roth
sits with Irving 'for a whole hour', as she comments sarcastically,
only to realise at the end as she returns to her editor that finally,
conclusively, what this is all about is a smokescreen for hubris that
has nothing but personal aggrandisement behind it. Irving makes an
overwhelming case for a military plan that cannot fail and will turn
the war around in Afghanistan, just as we the audience are privy to

the exercise going horribly wrong in the intercut scenes, in which we see the military planning being usurped by enemy retaliation. Roth's editor – played by Kevin Dunn – says simply that she should take the former – the official line – and forget the latter; 'no owners will buy it, you'll just get dismissed,' he concludes, really summarising the moral circumference of the picture and its central pitch. The media likes its exclusives but is too much in the pocket of officialdom to realise it is no longer an 'exclusive', merely another exercise in public relations by those in control of the press and wider media's agenda.

The final section is the fatally flawed, action-infused operation that Cruise's Senator Irving has approved to take place thousands of miles away at that very moment in Afghanistan. It goes awry as the helicopter gunship carrying personnel intent on taking a high ridge that will give cover and a base for attacks on the Taliban is attacked by a surface-to-air missile; one of the soldiers, Finch (Derek Luke), drops out of the back of the Chinook, his buddy Rodriguez (Michael Pena) following on behind trying to save him. The two are left on the mountain plateau they have been ordered to secure, surrounded by encircling Taliban, and their fate is viewed, via satellite, from the command post back at HQ as their comrades fail to make it back to them in time to launch a rescue mission.

These simultaneous events are linked by a number of factors that unfold as the movie develops, not the least of which is that Finch and Rodriguez were students of Malley's, who encouraged them to make something of their lives but did not expect it to be as patriotic exponents of the government's foreign adventures. The sometimes overbearing intentionality of the picture is a problem in some respects as eyes are opened and lessons learnt in each section of the plot. The galloping finale, alternating ever more quickly between each scene, does not quite convey the intent that Redford may have had either; but its significance lies in the fact that, more than six years after 9/11, longer than five years since actions in Afghanistan began, and after four and a half years of war in Iraq, here was a Hollywood film that told a tale of doubt, fear, apprehension and unaccountability in America itself and which questioned the wisdom of the public's complacency, if not support for the actions of the previous few years. As Mark Kermode's reassessment of the movie observed when it arrived on DVD, 'Redford's aims clearly echo those of Watergate thriller *All the President's Men*, retooling the contemporary news into contemporary drama, finding the personal at the heart of the political.' The aims might be 'quaintly dated', he noted, but they were also 'admirably apropos'.[16]

On a budget of $35 million, *Lions for Lambs* realised less than $7 million in box-office revenue in America, and little more than £500,000 in the UK. The figures would seem to be definitive. In an era when political awareness and galvanisation was more acute than it had been in thirty years, a series of mainstream Hollywood political movies could not seem to tap into the public clamour for answers to these issues. As Kermode concluded, suggesting that major box-office revenue was increasingly tied up in one demographic only, 'With its stagy settings and unflashy direction and editing, *Lions for Lambs* seems to have little to offer today's supposedly attention-deficit stricken teenage audience.'[17] But a deeper explanation than mere financial returns as a statement of impact is complicated by a number of factors. The first of these is less to do with the political ideas and messages on show in these movies than it is with the visual aesthetic they employ, at least in the case of *The Kingdom*.

Pursuing Pepper's argument about battle-conditioned realism still further, Garrett Stewart argued, in a 2009 article, that what the cinema-viewing public had been suffering from for most of the 2000s was 'digital fatigue'. First of all, he suggests that it is no coincidence that war movies during the decade appropriated Hollywood's own past (previous iconic war pictures) as a means to authenticate their almost temporal state of reality in the here and now of the newer features; war games are played out in all manner of digital images from TV to computer screen to mobile phones. Stewart cites a scene in Mendes's *Jarhead* as a particularly crucial example of the theory he is positing. The bored GIs spend their time watching *Apocalypse Now*, as though it were some kind of comparable drama, only replayed for their delight in a Hollywood movie. His point is that the choice of *that* war movie is really rather crucial in suggesting what is real, made up and/or apocryphal about war played out on screen. But the digital framing is the really key thing for Stewart. 'Narrative agency is subsumed to technology at every turn,' he argues, 'from aerial tracking, where characters are faceless pawns, to eye-level confrontation.'[18] The result is that there is no narrative drive, no immediacy to the characters and, critically, no certain closure from which audiences can derive meaning if not comfort in light of the events they have been watching on screen over the previous two hours.

Citing everything from the three films mentioned immediately above to *Syriana*, *Vantage Point* and Ridley Scott's *Body of Lies* (2008), Stewart argues that these movies are almost too ambitious in their parallel editing across hemispheric distances in what he calls the 'geopolitics of montage'. The audience has no frame of reference, no point-of-view shots on which to engage actively with the principal (read righteous or heroic) protagonists. Instead, 'the panoptic model [gives the] idea of a central point of view circumscribing all visible space under a mobile and pinioning gaze.'[19] Stewart concentrates particularly on the final moments of Scott's film to amplify his point. Roger Ferris (Leonardo DiCaprio) is a CIA operative working out of Jordan who is on the trail of a terrorist cell, but gets caught up in double-dealing, sees his Iranian girlfriend kidnapped, and then hatches a plan to expose a Muslim cleric that goes wrong. At the end of all this, Ferris is so disillusioned by his work that he resolves to excuse himself from further government service, and extricate himself from the control of his 'handler', Ed Hoffman (Russell Crowe), based in Langley.

The denouement sees Ferris wandering through a bazaar, being observed by drones in the sky and watched in Washington. Hoffman has the drones 'clear off target' and his screen clicks off, a two-fold paradigm for Stewart that is meant to exemplify an omniscient narrative running through everything, and doing so continuously, not just a hermetically sealed plot resolved for neatness and the audience's satisfaction. The closedown of the surveillance is, he asserts, 'the closest thing we get to narrative resolution'.[20]

For Stewart, then, these films are doing a combination of things that might well be very clever for the critic or scholar, but which seem almost as imponderable to the average cinema-goer as the government's own policy on combating terror and pursuing hi-tech wars via mobile phones, satellite technology, unmanned aerial vehicles and the like. Plots are multiple entities following several paths, characters are unusually ambiguous and even dislikeable, and closures seem not to offer redemption or hope wholly or even partially. In movies like *Rendition* and *Vantage Point*, as we have seen in this and previous chapters, Stewart even goes so far as to suggest that the temporal replay and digital framing in each film actually stand in as the narrative component rather than acting as a technological function that aides narrativity; it is, if you like, the movies' engine in these instances and is deliberately conceived as such.

So, just as Pepper is interested in audience engagement with visual dynamics scene to scene in modern combat stories, Stewart's concern is to point out the bewildering complexity of the modern foreign policy, militaristic movie in Hollywood and its likely appeal to audiences conditioned to political films of a simpler construction. The second reason, though, as a likely explanation for the disappointing returns of these movies over and above their cinematic style, is to do with the rise of the competition, most especially the extraordinary renaissance of documentary films in the 2000s built upon the considerable success of Michael Moore's features.

DECODING THE DOCUMENTARY

In *Mass Media and American Politics*, Doris Graber comments on the way fictional productions and/or docu-dramas can act as an influence upon wider public policy in the United States. Graber highlights movies like *Schindler's List, Mississippi Burning* and, inevitably, *JFK*, as films that not only unveiled periods and events in history that were re-opened to debate and interpretation, but which also influenced federal policies and discourse about continuing perceptions of, as these examples display, the Holocaust, civil rights and racism in the Deep South, as well as political assassination. But in mentioning *DC 9/11* (a made-for-TV drama about the aftermath of the attacks in 2001, by British director Brian Trenchard-Smith and starring Timothy Bottoms as George Bush) and especially *Fahrenheit 9/11*, Graber also pointed to a transformation in the reception and influence of documentaries and documentary-type pictures in the 2000s.[21]

In a special edition of the journal *The Velvet Light Trap* in 2007, Jeanne Lynn Hall commented on a 'remarkable renaissance in documentary filmmaking', particularly following the 2004 presidential election, a watershed for film and its relations with politics, as already indicated. Hall equates this revival with a major push by independent filmmakers and companies wishing to bring their work to a wider audience. But she also emphasises a link to a period in the mid-2000s when much of the mainstream media, Hollywood included, had suffered a 'dereliction of duty' with regard to political events at home, but especially abroad.[22] The irony of the two pieces that Graber refers to, for example, is how *DC 9/11* and Moore's film were polar opposites in outlook: the former a rather flattering portrayal of Bush's capacity to lead, as the movie perceived it; the latter a wholesale condemnation of the administration's tactics, philosophy and manipulation of the voters, of the system and of power more generally. Here was, in fact, an indication of the changes starting to take place among filmmakers and in Hollywood during the year or so between the making of each. In the same issue, Diane Waldman suggests that, in periods like this, when the American media becomes timid, there is always space for documentaries to fill the void.[23]

Both Hall and Waldman seem clear that what the rising number of factual films offered was a reminder that all was not well in American politics and society. Whether it was criticism of the Bush Administration itself, the war, the military industrial complex, or media portrayal and production of all these elements, a series of documentaries rifled through the controversies and contradictions at the heart of American life in ways Hollywood movies had appeared reluctant to do immediately after 9/11. And if pressed to assess the reach of these films at the box-office, then the answer lay in the fact that events appeared to be doing the work for the filmmakers. As Waldman asserts, the fact that the much-promised Weapons of Mass Destruction (WMD) never materialised in Iraq after the invasion in 2003 only made *Fahrenheit 9/11*, Jehane Noujaim's *Control Room* (2004), and Jarecki's *Why We Fight* all the more popular and pertinent.

Furthermore, initial reaction to this new breed of documentary that saw the very reticent mainstream media criticise such films for their use of reconstruction and docu-drama tactics, as well as fast editing and insertion of non-contextualised material for aesthetic effect that debased their 'factual' premise, was perceived to be a red herring by Walden. All films are subject to scepticism, she argues, but we should be wary of outright cynicism from the off.[24]

An additional contention, if not tactic, of these films was their willingness to explore all kinds of avenues in the modern media environment in order to have their work seen and discussed. While Michael Moore, Noujaim and Jarecki achieved mainstream releases for their documentaries and/or rich acclaim and awards at high-profile festivals and gatherings, long-time TV executive and producer Robert Greenwald made a series of movies throughout the 2000s that could be accessed cheaply through DVD outlets, and which used grass-roots organisations like MoveOn.org as promotion; they have subsequently been made available directly from internet sites like iMDB (Internet Movie Database). *Unprecedented* (2002) on the presidential election of 2000, *Uncovered* (2003) about the war in Iraq, *Unconstitutional* (2004) on American civil liberties and their violation, and especially *Outfoxed* (2004) concerning the media empire of Rupert Murdoch – which did,

in fact, receive a theatrical release – all generated acclaim, denuncia-
tion, commentary and debate using tactics that the *New York Times*
described as 'guerrilla documentary filmmaking'.[25] In other words,
new documentarians were no longer prepared simply to accept conventional distribution deals for pictures, wait until a major studio was
prepared to back them, or put up with doors being closed because the
content of the films did not look or sound right.

Two more points also seem critical in assessing the impact and
import of these films in the 2000s. Each of the documentaries focused
on extraordinarily big issues and did so within a comparatively tight
framework. Few of the films ran over two hours and some not much
longer than ninety minutes. One reason why this measure of their
scale and attention to detail is important comes back to the question
of aesthetics and visual construction again, which we will deal with in
a second. An interesting ideological and cultural point, though, is the
films' ability to measure some of the scale of media coverage in the
modern era and the huge amount of it that was and is never seen or
shown.

Hall, for example, tells the tale of a *New York Times* luncheon, at
which the host of Comedy Central's enormously successful political
satire, *The Daily Show*, was guest of honour. Jon Stewart was asked
how he managed to get such damning clips of politicians and of
President Bush in particular to air on the show. 'A clerk and a video
machine,' Stewart replied succinctly.[26] In other words, if you were
prepared to sit in a room with the miles of footage that is recorded
literally every day but almost never shown to the watching audience,
finding inaccuracy, inconsistency and downright falsity was not such
a hard task.

For Hall, then, modern watchers of media presentation and public
relations are increasingly aware of what that other great contemporary
entertainment satirist, Stephen Colbert, calls 'truthiness' at work in
American life. There is such a welter of information out there that (a)
it is not surprising how little of it reaches the eyes of the viewers, and
(b) much that does get shown has only a moderate relation to fact
because it has already been ciphered and contextualised and/or offers
a talking head or event that is not willing to convey the truth as it is,
only the reality as it appears. As critic Frank Rich's best-selling *The
Greatest Story Ever Sold* puts it, and Hall re-affirms, the 'new media-
thon environment' sees current affairs not defined, observed and cri-
tiqued on the news, but increasingly on entertainment shows which

now go further, and investigate more widely, into where stories and inconsistencies lie.[27]

But for that weight of material to work, the documentary filmmaker cohort of the 2000s has increasingly used a large array of cinematic styles to convey their message. Jerry White argues that their impact on the public, and belatedly on critics too, has been exacerbated by a new interest in aesthetics. White is not talking of the visual set-ups that Hollywood military movies employed, as discussed above, but a more hermetically constructed scenario for documentaries as a whole.[28] His examples include the montage sequence at the beginning of *Fahrenheit 9/11*, which is a rolling edit of perfectly fitted together video-feed footage of Bush and his cabinet/advisors being made up for various speeches and interviews, set against the backdrop of Jeff Gibbs's memorable musical score.

White makes the point that, in fact, the idea is taken almost in its entirety from Kevin Rafferty's *Feed* in 1992, a film that enlisted all of these discarded video clips used as set-ups for camera and lighting before shooting officially begins, which he then knitted together as a commentary on the issues and debates surrounding the New Hampshire primaries that year. Rafferty was cinematographer on Moore's freshman film, *Roger and Me,* so the link should not be so surprising. What White and fellow critic Gary Watson are emphasising with the comparison is not that Moore is parodying or even stealing effects from elsewhere, but that by simply alluding to the scene they are precisely reaching out for that which is little talked about when it comes to Moore: his cinematic deployment. The aesthetic style he places front and centre as a way to construct the parables that surround the story is, White suggests, crucial, and unless you talk of the aesthetics of Moore, you are losing some of the politics.[29]

And it is the further encoding of aesthetics that has mattered so much to the way high-profile documentaries have impacted upon the political and especially foreign policy scene in the 2000s. Alex Gibney's Oscar-winning *Taxi to the Dark Side* (2007), like his previous *Enron: The Smartest Guys in the Room* (2005), employs Oliver Stone-like editing techniques, enormous amounts of evidence flashed up on screen, and talking heads supported by reconstructed and actual footage that create a cacophony of visual signifiers for the audience to remarkable effect. Likewise, the use of his Interrotron machine was the selling point on which Errol Morris's powerful assessment of one man's contribution to post-World War Two American foreign relations, *The Fog of War* (2003), starring former Secretary of Defence Robert McNamara, was constructed and effectively moulded as a vehicle of historical and theoretical consideration.

Documentary has, therefore, driven the conscience of Hollywood towards greater and greater critiques and investigation as the decade progressed. Perhaps its harshest indictment and most blatant apparition came not with a Hollywood or even an American presentation, however, but with the Channel 4– and Film 4–backed *Death of a President* (2006). Gabriel Range's film uses every conceivable documentary motif from reconstruction of events to constant talking-head shots, and voiceover narration piecing together the action and issues. But it is all fiction: the fictional assassination in Chicago during 2007 of George W. Bush.

Range produces a movie that brings together all the anxiety of the Kennedy assassination with Bush-era protests on the environment and war, together with remarkably plausible characters who seem at first sight to be doctors, aides, Secret Service personnel and the like. In fact, their inscrutability came from the fact that, as actors playing parts, they were told little about what the production was doing or who it involved, and were not really kept in the loop about their scenes, almost as though they could not anticipate or react to the wider implications of the narrative; the performance, therefore, became that much more real and heightened.

Unsurprisingly, the controversy that the film caused in America, where it had a theatrical showing, as opposed to Britain, where it was initially shown on satellite and then network TV, was fairly pronounced. Members of the Bush Administration criticised it and even parts of the media in the US were sceptical about its message and metaphoric perception that Bush's fate awaited him somewhere beyond the movie in a similar real-life scenario. *Death of a President* merged fiction, assassination thriller techniques and documentary motifs to conjoin the realistic and reconstructed into a plausible and extraordinary film pushing the boundaries of documentary's mission and extending the critiques and observations about one of America's most dramatic and traumatic decades.

CONCLUSIONS

J. Hoberman sees Steven Spielberg as the doyen of the post-9/11 movie in the 2000s, not least because his series of historical, thriller and social melodrama pictures highlight for Hoberman the contesting terrain and public debates that characterised so much of the Bush era. Interestingly, he does not include *Minority Report* in his trilogy, but with *The Terminal*, *War of the Worlds* and *Munich*, Spielberg covers most of the ideological bases for Hoberman.[30]

Most of these films are linked by their recognition, appropriation or even actual setting that is relative to, or axiomatic of, the post-9/11 world. Whether through social allegory, contemporary sci-fi adventure or foreign policy interventionism, the films seek to conceive of America's place in the early twenty-first century. And on the face of it, like many of the films discussed during this chapter, they are relatively condemnatory. Whether networks of spies, leaks and conspiracy back home, military actions abroad that are at best ill conceived, or historical lessons not learned from past eras and times: all of the films have a critical agenda to portray. But is that the whole story on offer? Are all these films exposing American misadventure, misdirection, and lack of moral and justifiable leadership? Are there differentiations to be made between each? In what ways is this a different era from, say, the 1980s and 1990s of *Top Gun*, *Rambo* and others?

Douglas Kellner's slightly different take on Hoberman's idea is to see the 'allegories of catastrophe', as he calls these movies, as indictments of the Bush–Cheney era and prophecies of impending doom, played out in *The Day After Tomorrow* (2004), the *Resident Evil* franchise (2002 onwards), *28 Days Later* (2003) and *Children of Men* (2006). Interestingly, Kellner remarks that every time there are two consecutive Republican terms in the White House, Hollywood goes mad for end-of-the-world narratives. From the Reagan era twenty years before, he cites the *Mad Max* collection, *Escape from New York* and *Blade Runner* as proof that dystopian fantasies bring out levels of political alienation and critique in Hollywood circles that are not as swiftly realised during Democrat-controlled periods.

Hoberman and Kellner have interesting and provocative points to make about Hollywood's response to 9/11, to the political direction of the Bush years, and to the state of American society as a whole. It is certainly true, as we will continue to examine in the final chapter, that the film industry in all its forms woke up to the state of American life, and the nation's position in the world, in a major way in the 2000s, and especially after the initial shock and then complicity with the White House agenda immediately following September 11th 2001.

But, as this chapter outlines, the film industry as a whole was also

changing in the early twenty-first century; its themes, style, practitioners, outlets and ideological appraisal were taking on new forms and
directions that, as the final chapter makes plain, distanced it from the
1990s certainly, in a great many ways. Whether documentary renaissance will last through the second decade of the new century is hard
to predict, and certainly whether another crop of films can capture
some of the commercial and critical attention of a *Black Hawk Down*,
Fahrenheit 9/11 or *Good Night, and Good Luck* remains to be seen. But
ideological engagement, stylistic and cinematic veracity, and refusal to
bow to conventional studio logic and perceptions have thrown military, diplomatic and foreign policy films into a new era, the legacy of
which is only just starting to be mapped out.

NOTES

1. Trevor McCrisken and Andrew Pepper, *American History and Contemporary
   Hollywood Film* (Edinburgh: Edinburgh University Press, 2004), p. 188.
2. J. Hoberman, 'Unquiet Americans', *Sight and Sound*, October 2006, p. 20.
3. J. Hoberman, p. 20.
4. J. Hoberman, p. 20.
5. Andrew Pepper, 'The New Face of Global Hollywood: *Black Hawk Down*
   and the Politics of Intervention', unpublished paper presented at the
   British Association for American Studies Annual Conference, Manchester
   Metropolitan University, April 2004. See also Jon Lewis, 'The End of
   Cinema as We Know it and I Feel . . .', *The End of Cinema as We Know It*,
   ed. Jon Lewis (London: Pluto, 2002), p. 3.
6. Trevor McCrisken and Andrew Pepper, p. 189.
7. Philip French, Review of 'Tears of the Sun', *The Observer*, 14 September
   2003.
8. Peter Bradshaw, Review of 'Tears of the Sun', *The Guardian*, 12 September
   2003.
9. Glenn Whipp, 'War can be Hell, but as Portrayed in *Jarhead*, it's just
   Boring', *Daily News.com*, 11 March 2005.
10. Unattributed article, 'Bush Approval Hits New Lows in Poll', CNN.com,
    11 May 2004 at: http://edition.cnn.com/2004/ALLPOLITICS/05/10/war.
    bush.kerry/index.html.
11. Unattributed article, 'Poll – Bush Approval Mark at an All-Time
    Low', CNN.com, 14 November 2005 at: http://www.cnn.com/2005/
    POLITICS/11/14/bush.poll/.
12. Douglas Kellner describes the film as providing 'critical reflections on the
    Bush–Cheney right-wing extreme regime' in the form of similarly politi-
    cised agencies in the contemporary era, such as the Justice Department

and the Environmental Protection Agency (EPA). See Douglas Kellner, *Cinema Wars: Hollywood Film and Politics in the Bush–Cheney Era* (London: Wiley-Blackwell, 2010), p. 28.
13. Matt Hoey, 'Inside the Beltway', *Written By*, vol. 11, no. 8, November 2007, pp. 24–5.
14. Matt Hoey, p. 28.
15. Matt Hoey, p. 25.
16. Mark Kermode, 'The Battle for Mind and Soul', *The Observer Review*, 20 April 2008, p. 20.
17. Mark Kermode, p. 20.
18. Garrett Stewart, 'Digital Fatigue: Imaging War in Recent American Film', *Film Quarterly*, vol. 62, no. 4, Summer 2009, p. 45.
19. Garrett Stewart, pp. 47–8.
20. Garrett Stewart, p. 50.
21. Doris A. Graber, *Mass Media and American Politics* (Washington: CQ, 2006), pp. 172–3.
22. Jeanne Lynn Hall, 'The Role of Documentary in the Contemporary American Political Scene', *The Velvet Light Trap*, no. 60, Fall 2007, p. 80.
23. Diane Walden, 'The Role of Documentary in the Contemporary American Political Scene', *The Velvet Light Trap*, no. 60, Fall 2007, p. 86.
24. Diane Walden, p. 87.
25. Jeanne Lynn Hall, p. 81.
26. Jeanne Lynn Hall, p. 81.
27. Jeanne Lynn Hall, p. 81.
28. White argues that the same point may be made about the 2000s in America as Francois Truffaut made about the 1950s in France. He and other auteurs became interested in movies, argues White, because the films of the 1940s were bourgeois and visually wooden; they offered no aesthetic, cinematic pleasure or interest. See Jerry White, 'The Role of Documentary in the Contemporary American Political Scene', *The Velvet Light Trap*, no. 60, Fall 2007, p. 89.
29. Jerry White, p. 90.
30. J. Hoberman, p. 22.

Chapter 7

HOLLYWOOD AND CONTEMPORARY
DOMESTIC POLITICS

> Ask not what your country can do for you, you have nothing to
> fear but fear itself, if you can't stand the heat get out of the kitchen,
> live free or die, and in conclusion, read my lips.
>
> Acceptance speech, Thomas Jefferson 'Jeff' Johnson in
> *The Distinguished Gentleman* (1992)

WHO TOOK THE POLITICS OUT OF POLITICAL MOVIES?

In late April 2006 two new films with 'political themes' landed in the multiplexes of America on the same day. Paul Weitz's *American Dreamz* was, on the face of it, a not-so-subtle deconstruction of the *Pop/American Idol/X-Factor* cultural phenomena that had haunted the primetime schedules of Britain and the US for the previous few years. Starring Hugh Grant and Mandy Moore, it was on one level an obvious lambasting of the cut-and-paste world of modern TV pop music that adds dollops of every right ingredient just to try to flavour the taste of a group or lone singing 'sensation' to the satisfaction of all in an excruciating week-by-week vote-off. If anything, this format, far from feeling the force of criticism and pastiche, became even more popular subsequent to the film's release, with the changing music and pop chart industry of the late 2000s ushering in downloads as a replacement for actual records and where manufactured TV pop stars rule in the online world.

So Weitz's film tapped into a zeitgeist that delighted and infuriated different sections of the public in equal measure. But it did not captivate audiences enough to recoup much of its modest $19 million production budget. After an opening weekend of $3.6 million in April 2006, the film spluttered to a gross in America of $7.1 million by the close of its run in June. In Britain, *American Dreamz* captured £2.1 million in ticket sales, as well as moderate reviews, but few made much of a connection between the pervasive attraction of certain TV formats and the way such programmes could mould and influence the contemporary political culture.

In actual fact, *American Dreamz* did have a sub-plot working underneath its main agenda that was far more reflective and integral to the way domestic politics was changing on both sides of the Atlantic during these years than anyone seemed willing to acknowledge. In the movie, the show of the title manages to 'sign up' a recently re-elected American president (played by Dennis Quaid), who is looking to change his image and relate to the public with a just-happened-to-be-in-the-neighbourhood slot on the climactic season finale. Two years later, in April 2008, British Prime Minister Gordon Brown made the same self-serving move (albeit by satellite link) when he appeared on *American Idol* in what was ostensibly a plea to support plans for malaria nets in Africa to protect children and other vulnerable people. 'All year on *Idol*, it's the talent of the American people we admire. But tonight, it's your generosity,' he observed, openly admitting to being a talent show 'junkie' himself.[1]

Brown's guest slot had more conventional political applications to address than fictional President Staton's in the movie, of course. The appearance just happened to preface the Prime Minister's tour of America that month and his key meetings with President George W. Bush and the aspiring candidates in the US presidential election, Messrs McCain and Obama, and Hillary Clinton. But even so, here was a sitting world leader endorsing the power of TV culture and associating with its premise and demographic as a way to spotlight policy, character and ideological resonance with a perceptibly and increasingly dissolute and remote audience as regards politics.

Two years before, on the same day *American Dreamz* was released in America, a more conventional and recognisable genre re-entered the mainstream cinematic fray in the guise of *The Sentinel*, a political thriller starring Michael Douglas and Kiefer Sutherland (who was playing on the character recognition established within this genre with his role as Jack Bauer on the Fox TV hit, *24*). Directed by Clark Johnson, Douglas plays fictional Pete Garrison, a veteran agent who is so full of remorse for letting real-life would-be assassin John Hinckley get to Ronald Reagan in 1981 that, when he hears of an inside plot to assassinate the latest incumbent (President Ballentine, played by David Rasche), you just know that he has to stop it at all costs. If all this sounds a bit like the storyline to Wolfgang Petersen's 1993 hit film, *In the Line of Fire* (see Chapter 4), starring Clint Eastwood, that is because it mimics that movie in a whole variety of ways, even before it begins to exhume an array of other past films (*The Manchurian Candidate, Three Days of the Condor, Murder at 1600*) from which Johnson laid out the formulaic narrative.

The twist in *The Sentinel* is that Garrison is having an affair with the President's semi-estranged wife (Kim Basinger), and when this is uncovered, it is he who becomes implicated in the conspiracy to kill Ballentine, having a motive and all, only for the nail-biting conclusion to unveil the actual perpetrators. In the final couple of years of the Bush presidency, Johnson's film inspired more imitators flirting with much the same ground. In *Shooter* (2007) Mark Wahlberg is a Special Forces marksman coaxed back from exile to protect the President from an assassination attempt. When Wahlberg is set up as the assassin himself, the film gets interesting. But as he goes on the run to avoid all sorts of rogue, official and out-of-control government personnel on his tail, the conspiracy becomes silly and the crooked political plotting behind the scenes is obvious and clichéd all the way down to the final, violent denouement. Wahlberg's character, with the unlikely name of Bob Swagger, finally tracks down shady Senator Meachum (Ned Beatty), the man who is responsible for the whole conspiracy, at a log cabin somewhere in the woods, and the gunfight that follows is every bit as exaggerated as it is out of sync with the tone of much else in the picture.

Vantage Point (2008), on the other hand, does not offer a particularly original assassination narrative as its selling point, but it does have a structural composition that reminds us of techniques used by Oliver Stone in his own political movies and which date back to Constantin Costa-Gavras's *Z* (1969), as well as to this type of sub-genre's original progenitor, Akira Kurosawa's widely acclaimed 1950 film, *Rashômon*. In this newer homage, directed by British filmmaker Pete Travis (responsible for the award-winning drama-documentary *Omagh* in 2004), President Ashton (William Hurt) is seemingly the target of an assassination attempt by Middle Eastern extremists at a counter-terrorism conference in Spain. The shooting takes place in a giant square filled with onlookers and appears to have been caught by camera crews, tourists with cine-cameras, and photographers. But, like its inspirations, the film then rewinds to the same timeframe every fifteen minutes, looking at the events from different perspectives seen through the eyes of various witnesses, and a more confusing and disturbing picture emerges. Finally, we are required to observe Dennis Quaid's Secret Service agent, Thomas Barnes, moving beyond this repeated narrative sequence as the climax approaches and he tracks down what turns out to be a plot from within his own agency.

If these latter two movies were at least exciting, if not original, both the 2006 films were at best moderate fare and neither was that well received, even given the increasingly low expectations of mainstream Hollywood releases. Yet intriguingly, Manohla Dargis and Stephen Holden, both writing in the *New York Times*, effectively offered the same critique in their respective reviews of the time. Where is the politics? they asked. And what were both these films meant to be signposting in this post-9/11, post-*Fahrenheit 9/11* world, when dealing in the most creaky and obvious of clichés for political figures and rhetoric? As Dargis said of *American Dreamz*:

> What gives the film its topicality is that it sends up both the Bush presidency and 'American Idol,' those twin pillars of contemporary homespun populism. The problem being that, as Jon Stewart habitually reminds us, both surrendered to self-parody some time ago.[2]

Holden was even more scathing of what might laughingly be called the conspiracy in Johnson's *The Sentinel*:

> Those dang foreigners behind it all are the usual vague assortment of acceptable scapegoats: former members of the K.G.B., neo-Nazis and members of a drug cartel. The movie is too timid to name names or to identify grudges. The words Al Qaeda, mentioned only once in passing, are the only indication that we are living in a post 9/11 world.[3]

And so, one assumed, here was yet another by-the-numbers thriller complemented by an offbeat comedy that rose and disappeared from view in relatively short order. It was a sign of the mood of the times that movies of the mid-2000s and the reviewers assessing them should cast such a weary eye over films that appeared lightweight and uncommitted in their domestic political stance, especially considering the more forceful moves in foreign policy, documentary and military features. Even the later two films found it difficult to turn their graver and bleaker outlooks into something more demonstrable. As we moved through 2008, the war in Iraq (and with more force now that in Afghanistan too) rolled on, the implications of a second term in office for George Bush had taken hold, and the almost pulsating excitement of the closest and most compelling US presidential primary election season in recent memory was galvanising thought and opinion. In this context, *Vantage Point*'s bold but imitative structural presentation of replaying each scene from different viewpoints did at least convey a sense of multiple perspectives that, in and of itself, hinted at the political and ideological deception on offer in the 'post-9/11 war on terror' world. But even though the scenarios in both this movie and *Shooter* linked them to private corporate interests and anti-terrorist initiatives that should have brought the pictures' contemporary affiliations to the current climate in a way that films from the 1970s did, for example, the reality was that they were never contemplated as anything more than parodic replications of earlier and better conspiracy pictures. And Brown's subsequent appearance on *American Idol* (co-creator Simon Cowell having been invited the previous December to Downing Street, where he extended the return invitation) demonstrated an equally wearying acceptance that this is what politicians now do. A man who claimed to be about as fiercely intellectual as it gets in the modern political world could confess to being an addict of reality shows and not be firmly rounded on by the world's media, to say nothing of wider public opinion. The PM's agenda reflected just how difficult it now was to distinguish satire from reality. As film and TV critic John Patterson remarked at the time, quoting director Joe Dante, 'Have you seen *Network* lately? It looks like a goddamn documentary now.' Sidney Lumet's 1976 thriller exposing the manipulation of the audience and the politics behind the TV culture of the era highlighted a moment when satirising what would later emerge as 'reality TV' was possible. Peter Finch's raving host attempts to stir up the populace to believe in something and someone again to gain ratings for a struggling network. More than thirty years later, as Patterson hints, 'Reality TV long since ceased to entrance us, and satire can't put a dent in it anymore [either].'[4]

Political movies during much of the 2000s, therefore, recaptured a succession of styles and premises played out in other eras. But at the same time they also reflected on change and differentials that existed between movies of the post-9/11 Bush era and those from the post-Cold War Clinton years. How the two eras altered, shaped and redirected Hollywood presentations of domestic politics particularly is worthy of discussion and tells us a considerable amount about the shifting focus of the industry in these years as well as the groundswell of opinion towards politicians and public life more generally in the United States.

POLITICAL FILMS IN THE 1990s

When I tried to take stock of political films in the 1990s in the first edition of this book, it seemed natural to go straight to Bill Clinton as an initial port of call. Just as Franklin Roosevelt appeared to be a clear influence on and signifier of Hollywood's political discourse in the 1930s, as was John Kennedy to some lesser degree in the 1960s, so William Jefferson Clinton suggested that, in order to take stock of the Hollywood/Washington connection by the last decade of the century, one had to garner an impression of the man from Arkansas and his cinematic predilections.

In fact, Clinton's taste for cultivating the 'celebrity' candidate/ president image was not very hard to spot from early on. From that famous saxophone-playing appearance on the *Arsenio Hall Show* in the 1992 campaign, to publicity photo calls with Oprah Winfrey and Steven Spielberg, Clinton understood how to connect with his core voting constituency right from the off. He took his cue from John F. Kennedy's liaison with Hollywood stars in the 1960s, of course, but he also maximised the brief association the two had with each other in those halcyon years. Clinton visited the White House on 26 July 1963 as part of a cohort of outstanding students sponsored by the American Legion. The photograph and short footage of the handshake between the President and the youthful provincial protégé became, as Luc Herman observes, a 'mandate for future leadership' adopted through-out Clinton's 1992 campaign and a visual metaphor for debates that surrounded the entire election. 'Bill and Jack would be regarded as young and energetic warriors for the same good cause that is America,' surmised Herman.[5] As Clinton's subsequent presidency sought to mimic Kennedy's in more ways than one, especially with regard to the later revelations over Monica Lewinsky, he made less of the affiliation between himself and J. F. K. But the connection had been made, the comparison established.

Back at the beginning of Clinton's time in office, indeed, Michael Coyne makes the important point that surreptitiously the Arkansas Governor was helped along by this mythic construct of a natural succession between his candidacy and Kennedy's, and with his accli-matisation to the presidency, by a series of timely movies that nostal-gically harked back to the Kennedy years in tone as well as political optimism. From *Love Field* (1992) with Michelle Pfeiffer, through the aforementioned *In the Line of Fire* by Wolfgang Petersen, to Eastwood's own directed feature – the underrated *A Perfect World* (both 1993) – the 1960s, American idealism and Kennedy's New Frontier are all invoked in a series of narratives that preface and yet also partly challenge the collapsing liberal consensus later in that decade by focusing on char-acters and events that incur the wrath of authority and bear the brunt of tragedy and loss.

Whether it is Pfeiffer's grief-stricken heroine making her way to the state funeral in the aftermath of Kennedy's assassination, Eastwood's Secret Service agent haunted by the shooting in Dealey Plaza that he could do little to prevent, or Kevin Costner's desperate killer pour-ing his feelings out to the innocent child he kidnaps on his road trip to avoid the authorities, these were films, as Coyne points out, that showed 'the last time, according to '90s mythology, that "a perfect world" was possible'.[6] The films hint at what we now know was just around the corner in the 1960s, but at the same time they ache with a feeling of loss for the idealism and optimism about to vanish before the eyes of their protagonists. And one might further add to this list Oliver Stone's slightly earlier *The Doors* (1991), as well as Joe Dante's affectionate parody, *Matinee* (1993), for their clashes of innocence and inanition in the American condition of the time.

And Herman too moves swiftly to conclude that it was not just the convenience and symbolism of the image of Kennedy and Clinton on that Summer's day in the Rose Garden that struck a chord with the public thirty years later; another film also added piquancy to the mix. For, in addition, during the year leading up to Clinton's election, the debate, controversy and astonishing success of Stone's *JFK* (see Chapter 4) contributed mightily to analogies unfolding between the two of them. Thanks to this three-hour epic,

> it almost seemed as if Kennedy was being marketed again in 1992, and [explains] why the Clinton team strategically tapped into the suddenly revived vein of Kennedy's popularity in order to multiply Clinton's own chances as the Democratic contender for the White House.[7]

Ultimately, Clinton's salvation was at least partly forged on a machismo and political astuteness that many associated only with Kennedy, and it was this comparison that arguably saved him his job in early 1999 when scandal and controversy engulfed him.

But Kennedy was not the only template for Clinton's style of governance in the 1990s. Another figure of influence – one who cropped up again for a subsequent occupant – also filled in the style and performance quotient that a modern chief executive seems to require. For Clinton had also observed how a real-life actor like Ronald Reagan could almost adopt a constructed persona within the White House and thus readily appropriate the language of Hollywood film – sometimes literally taking his cue from characters in movies – as a means to make the whole political business seem that much more glamorous and larger than life. As Gary Wills reports in his famous assessment of the man, *Reagan's America*, the handlers were often keen to deflect attention from what they perceived to be the soft underbelly of Reagan's political appeal. After all, if the scrutiny became severe enough, how was a 'B' movie actor going to come across as serious and resolute in times of crisis? 'Reagan, with surer instinct, cheerfully emphasis[ed] what others feared to bring up,' counters Wills. 'He underst[ood] that a show-business background [was] part of his political resonance.'[8]

But even allowing for Clinton's studying of the Kennedy and Reagan art of leadership, as well as motion pictures that appeared to tap into the same lost innocence he himself wanted to recapture for the American people, voters also discovered in Clinton a student of Hollywood stardom and personality who understood exactly how to shape the mythology of the contemporary film industry for his own indefatigable ends. And it is for that reason, as much as any, that a link between Hollywood's and Washington's approach to politics in the 1990s has such strong resonance not only with Kennedy in the 1960s, but with FDR back in the 1930s too.

Once Clinton was in the White House, not only Winfrey and Spielberg, but also Michael Douglas, Rob Reiner, Ron Howard and Barbra Streisand made regular appearances in the roll-call of Hollywood's glitterati. They supported the President's initiatives and consolidated his support with ordinary voters as he swept to re-election victory in 1996. But they also probably sustained him for longer than might have been thought possible when so much of the administration's agenda ran aground in his second term and his job approval ratings, as opposed to personal appeal, were not so healthy, even within Hollywood circles. Activist and actor Ed Asner cited land mines, homosexuality, the Kyoto climate treaty and welfare policy as areas where Clinton could have been far more liberal during his terms in office but at the last moment stepped away from bolder initiatives. When the President reneged on further policies, such as the tax breaks that members of the Hollywood fraternity in particular were led to believe were coming their way, and more especially when the Monica Lewinsky scandal blew up in early 1998, even the parts of Hollywood that were used to titillation and gossip were disappointed.

As Ben Dickenson retorts, quoting Asner above, 'the betrayal was heightened by the continued support that many on the left showed for Clinton, even when his integrity was being called into question.'[9] In December of that year, however, Tom Hanks, one of the President's biggest and most vocal supporters until that point, publicly announced that he regretted contributing the maximum $10,000 to Clinton's legal defence fund that was fighting the allegations made by the former intern, after the President was forced to testify that, in fact, sexual impropriety had taken place between the two of them within the Oval Office itself.[10]

It was not only Republican commentators and political opponents, therefore, who at one stage felt that these revelations were so damaging that Clinton might be forced into resignation. In fact, despite the ignominy of an impeachment trial, his personal approval ratings did not waver too far in the final months of the scandal. Some of that was down to the almost religious – and counter-productive – zeal that was employed by Special Prosecutor Kenneth Starr in his pursuit of Clinton, a crusade which came to be seen by some as dangerously close to persecution and, worse, a McCarthyite witch-hunt.[11] In the end, Starr came to be vilified for his tactics almost as much as Clinton had been for his behaviour. Economically, too, the President's credibility and popularity remained largely intact because the United States continued to prosper from the sort of Clintonian 'third-way' economics that had already condemned the major budget deficit he inherited from the Reagan/Bush years to history.

But for all this hard-nosed political credit that Clinton stored up, one should neither forget nor underestimate that continuing Hollywood connection. It was not just his showbiz buddies and their aura that rubbed off on the President and sustained him through eight years. It was Clinton's language, demeanour and conduct that found commentators naturally linking his performance in the job to Hollywood replications of presidential character emerging in a new wave of off-beat, likeable and heart-warming narratives in the early 1990s. True, this revived interest in political comedy dramas did not begin as promisingly as it might have. As Clinton's first campaign for the White House got under way in 1992, two overtly political films, *Bob Roberts* (discussed in Chapter 3) and *The Distinguished Gentleman*, were released and were seen as less than flattering appraisals of contemporary politics in general, of how candidates run for office in particular, and why the public had become so jaded about the political culture around politicians. Yet Tim Robbins's clever 'mockumentary' might conceivably be seen in retrospect as a lever for Clinton because, for all its satirical tone as regards the right *and* left wings, much of the force of its attack – through images that linked the eponymous character back to the first Gulf War as well as the Iran-Contra arms scandal – concentrated on the fallibility and duplicity of the Reagan/Bush agenda. The film thus appeared as a call to arms for a brand new start and perspective on politics at the time and Clinton could claim to be handily filling that void.

The Distinguished Gentleman was a different matter, however. British director Jonathan Lynn's light-hearted comedy, set up as a vehicle to showcase Eddie Murphy's talent for comedic impersonation, was more of a harsh critique of slick candidates, morally dubious politicians, and the soft rhetorical reheating of old clichés and faded memories – in other words, hints of just the kinds of accusation that Clinton's own 'Slick Willie' persona was having to counter in the early months of the 1992 campaign. Here Murphy plays Jeff Johnson, a small-time crook from Miami, who just happens to have the same name as the recently deceased Congressman in his district (a cameo by James Garner). Announcing to his friends that this is going to be his greatest con, Murphy's Johnson declares that he is going to run for office – on name recognition alone. Because he cannot generate enough signatures to get his name on the ballot, Jeff cleverly ingratiates himself with the Silver Foxes, a pseudo-independent party representing Florida's retirement community who already have an official allotted space on the ballot paper. Tapping into every diverse community in the district that he can – and using his uncanny knack of impersonation along the way – Johnson wins because incumbency and recognisable names play to the re-election cycles. 'Who do we usually vote for?' asks a man of his wife, as they enter the voting booth in one scene. 'Isn't it always Johnson?' she replies, not realising the incumbent has passed away, and Murphy/Johnson's victory is thus assured.

Director Lynn worked as a writer on the British *Yes Minister/Prime Minister* political comedy series of the 1970s and 1980s and is joined here by screenwriter Marty Kaplan, himself a veteran of real political campaigns in the States. Together they concoct a story that allows Murphy the freedom and space to perform his stock comedic routine, but add quite specific and unflinching sideswipes at the repetitive and accepted monotony of modern politics. The premise of 'voting for the name you know', as Jeff's face never appears in his mocked-up campaign adverts which instead deliver that campaign phrase over and over, as well as an acceptance speech that name-checks every political sound bite of the previous sixty years and is lost on an audience who vaguely remember the words but not the context, taps into a rich vein of satire and cynicism about the whole process that points towards a culture tired of the way politics was becoming professionalised and empty of inspired or inspiring rhetoric.

Rather as with the pompous officialdom of civil servant Sir Humphrey Appleby (Nigel Hawthorne) in *Yes Minister/Prime Minister*, Lynn mocks the absurdity of American politics just like its British counterpart – not for its tradition and imperviousness to change and modernism, as with Appleby's character, but for its brashness, false glamour and empty bravado. Johnson succeeds merely by rebranding himself, and even then, only in the vaguest of terms. Anybody can be elected to office, the movie claims, and the duplicity and false accounting have then only just begun.

If *Bob Roberts* could perceptibly be seen as a plea for the rise of a new baby-boom generation of politicians like Clinton to inherit and change the mantle of politics, *The Distinguished Gentleman* was wary of how each succeeding generation had approached office and then been inculcated into the 'system', and how the privileges and responsibilities that went with serving the electorate inevitably skewed people's idealism. Clinton promised change in 1992, and Washington politics conducted differently from how they had been for several decades, and his was an outsider perspective that he believed could shake up the beltway mentality. Indeed, he had an agenda that, rather than harking back just to the promise of Kennedy's Camelot, actually went still further than that: to the Hollywood narratives of the 1930s, and the lone, crusading individuals who inhabited those timeless tales. And no sooner was Clinton in office than Hollywood proceeded with a series of films that left some of the satire and humour of Robbins's and Lynn's films intact, but otherwise attempted to restore a similar sort of faith and hope – to bring a bit of common-sense character back to Washington and in the process restore and relive some of the idealistic principles established by Hollywood's earliest classic takes on democracy, such as *Washington Merry-Go-Round* and *Mr. Smith Goes to Washington.*

Thus a linkage between Clinton and Hollywood that suggested the new President could become an embodiment of an earlier idealistic vision of politics took hold as early in his first term as September 1993 when, in an article for *Sight and Sound*, *The Guardian*'s then Washington correspondent, Martin Walker, wrote of the emergence of what he termed 'Clinton's Hollywood'. Walker's argument was that a number of films in general, but the recently released Ivan Reitman vehicle for Kevin Kline, *Dave*, in particular, had real and metaphoric connections to the Clinton White House. Not only was Dave Kovic, the man who impersonates an ailing, incapacitated President, a good-looking, free-thinking Waspish liberal who becomes a public relations godsend, much as Clinton had positioned himself as the outsider candidate; but the film also featured literal connections to the President in the appearance of, for example, Ruth Goldway, former free-thinking liberal mayor of Santa Monica and a 'genuine Friend of Bill', as Walker put it.[12] More than this, *Dave* represented the sort of 'doppelganger' storyline so beloved of Capra and his contemporaries such as Preston Sturges, and forever associated with the 'screwball' tradition of films from that time. Hollywood could solve the problems of graft and deceit, in other words, by returning to base principles and classic characters.[13]

Dave Kovic is a happy-go-lucky guy who runs an employment agency and just happens to look like incumbent President Bill Mitchell (both roles played by Kevin Kline). When the President falls into a coma whilst in mid-liaison with his secretary (Laura Linney), Chief of Staff Bob Alexander (Frank Langella) and advisor Alan Reed (Kevin Dunn) take it upon themselves to dupe the public and the Cabinet by inserting Dave into the role of Mitchell until Alexander can find a way to succeed the comatose President, bypass the weak Vice-President Nance (Ben Kingsley), and become Commander-in-Chief himself.

With a directorial background making such sizable mainstream hits as *Ghostbusters* (1984), *Twins* (1998) and *Kindergarten Cop* (1990), Ivan Reitman might not have been the first name to spring to mind when talk of reviving the Washington feel-good political comedy emerged. Much of the film's clever, somewhat knowing and not a little subversive commentaries, however, really fall from the pen of writer Gary

Ross. Having worked as a speechwriter for Democratic contenders such as Walter Mondale, Ross conceived a fable that had all the
ingredients of an iconic Capra classic. Intimating more than a passing
fascination for the legendary director, Ross subsequently showed his
capacity for relaying history, contemporary pop culture and ideological reminiscence with his own hits, which, either by their quirky and
persuasive time-travelling or their 1930s setting, continued to demonstrate his intuitive feel for studio-era filmmaking updated to the
present. Directing movies such as *Pleasantville* (1998) and *Seabiscuit*
(2003) brought Ross a collision of nostalgic, sepia-tinged recollections
allied to contemporary, modern sensibilities.

In a not dissimilar manner in *Dave*, Ross and Reitman self-consciously
insert real people and television programmes into the action, authen-
ticating the premise of the picture – as Capra did with the inclusion of
legendary radio announcer H. V. Kaltenborn in *Mr. Smith* – but at the
same time self-consciously undermining its whole logic. A recording
of *The McLaughlin Group* lambastes Dave as Mitchell for being only
one step away from a 'return of the zombie' who inherited the White
House before this seemingly humane transformation. The new Dave,
therefore, is almost too good to be true. Who in politics could be this
likeable, have this much common sense?, the 'real' commentators
playing themselves in the fictional movie intimate. Meanwhile, Arnold
Schwarzenegger, rehearsing his role as consultant to the presidential
task force on physical fitness, which he then was in real life, gets to
preach about healthy food and proves to be a good photo-op for Dave/
Mitchell. How could one know at the time that it would be a role perfectly positioned, we see now, as a stepping-stone to the governorship
of California? And yet Ross sort of authenticates this scenario in the
movie, makes it somehow seem natural, and real history went on to
take care of the rest. In more tongue-in-cheek fashion, Oliver Stone
plies his trade on *Larry King Live*, telling the host that something is
clearly amiss in this transformation of the 'post-coma' President, and
if you look closely, he does not look like the real Bill Mitchell.

Dave, with this knowing self-reflection on the media politics of
the age and sly dig at everything and everyone, from the conspiracy
theories of Stone to the ethical judgement of former speaker of the
House of Representatives, Tip O'Neill – who congratulates Alexander
and Alan on their boss's recovery when they bump into each other on
the street – was thus a sunny, airy re-assessment of how optimistic,
upbeat and genuinely warm political movies could be. '[*Dave*] reverts

to a Hollywood tradition of presenting the American political system as inherently good as long as it's in the hands of plain, decent folk,' claimed Walker, naturally citing Capra and *Mr. Smith* as one of the film's chief antecedents.[14]

Dave saves the day by creating a scenario which allows for the real and the constructed President finally to pass away as one and the same person – Dave, like Jeff Smith, collapses on the floor of the Senate – and this paves the way for the goodly Vice-President Nance to inherit the White House and for Bob Alexander to be excommunicated by all and sundry for his Machiavellian scheming.

If all this were a one-off, it might explain the mood of optimism surrounding Clinton's presidency in his first year of office, as well as expand on the reasons for Hollywood's unassailable commercial renaissance by the early 1990s with films that were as easy on the eye as this. But the Clinton political agenda and subsequent legacy on celluloid certainly did not stop there. If Dave Kovic *and* Bill Mitchell had something of the Clinton gene about them, then in 1995 Clinton's friend, Rob Reiner, took this premise a step further and created a White House that had not only Clinton's character built in, but its policy wish fulfilments too.

Reiner's connections gained him privileged access to look inside the Oval Office and study the layout and the work of staffers in preparation for his film, *The American President*. The movie was scripted by the man who subsequently went on to become the doyen of political fiction for most of the next decade: Aaron Sorkin. Starring Michael Douglas and Annette Bening, *The American President*, like *Dave* before it, proved an attractive hit with cinema audiences, offering smart dialogue, intelligent plotting and likeable performances from its two stars.[15] Indeed, it became the template from which Sorkin would go on to manufacture his stupendously successful and award-winning series, *The West Wing* (1999–2006), which would include some of the stars of the film in other roles, notably Martin Sheen and Anna Deveare Smith.

Andrew Shepherd (Douglas) is a Democratic president (a self-conscious acknowledgement of party affiliation here) who is a widower with a young daughter. He is battling with complex policy initiatives like gun control and greenhouse gas emissions while feeling lonely in the White House and wondering whether his career and political legacy will be determined by the public's sympathy for his plight at losing his wife only months before he was elected. Sidney Ellen Wade (Bening) is a tough Washington insider, a lobbyist with strong credentials and political ability who is hired by an environmental group to campaign for a greater reduction in emissions from a climate bill that is being sponsored by Shepherd's Administration on Capitol Hill. When the two meet, the connection is clear and the relationship they enter into begins to have ramifications for both, as personal associations and political loyalties are put to the test.

Where Reitman and Ross made modern media influence and its profile the centrepiece of their gentle political satire, however, Reiner and Sorkin saw the Hollywood legacy of political movies themselves as the cultural and ideological touchstone upon which to create a modern fable rooted in film folklore. In one scene Sidney attends her first ever meeting at the White House with her colleague, Susan Sloan (Wendie Malick), whereupon she introduces herself to the security guard at the entrance gate.

> SIDNEY: 'I'm Sidney Ellen Wade, I'm from Virginia.
> SUSAN: He doesn't care where you're from.
> SIDNEY: I'm sorry I'm so excited; this is my first visit to the White House. I'm soaking up the Capraesque quality of it.'
> SUSAN: 'He doesn't know what Capraesque means.'
> GUARD: 'Sure I do. Frank Capra, great American director. *It's a Wonderful Life*, *Mr. Smith Goes to Washington*. Sidney Ellen Wade of Virginia, have a great day!'

In a later scene Shepherd is playing pool with his Chief of Staff, A. J. (Sheen), and further equates the reality of modern campaigning and governance with its 1930s equivalence. If there was this much scrutiny and this many photographers back then, 'no one gets elected in a wheelchair,' Shepherd reminds his friend and colleague, who asks whether he would like to see some poll numbers. Exasperated, Shepherd says, 'No, I don't want to know whether I poll well to ask a woman out on a date.'

When Shepherd finally does resolve to ask Sidney out – in one of the film's funniest sequences in which she refuses to believe he is calling her on her sister's phone, and how did he get the number anyway? – and the two of them then become a couple, Shepherd's nemesis in the Senate, Republican Bob Rumson from Kansas (Richard Dreyfus), pursues their relationship in a manner uncannily similar to what Bill Clinton might later describe as Kenneth Starr-esque! Rumson publishes old pictures of Wade at a protest rally, where she just happens to be in frame when an American flag is being burnt, and then accuses her on national television of having traded sexual favours for political gain while she worked in the Virginia state legislature. Meanwhile, the deal that Shepherd has made with Sidney, for her lobby group to chase up the missing votes in Congress that will mean a 20 per cent emissions target will be written into the bill and passed, falls apart as Shepherd is forced to play reality politics and accept the conditions of what is achievable in office and when. 'We fight the fights we can win,' he sagely reminds his idealistic policy aide, Lewis Rothschild (Michael J. Fox).

But Sidney then unwittingly lets slip that certain Congressmen in the heavy manufacturing districts of Michigan, under pressure not to accept a high-profile environmental bill in their district – the so-called 'Motown three' in the film – would rather put their weight behind Shepherd's crime bill than the environmental legislation and thus can have their loyalty traded one for the other. Sidney gets the votes to hold up her end of the bargain but Shepherd makes the deal with the 'Motown three' in any case, thus ensuring passage of the crime bill, even though he knows it is a watered-down, rather anaemic version of the law he really wants to see enacted. All this does not necessarily seem comedic, or indeed straightforward as a narrative, and yet that is Sorkin's gift as a writer, which he later explored on *The West Wing*. The film does not pander to its audience about the realities of how bills reach the floor, never mind how they are passed, and the technical, often colloquial language feels authentic as the movie unpicks the wheeler-dealing of the beltway game.

The politics and Shepherd's preachy final-act speech to the assembled press corps allow for some of the convenience that is the hallmark of closures in the 1930s movies from which *The American President* takes its inspiration. But in Sorkin's words about 'kinder and gentler times', as well as Shepherd's mentions of 'nostalgia' in his soliloquy, there are recognitions of a 1990s mood and a way with the past that Hollywood wished to reclaim as its own.

The third in this trio of smart and savvy political comedies was Jon Peters and Peter Segal's *My Fellow Americans* (1997), which places much of this nostalgia in the hands of its protagonists, former Chief Executives Russell P. Kramer (Jack Lemmon) and Matt Douglas (James Garner once more). In a snappy and very funny opening prologue, Kramer and Douglas swap electoral victory and defeat against one another in each four-year cycle, only for both to find themselves as ex-politicians doing the after-dinner speaking circuit for Japanese businesses (Kramer dancing with people in panda suits!) or else writing their less than engaging memoirs (Douglas, while sleeping with his glamorous editor). They hanker after the limelight that was once theirs in times that seemed more comfortable and easy-going than they are now under new President Haney (Dan Ackroyd). But when the two become the intended victims of a conspiratorial plot that tries to blow up a helicopter they are both travelling in, their mutual antagonism towards each other is set aside as they take a road trip – after the helicopter crashes in wilderness – through the eastern United States and attempt to find the enemy within the administration who is attempting to do away with them.

Along the way, Kramer and Douglas's political philosophy is mildly examined to the point that both realise, in their own 'third way' sense, that the Republicans and Democrats have quite a lot in common and that tyranny and conspiracy are the foes they have to defeat. At each small town and pre-arranged comedic moment, they meet with 'ordinary' people who express their hopes and fears, and their exasperation at government, and they realise how talking to each other and communicating with the voters can achieve more than they ever contemplated. In conclusion, it is the rather simplistic, Dan Quayle-like figure of Vice-President Ted Matthews (John Heard) who turns out to be the architect of the conspiracy to kill Kramer and Douglas so that he can displace Haney without the two ex-Presidents asking publicly difficult questions, and it is this that gives the film its sharper contention as to who can and cannot become president, and that posits a certain acknowledgement of character and personality once again at the fore of political leadership.

All three films offer a critique of 1990s politics that was broadly an object lesson in communication with the voters and the distance that had been expanding over the century between the Washington elite and the ordinary people of America. If Clinton himself saw any lesson in these movies, then his further inculcation into Hollywood circles suggests that he thought this was the route to maintaining popularity and standing with his film-literate constituency. It was the President who suggested and publicly helped Wolfgang Petersen to cast Glenn Close in the part of Vice-President Kathryn Bennett in the German director's 1997 action film *Air Force One*, had his actions over Lewinsky and the administration's response to the emergence of terrorist organisation Al Qaeda in Africa raked over in Barry Levinson's amazingly prescient take on the events of 1998 in *Wag the Dog*, and finally was thoroughly impersonated by John Travolta for Mike Nichols's thinly disguised film of Clinton's 1992 campaign in *Primary Colors* (1998). Had any president ever crossed, blurred and generally implicated the worlds of Washington and Hollywood in each other's business in quite the same way and with quite the same measure of influence as Clinton? As I noted in concluding the 1999 edition of this book, Dreamworks Pictures reportedly had an eye on Clinton at the time for an executive producer slot once his final term in office was up, an outlandish piece of rumour-mongering that significantly would not go away for a long period of time, even though it never came to pass.

In the second half of the 1990s, the President became something of a macho figure and, in Summer blockbusters like *Independence Day* (1996) and *Deep Impact* (1998), the leader of the free world got to exercise that role most conspicuously. Pushing the limits of this high-octane version of presidential performance was Peterson's *Air Force One*, where Harrison Ford as President James Marshall re-affirms his macho, action-man credentials in a preposterously plotted and yet preternaturally exciting yarn, in which breakaway Russian nationalists have hijacked the President's plane on a flight back from a Russian summit and are demanding independence for their homeland. Gary Oldman's familiar over-the-top persona is ideal for lead Ivan Korshunov, while Ford as Marshall, in the film's memorable if equally implausible ending, invites the terrorist to 'get off my plane', having shown the same kind of military fortitude that allowed Bill Pullman's James Whitmore to defeat alien invasion in the aforementioned *Independence Day*.

Somewhat more carefully crafted, if rather less exciting, were Nichols's *Primary Colors* (see Chapter 3) and Levinson's *Wag the Dog*. In the latter, dramatist and screenwriter David Mamet (adapting Larry Beinhart's book) comes up with a tale that not only brings the worlds of Hollywood and Washington together, but which also prompted accusations of real-life similarity from the floor of the United States Senate itself. Senate Majority Leader Trent Lott accused Clinton, in the Summer of 1998, of behaving as duplicitously as Hollywood producer Stanley Motss (Dustin Hoffman) and Washington spin doctor Conrad Brean (Robert De Niro) when he ordered air strikes in the Sudan amid the chaos of the impending Lewinsky impeachment trial, and then approved a seventy-eight-day bombing campaign on behalf of NATO in the former Yugoslavia immediately after he was acquitted. In the film, the barely seen President (Michael Belson) is accused of improper relations with a 'firefly' girl (a young scout) in the White House just weeks before re-election. In a bid to kill the adverse publicity before it starts, Motss and Brean are hired to come up with a deflecting strategy, eventually settling on a mock war with Albania, the news footage of which is entirely constructed in a Hollywood studio and directed by Motss himself.

With a plot that involves old songs being rediscovered in the National Archive – but which really have only just been written and inserted there by singer Johnny Dean (Willie Nelson) and 'fixer' Fad King (Dennis Leary) – and returning war veterans from the 'Albanian front' – Woody Harrelson's psychopathic Sergeant Schumann, who is actually released from military incarceration and is then killed before he receives his hero's welcome – the film is both funny and eerily prescient for the times. Satirical TV ads appear on screen, which are at once ludicrous and yet plausible. The slogan 'Don't change horses in mid-stream'[16] is fatuous but credible; the rumour surrounding Brean's made-up comment about the existence of a new, hi-tech B-1 bomber is laughable and yet possibly truer than is being contemplated. It all adds up to a construction of a publicity campaign in a construction of a movie that has been equated with real political actions and decisions throwing up the usual slice of sex, sound bites and technical wizardry, and so asks the question, if this could be done, what else is possible?[17]

Wag the Dog puts forward the notion that, by the end of the 1990s, spin really was king, and after that anything *is* possible. When Motss is asked whether he can keep coming up with ever more ludicrous scenarios to deflect from the President's indiscretions, his reply sums up the movie: 'This is NOTHING!' Stanley sees the fake Albanian creation as his greatest moment, but like all epic Hollywood moments and all ambitious producers, he wants the credit. 'You can't tell anyone, Stanley,' warns Brean, who has an agent follow him out of the door; a week later we wind up at Stanley's funeral, with the crisis averted and the President's re-election campaign back on track.

These three pictures were the most apparent but, along with a raft of new conspiracy/paranoia movies that emerged at the same time (see Chapter 4) – *Absolute Power, Enemy of the State, Murder at 1600, Shadow Conspiracy, The X-Files: Fight the Future* – and then late on in his presidency, melodrama *The Contender* (2000), Clinton connections to Hollywood political tracts abounded in all manner of sub-genres all the way through the 1990s and into the new decade. In a way, it is easy now to look back and say that any president is what is filmed and written about them. Cinema, especially, is more apt to conform to certain stereotypical analyses of time and place; movies define eras in a way that suits what Fredric Jameson called our 'nostalgia mentality'. In other words, they provide a shorthand historical notch for remembering our own past, as well as contextualising it within wider events, even if the substance of the memory is vague or even false.

Nevertheless, even allowing for the convenience of Hollywood cultural signification, the 1990s did, for a time, have the easy sway of nostalgic excess and post-Cold War reverie that was fittingly apposite to Clinton's own baby-boom mentality. There was a mixture of retrieved 'swinging sixties' chic with the President's 'third way' political agenda that seemed to signal prosperity, peace and a new conviction about America's relations in the world. Clinton also managed to be a president who could effortlessly recreate the screwball, comedic charm of Capra's films, on the one hand, and then, on the other, confound us with conspiratorial and sexual shenanigans, the like of which Alan J. Pakula was showing us in the 1970s.

Clinton brought glamour, rhetoric and intellectualism back into White House politics, as well as – dare one say it? – something exotic to public life. It should not be forgotten that, as the basis for Joe Klein's best-seller and Nichols's film of dirty tricks and illicit deceit, he was a character exposed to compulsion, obsession and occasionally very bad judgement. And in foreign policy terms, he helped establish the plot for Ridley Scott's *Black Hawk Down*, the tale of America's (albeit under the UN banner) disastrous misadventure in Somalia in 1993 that was every bit a miscalculation of America's philosophical and military capacity to 'do good' in the world as was the attack on American marines in Beirut under Reagan's watch a decade before.

So Clinton on film certainly showed the way towards the solidification of Hollywood and Washington as integral partners. But that partnership was also prevalent in the way Clinton did politics too. The conduct of politics, the manner of getting elected, the finances being gathered for political campaigns, and the way of behaving in the political environment – whether it was speeches, press conferences, photoops and so on – all suggested that the two powerful cultures at the root of American life had a vested interest in each other's operation and future. And Clinton played host to this marriage of ideals and aesthetics as the 1990s progressed with an affability and charm that made it hard to distinguish which camp he was in sometimes.

The Clintonian legacy thus played host to the return of the comedic screwball narrative in films of the 1990s. But it is also important to offer up some explanation, context and connection to other movies that do not wholly fit into the characterisation discussed so far. There is a further distillation of political feelings about the era to be considered before we move on to the 2000s but there are also quixotic, slightly odd analytical pauses to be interpreted too, not least to do with audience reception and popularity.

Bob Roberts, Wag the Dog, Primary Colors, Bulworth (discussed in Chapter 3) and, to a lesser extent Andrew Fleming's teenage slacker movie *Dick* (1999) are all films that took satirical, postmodern side-swipes at politics in the 1990s. Each courted the idea that political idealism and principles had either been dissolved by the modern process or were easily manipulated and countered. Music, the sixties, popular culture and media technology could all be utilised, rewritten or even dismissed, each film reasoned, by a collection of scheming, ambitious, hyper-politicos whose only goal was to win and keeping on winning. Jim Emerson, writing for MSNBC on the net, thought that both *Wag the Dog* and *Primary Colors* featured 'some delicious performances and some piercing insights into the political process'.[18] John Harkness in *Sight and Sound*, on the verge of Clinton's election in 1992, called *Bob Roberts* 'astute and funny', remarking that it conveyed a better understanding of the political system than many so-called experts could muster.[19] Todd McCarthy commented in *Variety* that Tim Robbins's film was so successful at stating current truths about politics that it made for a 'sorrowful spectacle indeed'.[20]

Most of the films won plaudits, even when tough questions about the implications of their comedy and wholesale debunking of the political system – minus any answer to the problems – seemed to open up debates about their credibility. But more importantly, and very rarely spotted in much of the work on the 1990s, is the fact that the films were really not that successful. Unlike a movie such as *Mr. Smith Goes to Washington* in 1939, which, as Eric Smoodin demonstrated in Chapter 2, resonated so deeply with audiences as to be the main point of reference for the way the genre operated from thereon in, the nineties films were sometimes well received, and were occasionally compared to earlier works, but more often left audiences ambivalent about their take on the political process. Outside of the two main political comedies discussed above, *Wag the Dog* achieved the best and indeed very creditable returns ($43 million on a budget of only $15 million), while *Primary Colors* recouped a mere $39 million at the box-office (on a $65 million budget), *Bulworth* $26.5 million (budget $30 million) and *Bob Roberts* $4.5 million (on a budget around double that). Of course, they did subsequently pick up on video and DVD rentals and all achieved some of the cult status afforded Robbins's movie. But even so, why, given the more solid success of mainstream, mildly polite comedies like *Dave* and *The American President*, would this be so?

The answer might lie in the political psyche of the American public at the time. The familiar mantra, 'like politics, hate politicians', often came to mind. Americans respect their institutions but do not respect the people they put in them; with an incumbency rate of more than 90 per cent in the 1990s, that contradiction was borne out by the fact that electors' attitudes held true until election day, when many millions of Americans did appear to go and vote for the self-same politicians of whom they were highly critical. It is a truism, if only a clichéd one and one that only gets to part of the truth, but Americans in this era, like the British before 2000, were turning out less and less to vote. The feeling that politics did not connect with any kind of voting demographic, let alone new young voters coming into the system, was endemic. Political campaigns were and continue to be cited as too long and too drawn out, and to feature too much mud-slinging and not enough focus on the issues. It is easy to see, therefore, why condemnatory exposés of American politics would receive less endorsement from voters. The only shock was how close these fantastical tales were to reality – and even that was becoming less of a shock by the close of Clinton's Administration. For the reaction of the voters/audience to these movies, there is the crux of the matter. How complicit did the voters feel in bearing the brunt of the joke behind some of these narratives? Did they feel Hollywood was equally, if not more, to blame for the state of modern politics, with its sound-bite logic, iconic imagery and spin-doctoring mentality, and therefore rejected its self-righteous condemnation?

All these points are probably true, to some extent. Rather like other political movies down the ages, these pictures were also vilified in some quarters and praised in others for their portrayal. Prominent Republicans condemned Robbins's movie, a number of Democrats disowned Nichols's and quite a few from all sides, as well as original backers Disney who refused to market the picture, completely trashed Beatty's *Bulworth*. For all Hollywood's liberal credentials, the lesson, dating back to the 1930s, is that it can be a pretty conservative place when it wants to be. But that did not mean that there were no political films around at the end of the decade whose cause amounted to more than an understanding of the relationship between Washington and Hollywood, or indeed more than a portrayal of politics at the national level.

When I first analysed Harold Becker's film about New York politics, *City Hall* (1996), I commented that it was practically the only mainstream political drama of the era that went beyond a critique of the 'federal' system. Starring Al Pacino as the city's mayor, John Pappas, a Greek-American with an almost evangelical zeal to his politics, this story of bribery, corruption and recurrent 'graft' is constructed in much the same vein as earlier stories like *All the King's Men*. But with a screenplay that included contributions from Paul Schrader and Nicholas Pileggi, the story is far richer in complexity than Rossen's tale, heavily nuanced by colloquial, what I described as circumlocutional, dialogue at times, and held together at the centre by the paternalistic relationship of Pappas with the man he is grooming to be his successor, Kevin Calhoun, played by John Cusack. The film owes much to the gritty, down-at-heel institutional examinations that interested a director like Sidney Lumet so often in his career, all the way from *Prince of the City* (1981) – hard-boiled cop becomes informant – through *Q+A* (1990) to *Night Falls on Manhattan* (1996) – both with an accent on racism, corruption and murder at the heart of the New York judicial system – as well as the streetwise, edgy TV cop series of the 1990s such as *Homicide: Life on the Street* and *NYPD Blue*, this latter show being one that Pileggi wrote for in its first couple of seasons.

But the reason why *City Hall* is worth another look is because it tends to do what a show like *The West Wing* three years later set out to achieve over a whole season: it never panders to its audience nor takes it for granted. Indeed, watching Becker's film all the way through for the first time, you are not altogether sure whether you have 'got it'. A shooting takes place in a black neighbourhood that involves a young boy and an undercover cop; but the two deaths have wider ramifications for relations between law enforcement, mafia bosses and the mayor's office. Calhoun is persuaded by the cop's widow, whose pension is being withheld, to investigate further and the array of complex and conspiratorial leads him into the less than transparent hinterland of the city's politics.

Can the viewer follow all the characters' actions and motivations? Do all the loose ends tie up? The genuinely underplayed finale leaves one feeling uneasy about the pull and push of brokering and negotiation, the adrenaline rush that comes from power and the exercise of authority. Pacino's tour-de-force performance makes Pappas utterly credible and partly sympathetic, yet at the same time signifies to the audience a driven, uncompromising force at the heart of office. Has he been ousted from his platform, you find yourself asking at the end, or was he just unlucky? It is rare that a film can arrive at such important considerations for the way modern politics is construed without feeling the obligation to tie up loose ends and provide comfortable lessons and epilogues. And yet *City Hall*'s worth lies in asking those questions of its audience and looking for the reasons why accountability and transparency have evaporated from the modern system, as though a return to earlier, more compromised political eras has transpired.

If *City Hall* offered up a slice of the viper's den that is New York politics, Rod Lurie's 2001 film, *The Contender*, returned to the comparatively normal environment of the US Congress. But while Lurie's film too owes its inspiration to earlier political tracts such as *Mr. Smith*, Otto Preminger's *Advise and Consent* (1962) and even films like *The Candidate*, its treatment of partisan politics, and most especially sexual and gender politics in the last decade, makes it stand out as a text worthy of consideration.

Joan Allen plays Senator Laine Hanson, a former Republican who has recently switched sides to the Democrats; now, with the death of the sitting Vice-President, she finds herself in line for the number two job in government, next to Democrat White House incumbent Jackson Evans, played by Jeff Bridges. While it is undeniable that the strength of the film, rather like Pacino's performance in *City Hall*, is measured by the brilliance of Allen's acting and Bridges's rather pointed adoption of a certain incumbent's traits, the film does suggest that political discourse, the patriarchal legacy of Washington politics, and the character of female public officials all remain obstacles to women's progression within US federal politics.

The Washington press corps is taken aback (as though the choice of a woman remains very much a huge political gamble) when Hanson is revealed as Evans's chosen successor rather than the popular governor, Jack Hathaway, played nicely against type by William Petersen. Hathaway, we learn, has actually staged the attempted dramatic rescue of a girl from a sinking car after it has dived off a bridge near to where he is fishing on vacation. The girl loses her life and Evans remains suspicious of the whole exercise. Hanson is a bolder choice but her confirmation hearings almost immediately run into a minefield of controversy when pictures of her involved in a sexual orgy while at college emerge, and her political nemesis, Senator Shelley Runyon, played by Gary Oldman in McCarthyite mode, sets out to destroy her credibility.

Elizabeth Hass is very complimentary of the film and the construction of Hanson as a character but the solution to the denouement is, in Hass's words, a film 'having it both ways'. Hanson's refusal to entertain an outright rebuttal of the allegations about her sexual conduct many years before only seems to reinforce the stories, but paints her into a corner where she must maintain the moral position that privacy, especially as regards sexual activity, should be respected in political life, she and the film suggest. But when all is over and Hanson has triumphed against the odds, she confirms to the President that the pictures are fake and the stories untrue, and thus her 'rehabilitation as a loyal wife and model mother' is complete, even if sexually promiscuous women appear undermined in their bid for high office.[21]

The movie has some other uneven elements to it as well. Bridges plays Evans with more than a touch of Clinton about him. His politics are liberal, inclusive and pragmatic, but his world of bowling alleys, macho conversation and especially the nice recurring motive about how much different food he can have prepared for him is pure southern boy made good. Christian Slater's turn as a young Republican Congressman who muscles his way on to the hearings committee but then suffers an attack of conscience is pretty Capraesque, and Oldman – who fell out with Lurie when a good many of his scenes ended up on the cutting-room floor – is never less than his usual over-the-top self. But he does still convey a sound impression of a representative wound up in Washington beltway mentality. Runyon's sense of justice and accountability is a curious insider's view of the way politics works. His stance is partly about Hanson's morality and attitude towards issues like sex before marriage and abortion, but it is also born out of a need for revenge for her defection, as though a cardinal rule had been broken. Yet his is an inquisition that largely remains detached from the general public's attitudes to Hanson's past. If one suspects Lurie's intention was to signpost a commentary on Clinton's impeachment, then, as Jeff Bridges himself confirmed, that is probably not far off the mark.[22] Stephen Holden commented in his *New York Times* review of the film that '[*The Contender*] is essentially a pro-Clinton editorial in the wake of the Lewinsky scandal' and an angry brief against what it calls 'sexual McCarthyism'.[23]

While Hass and others have criticised the film's duplicity in respect of the central plot device, in a way it is also easy to see how it remains its strength. For much of the movie we are led to believe not only that the accusations and evidence are true, but also that Hanson somewhat revels in her sexuality. The first time we see her, for instance, is when the President is calling her about the job offer of Vice-President and she is 'making out' with her husband-cum-political manager. Her meetings throughout the film find Allen delivering Hanson's lines in a cool, almost sexually confident manner, as though it is this presentation, let alone her intellect, that is the most important political tool. Indeed, it is this very clash of styles – Hanson's slightly alluring persona mixed with a very striking, brilliant mind – that confounds the expectations one might usually have of a film and political character of this kind.

City Hall and *The Contender* were certainly not the perfect, all-encompassing examinations that politics and even Hollywood perhaps warranted by the end of the 1990s and turn of the millennium. Both faced problems in actually mounting their productions and getting themselves made, even before their lukewarm reception by critics and audience alike. And yet in retrospect they offered alternative critiques of the political values at work in contemporary America at the time that needed recognising. Between the comedic screwball homages of *The American President* and *Dave*, and the action-adventure cartoons of *Independence Day* and *Air Force One*, Hollywood did rediscover an arena in which ideology, institutional structures and public accountability could be analysed and made accessible to a cinematic audience. The lesson of the late 1990s was that Hollywood realised it did have the capacity for penetrating inquiry and it was a lesson that, if temporarily forgotten over the following half-decade, served the industry well when it came to more blatant critiques of the political environment and America's place in the post-9/11 world of the later 2000s.

THE 2000s AND BEYOND

If the 1990s reconsidered America's political legacy of the last forty years, the 2000s took that re-assessment to a more critical level when it came to foreign and diplomatic entanglements, as Chapter 6 illustrates. But domestically, Hollywood political movies shot back and forth between the here-and-now while trying to allegorise still further past political events and controversies. As Chapter 5 contends, films such as *Munich* and *The Assassination of Richard Nixon* returned politics and society to the 1970s and an era of social despondency and political schisms. In the 2000s, Emilio Estevez's *Bobby* (2006) took its audience back a decade further, to the 1960s.

With an extraordinary ensemble cast, the film takes us through the hours leading up to the assassination of Robert Kennedy on 5 June 1968 at the Ambassador Hotel in Los Angeles. Characters real and imaginary intermingle in Estevez's own original story as the Kennedy narrative, the 1960s, and the fading memories of hope and optimism that ushered in the decade are brought to bear on a group of people, each of whom is touched by the events late that night. One could not say that the film is anything but reverential towards its subject, and the documentary prologue shapes the mood from the off as iconic imagery shows the last great political hope of the 1960s. Yet the movie is also deeply depressing and downbeat at times, an episodic series of reflections that continually parades a decade, a political dynasty, and a society that have lost their way over the course of less than ten years. Marriages flounder and infidelity festers, while drug abuse, racism and the desperation of avoiding the draft to Vietnam occupy the minds of protagonists who cannot seem to wait for the decade to end.

The stellar cast recall their own lives as much as Kennedy's, each following a hopeful yet often tragic course. In the kitchen of the hotel lie the roots of dissatisfaction between the Mexican and African-American staff, each reflecting their disaffection with a system no longing ringing the changes or expressing their desires. 'You got no poetry, you got no light . . . all you've got is your anger,' Lawrence Fishburne's cook, Edward, tells Miguel (Jacob Vargas), the man who will eventually cradle the dying Kennedy in his arms at the climax. 'I was like you, I had anger. Then when Dr King was killed, well . . .'

Bobby is a well-conceived and interesting social commentary about both a bygone era and, in so many ways, the one the movie was made in. Disappointing political dynasties, a country unhinged by an unpopular war, and the threat of social and political dislocation just around the corner: the 2000s were etched clearly enough in the parable at work. *Bobby* reconditioned a key moment and event during these years, then, and stood comparison in many ways with Spielberg's earlier *Amistad* (1997), a re-imagining of the story of African slaves fighting for rights and recognition in the aftermath of the 1839 mutiny aboard the ship of the title, and against the backdrop of slavery and racism, and with Mike Nichols's later *Charlie Wilson's War* (2007), a recollection of the

Texan representative of the title's nearly single-handed attempts to help the Afghan Mujahideen oust the Soviet Union from the country in the early 1980s.

Just as the 1960s are re-examined by Estevez, so the early nineteenth-century position of America is aired in the competing arguments and philosophical musings of some of the nation's foremost leaders and scholars in Spielberg's film. Freedom and justice, isolationism and international involvement, political manœuvring and social principles: each contrasting stance has an exponent in *Amistad* and conceives of an America waking up to its responsibilities within the world, not least in the form of Anthony Hopkins's portrayal of former President, John Quincy Adams, who has returned to the US Congress and is making an impassioned plea in the Supreme Court in the closing moments of the film. In Nichols's picture, Tom Hanks gives one of his best-ever performances as a free-loading Congressional Republican with a passion for power and a taste for women. Encouraged by his rich benefactor and part-time lover Joanne Herring (Julia Roberts giving an equally startling performance), Wilson gains new political gravitas with his commitment to the Afghan cause, and goes from Washington hanger-on to influential foreign policy advocate during the Reaganite 1980s.

Bobby, *Amistad* and *Charlie Wilson's War* re-imagined America's past during the 1990s and 2000s but Hollywood was not finished in reconditioning its own history when it came to social and political movies. While one perhaps should not labour the comparison between Capra and Riskin's outstanding commentary on the 1930s and the Steven Brill and Adam Sandler remake of *Mr. Deeds* in 2002 (surely one of the worst remakes ever), Jonathan Demme's updated version of *The Manchurian Candidate* (2004) was more than serviceable, and Steve Zaillian's new adaptation of *All the King's Men* (2006) was arguably better than the original, if unfairly neglected by audiences.

When that era reached its zenith and the Bush years were drawing to a close in 2008, Hollywood made an intriguing move. Its adoption of British political drama reconverted into an examination of the American system was an interesting and perhaps not so surprising development in the 2000s. In both *State of Play* and *Edge of Darkness* (see Chapter 4) the sombre, cynical, often hopeless disaffection with the authority of the state is reconfigured to reflect Bush-era politics, as well as corporate power and unaccountability. In an adaptation of Paul Abbott's BBC drama, Kevin MacDonald turns *State of Play* (2008) into a morality story about the ambition of politics and the blunted nature of crusading journalism. The offices of Cal McCaffrey (Russell Crowe) bear many of the hallmarks of the journalists' locality inhabited by Bob Woodward and Carl Bernstein thirty years before, but allowed to grow dusty and unused, said MacDonald of the look for which he was striving. And the updated allusions to *All the President's Men* do not stop there. Private military contracts, unscrupulous political operators, unaccountable intelligence service personnel: they are all part of the mix in *State of Play*.

The film offers a similarly depressing last rites allegory of the Bush years in its story as *Bobby* does for the 1960s or even Pakula's films did for the 1970s. It also confirmed a film industry much more willing to elaborate on the troubling questions at large in society. When and why was there a block on the accountability of the state to its citizens and at what point did journalism have its stake in that oversight rescinded? *State of Play* is top-notch political thriller filmmaking, and unlike some of the conspiracy movies earlier in the decade, it is not prepared simply to reheat old clichés or inhabit tired narratives. The questioning of the role of the state is constantly foregrounded and the ambivalence and ambiguity of politicians like Stephen Collins (Ben Affleck) are acutely treated. Much of this is due to writers like Matthew Michael Carnahan (see Chapter 6) and Tony Gilroy, a new breed of screenwriter–directors who have been energised and engaged by the political developments of the last decade.

Gilroy's background and CV are virtually an object lesson in the evolution of the action/conspiracy film in the 2000s. From *Proof of Life* (2000), also starring Russell Crowe, to *Michael Clayton* (2007), by way of the 'Bourne' franchise with Paul Greengrass and Matt Damon (see Chapter 4), his interest in government surveillance, corporate politics and the corruption of institutional authority is subtly and completely brought to life in these scripts. Gilroy himself has stated that a film like *Michael Clayton* is not really a 'political film' but is about morality, and one can see how films like his, which have been ascribed political credibility in this era, are really dealing in worlds where some sort of value system is constantly being challenged or even denied.[24] Indeed, in 2009 he moved on to parody much of the drama he created in the earlier pieces with the not entirely successful spoof heist-comedy-corporate-dealings thriller, *Duplicity*, with Julia Roberts and Clive Owen. Ex-Secret Service, CIA officers fall for each other, then start working for separate multinational corporations who are trying to steal each other's secrets (to consumer products!), only for the pair to concoct a scam to steal millions of dollars for themselves. It all looks like a take on the spy-themed action thrillers Gilroy has become renowned for, only to end up as a piffling fight for market share among consumers.

Compatriot and like-minded action-helmer Greengrass has not only reinvigorated the spy-movie franchise with Bourne – he directed the latter two and is to direct the future fourth version – but with his astonishing pared-down vision of 9/11, seen in the claustrophobic and gripping *United 93* (2006), as well as his conspiratorial take on the non-existent WMD in *Green Zone* (2010), Greengrass is also yet another British filmmaker well attuned to the political dimensions and influence of Hollywood filmmaking who has provided caustic and subtle interpretations of America's so-called world-view under Bush. In the latter film, and teaming up once again with Matt Damon, Greengrass takes some of the immediacy of movies like *Battle for Haditha* and *The Hurt Locker*, and transforms it into a conspiratorial game that bridges the military and political worlds in his usual dazzling cinematic style with swift-paced narrative action sequences.

In a more serious manner, *Edge of Darkness* (2010) is director Martin Campbell's updating of his own BBC mini-series from the 1980s, here given a Boston setting and a tougher, grittier lead in Mel Gibson's Tom Craven. As in *State of Play*, the latter film's unapologetic attitude to the perspective of corporate involvement in politics, and the institutional corruption rife in all manner of agencies, is uncompromising and unassailable. As in *State of Play* too, the ending offers little redemption and the sense of disillusionment brought to post-Bush America is as taut and authentic as the despondency and displacement that Campbell's original series, and British movies surrounding it at the time like *Defence of the Realm* and *Hidden Agenda*, brought to Thatcherite politics in Britain in the 1980s.

CONCLUSIONS

In drawing the first edition of this book to a close, I cited a list of real political events, issues and controversies that linked the culture of the late 1990s with Hollywood in particular and with political filmmaking more generally. The election of such colourful figures as Jim Janos and Jesse Ventura during the decade appeared typical of voters' willingness to embrace celebrity as a positive attribute when it came to public service. Almost like the movies that had embraced innocents and outsiders, Janos and Ventura could be seen as emblematic of a society that wanted to shake up the complacency of electoral politics at least. Now we might see that these two only presaged the coming of a really major star to the political party, and one that voters took so seriously they believed that, as in his movies, he really could save the union's most economically important state from fiscal calamity. For Arnold Schwarzenegger's ascent to the governorship of California in 2003 was surely the end product of seventy years or more of Hollywood insurgency on the West Coast, if not the rest of the country.

But it was Prime Minister Tony Blair (ironically enough) who suggested just how amorphous and problematic Hollywood influence was upon wider political culture at the end of the century. Speaking at the time of his Foreign Secretary Robin Cook's resignation from the Cabinet, due to an affair with his personal assistant which resulted in Cook divorcing his wife, Blair commented that 'Britain could be heading for the same type of political agenda as they've now got in the United States, where everything is an extension of Hollywood.'[25] I said at the time that 'Hollywood' status wasn't easy to identify with or confer on the Cook case. This was not a story that was accompanied by outrageous or salacious gossip, and the man himself was never the embodiment of Hollywood glamour – nor would he ever have liked to be considered so. The Lewinsky affair that was going on at roughly the same time across the Atlantic, as well as later resignations in America and Britain that were accompanied by somewhat more dramatic headlines, did follow, however (and all were summarised in the BBC docudrama presentation, *The Special Relationship* (2010), starring Michael Sheen and Dennis Quaid), and reinforced the sense that Blair's vague sentiment had credence in some way.

In 2001, that credence was reinforced by events in Washington that were at once profoundly serious and tragic, and yet at the same time bore more than a passing resemblance to fictional movies of the late 1990s such as *Absolute Power* and *Murder at 1600*. In the Spring of that year, California representative Gary Condit was caught up in the mysterious disappearance of a political intern who came from his district, Chandra Levy. Condit claimed to know Levy when initially questioned about her disappearance but denied having an affair with her, only to renege on that statement some while later. These false claims to the authorities, as well as the unveiling of a series of revelations in the press that hinted at Condit's steamy private life, all appeared to implicate him seriously in the mystery during the course of the following, media-frenzied days and weeks. By the summer of 2001, Levy had not been found and neither had any hard evidence against Condit. But when he was discovered by police attempting to discard a gift box in an anonymous dumpster in the Virginia suburbs, and then went on national television only to be evasive about a whole series of pertinent questions relating to the case, it really did seem as if Condit was part of an elaborate scriptwriter's scenario for a tale of sex, murder and deceit that most Hollywood studios would have simply found too far-fetched to green-light.

Ironically, the denouement was even more unexpected. In the late Summer and Autumn of 2001, Condit's name disappeared off the front pages of newspapers and the headlines of TV nightly news altogether, to be replaced by somewhat more global events. While she was presumed dead, Levy's body had never been found to that point. More than a year after the last sighting of her, however, in the Spring of 2002, it was discovered by accident in a Washington park. As suspected, Levy had been murdered but still no evidence was found and no charges were ever brought against Condit. In May 2009, a prison inmate, Ingmar Guandique, confessed to the murder as part of a series for which he had already been indicted that took place in the area around the same period. Condit always protested his innocence and even attempted to win re-election to Congress in 2002 in a desperate bid to prolong his long service to the state. (He had already been a House representative for fourteen years spanning two California districts.) Perhaps unsurprisingly, he did not even get as far as the November general election, losing in the Primary to a former colleague, Dennis Cardoza.

It would be easy to forget that at the centre of this sensational and even unlikely story was an intelligent young woman with a sparkling future ahead of her and the promise and potential that come from the mixture of youth, ambition, idealism and a desire to serve. If Chandra Levy's brutal and horrific slaying was lost at times in the roll-call of gossip and innuendo that accompanied the case, one could hardly make the claim that this was the result of Hollywood's pervasive influence at the turn of the century on events surrounding the nation's political culture. In Washington as well as the film colony, tragic tales of this type had arisen before and the public reportage of such issues had been equally salacious and at times ill judged.

But the point is, rather like the events of 9/11 that the Condit–Levy case wrapped itself around, the story was persistently framed within Hollywood terms: as some larger-than-life, almost surreal take on the film world that captured the attention of the global media in all its twists and turns. Although only a part of the overall evolution of political culture in the 2000s, and how that culture has periodically been represented on big and small screens, this case, together with 9/11, the sometimes extraordinary behaviour of the Bush Administration, and the intertwining of politics, celebrity culture, Hollywood re-imaging, and personalities that crossed over and straddled both those worlds confirms the importance of both communities in American culture and society for good and ill, and made a Hollywood appreciation of domestic politics in the 2000s that much harder to come by.

As well as a greater Hollywood focus on foreign and diplomatic issues of the time, who could seriously contemplate a drama or even comedy that could outdo many of the real-life escapades that had afflicted the later Clinton and then Bush years for more than a decade? Yet Hollywood's fascination with political topics has not only continued but also intensified over the course of the last decade. Comedies such as *Head of State* and *Welcome to Mooseport*, pseudo-historical biopics like *Charlie Wilson's War* and *Bobby*, conspiracy films like *Spartan* and *Silver City*, and even comparative satirical comedies set in the US and Britain, such as the film version of *In the Loop*, have all added to the welter of political tracts, even if the influence and popularity of some of these have been slight compared to the movies focused on in other parts of this book.

But the political tale that achieved a greater sense of collective cultural and critical traction between the public, Washington and Hollywood in the late 1990s all the way through the mid-2000s was the Aaron Sorkin-penned, NBC-produced television series, *The West Wing* (1999–2006). When NBC commissioned the series in 1999, they had few hopes and even less ambition for it. Writer Aaron Sorkin had cut his teeth on Hollywood screenplays like *A Few Good Men*, *Malice* and *The American President*, but even with a major star like Martin Sheen commanding the role of the President in the series, Jed Bartlet, expectations were fairly low.

But *The West Wing* simply caught the public imagination like no other political series before it, and through the first four seasons it picked up awards, plaudits and, at the beginning of season two especially, some of the highest viewing figures in American TV history for a drama show. For four straight years, from 2000 through to 2003, the show won the Outstanding Drama Award at the Emmys, as well as numerous other acting, producing and directing accolades. Given the often-difficult commercial proposition that political topics have constituted in Hollywood and on television, one must be tempted to ask why the programme should have done so well. After all, ABC rival, *Commander-in-Chief*, created by Rod Lurie and starring Geena Davis, only survived one season (2005–6), even though it too was nominated for awards and received some respectable reviews.

A clue can be discerned from its treatment of certain topics and their insertion into particular episodes. The first-season story, 'Mr Willis of Ohio', for example, coincided with the new round of census data to be collected all over the nation at the close of each decade. The episode spent more than a third of its 44–minute run explaining the intricacies of census polling (mainly in a one-on-one conversation between deputy Communications Director Sam Seaborn (Rob Lowe) and Press Secretary C. J. Cregg (Alison Janney)) and why the process was important, while the news networks of major stations spent a total of 2.4 minutes *collectively* looking at the issue over a two-year period.[26] Conclusions suggested that *The West Wing*'s approach to and rhetoric around such 'dry' material were far-reaching enough to be grounded in educational procedure and high-minded civic duty, as well as plain old Washington beltway wheeler-dealing. The series may have subscribed to a forgotten time and place when the rhetoric of the Founding Fathers could be met by the dynamics of the New Frontier or the Great Society in the form of characters like Bartlet, Cregg, Seaborn and Deputy Chief of Staff Josh Lyman (Bradley Whitford), but it pointedly refused to believe that that world was closed off forever. Samuel Chambers argues that the show actually challenged the principles of political theory by offering not convenient 'teleological endpoints' that fit the episodic construction of the genre, but by 'grappling with questions of political agency, legitimacy, and the very space of the political'.[27] In other words, the language employed by the characters from the very beginning of the series did not automatically orientate itself towards the pursuit of consensus and resolution, but instead actually challenged the notions of political governance and legitimacy in a mainstream television drama.

As Christensen and Hass state, 'The image of politics reflects and reinforces popular prejudice, but it [also] helps to entrench alienation and apathy.'[28] No wonder, they observe, that some continue to see movies as a way of dictating the thoughts and feelings of the populace. The collection of films on offer in this book have re-affirmed some of that propaganda persuasion over the course of film history, but just as many have opened the eyes of the public to intolerance, malfeasance and flaws. The Hollywood model of political culture has also found ways to perceive hopeful, optimistic, if crudely patriotic visions of institutional rhetoric and behaviour as part of the norms in political life, and present these as adjuncts to a wider social debate about the health of democracy. At its most rarefied, a series like *The West Wing*, in Chambers's words, 'opens up those spaces of the political, to make the word politics itself less a term of derision and contempt and instead one of hope, of possibility'.[29] By season seven, when the worlds of *The West Wing* and American political life converged in the form of the electoral battles going on in the fictional campaign of Matt Santos (Jimmy Smits) and the real one of Barack Obama, it was clear that in contemporary society politics both needs and has become reliant on culture and art more than ever to convey its form, if not its content. Future political movies are already announced for the 2010s and if they can inform, educate and, yes, even entertain in the manner of their predecessors, the political movie will be in rude health, and the importance of this type of filmmaking will be assured and require even more inquiry and analysis.

NOTES

1. 'Brown Appears on American Idol' on the BBC News Site at: http://news.bbc.co.uk/1/hi/7339349.stm.
2. Manohla Dargis, 'Paul Weitz's "American Dreamz": An "Idol" Clone with a Presidential Aura', in *New York Times* on the Net, 21 April 2006 at: http://www.nytimes.com/2006/04/21/movies/21drea.
3. Stephen Holden, 'Michael Douglas as a Secret Service Agent in "The Sentinel"', *New York Times*, 21 April 2006 at: http//www.nytimes.com/2006/04/21/movies/21sent.
4. Jon Patterson, 'Film', *The Guardian Guide*, 13 September 2008, p. 17.
5. Luc Herman, 'Bestowing Knighthood: The Visual Aspect of Bill Clinton's Camelot Legacy', in *Hollywood's White House: The American Presidency in Film and History*, ed. Peter C. Rollins and John E. O'Connor (Lexington: University Press of Kentucky, 2003), p. 316.
6. Michael Coyne, *Hollywood Goes to Washington: American Politics on Screen* (London: Reaktion, 2008), p. 36.
7. Luc Herman, p. 312.
8. Gary Wills, *Reagan's America: Innocents at Home* (London: Heinemann, 1988), p. 4.

9. Ben Dickenson, *Hollywood's New Liberalism: War, Globalisation and the Movies from Reagan to George W. Bush* (London: I. B. Tauris, 2006), p. 75.

10. Michael Ellison, 'Wholesome Hanks Turns his Back on Clinton', *The Guardian*, 1 December 1998, p. 18.

11. Clinton hinted as much in his 2004 interview with the BBC, which heralded the arrival of his memoirs on the bookshelves. Groups like Artists United and MoveOn.org were instrumental in galvanising the Hollywood community at the time to oppose the impeachment. Later, though, they were part of an effort to criticise the President and his successor for a series of failed and/or mistaken policies right up to and including the start of the second Iraq War in 2003. See Ben Dickenson, pp. 75–6.

12. Martin Walker, 'Clinton's Hollywood', *Sight and Sound*, September 1993, pp. 20–1.

13. Michael Coyne, p. 89.

14. Ben Walker, p. 20.

15. Both films took almost exactly the same box-office (*Dave* $63 million and *The American President* $65 million) while going on to be sizable hits on video too, each passing $30 million in rentals in the US alone. Source of figures: iMDB.

16. 'Don't change horses in mid-stream' was actually a phrase attributed to campaign films in 1934 denouncing the candidacy of Upton Sinclair for governor of California. The films were made by Hollywood insiders and promoted by the likes of Louis B. Mayer.

17. Robin Dougherty, 'Wag the Dog' review, *Sight and Sound*, vol. 8, no. 3, March 1998, p. 57.

18. Jim Emerson, 'Audiences will Feel his Pain' at: http://www.msnbc.com/news/151991.asp.

19. John Harkness, 'Hall of Mirrors', *Sight and Sound*, September 1992, p. 4.

20. Todd McCarthy, Review of *Bob Roberts*, *Variety*, 18 May 1992.

21. Elizabeth Ann Hass, 'Women, Politics and Film: All About Eve?', in *Projecting Politics: Political Messages in American Films* (London: M. E. Sharpe, 2005), p. 274.

22. Bridges was quoted as saying that the references to Clinton and the Lewinsky episode were not really 'veiled' at all (Elizabeth Ann Hass, p. 274).

23. Stephen Holden, 'The Contender: Those Strange Bedfellows Haunt a Politician', *New York Times*, 17 October 2000 at: http://www.nytimes.com.

24. Interview with Tony Gilroy in the *Washington Post*, 27 September 2007 at: http://www.washingtonpost.com/wp-dyn/content/discussion/2007/09/25/DI2007092500910.html.

25. Michael White, 'Blair Backs "Superb" Cook', *The Guardian*, 11 January 1999, p. 1.
26. Jesse Oxfeld, 'Census Consensus: *The West Wing* Covered it Better', included in Matthew Miller, 'The Real White House', *Brill's Content*, March 2000, p. 94.
27. Samuel A. Chambers, 'Dialogue, Deliberation, and Discourse: The Far-Reaching Politics of *The West Wing*', in *The West Wing: The American Presidency as Television Drama*, ed. Peter C. Rollins and John E. O'Connor (New York: Syracuse University Press, 2003), p. 84.
28. Terry Christensen and Peter J. Hass, *Projecting Politics: Political Messages in American Films* (London: M. E. Shape, 2005), p. 288.
29. Samuel Chambers, p. 100.

INDEX